PRAISE FOR THE HOLINESS OF

"One of my best Talmud teachers told us that the questions in the Talmud were often better than the answers. A professor of mine told us graduate students in philosophy that a philosopher is a five-year-old child who never stopped asking 'Why?' Being willing to ask questions and not expect totally satisfactory answers is the mark of the epistemo-logical humility that we all should have, for God may know everything, but no human being does. This does not mean, though, that we should not ask questions and seek answers. On the contrary, questions are abso-lutely critical in seeking meaning in life, as this book amply demonstrates. So ask away, and let Rabbi Hoffman and the Torah itself spur you to more questions!"

—**Rabbi Elliot N. Dorff**, rector and distinguished
service professor of philosophy, American Jewish University

"This is a wonderful book for anyone who wants a deeper mode of Torah study. Rabbi Hoffman explores the world of the Torah through the questions found in the text and helps us ask our own questions of ourselves, God, and the world."

—**Rabbi Denise L. Eger D.D.**, founding Senior Rabbi of
Congregation Kol Ami in West Hollywood, CA, author, and
past president of the Central Conference of American Rabbis

"The one who questions and doubts is a person of faith. Scattered throughout the Torah are prompts—questions that help guide our lives. In Rabbi Joshua Hoffman's masterful book, he seeks to answer those questions. And in doing so, he provides us with direction for our own lives while also helping us to probe the depths of wisdom that Torah has to offer. At the same time, Rabbi Hoffman offers us his own torah so that we may deepen and widen our learning even further."

—**Dr. Kerry M. Olitzky,**
former executive director of Big Tent Judaism

"In the sacred text of the Torah to which so many turn for answers and clarity, the presence of abundant questions challenges us to probe deeper. Hoffman's book thoughtfully and insightfully invites us to embrace the blessing of uncertainty in our studies and spiritual life journey."

—**Rabbi Ari Sunshine**, Senior Rabbi,
Congregation Shearith Israel, Dallas, TX

THE HOLINESS OF DOUBT

A Journey Through the Questions of the Torah

RABBI JOSHUA HOFFMAN

ROWMAN & LITTLEFIELD

Lanham • Boulder • New York • London

Published by Rowman & Littlefield
An imprint of The Rowman & Littlefield Publishing Group, Inc.
4501 Forbes Boulevard, Suite 200, Lanham, Maryland 20706
www.rowman.com

86-90 Paul Street, London EC2A 4NE

British Library Cataloguing in Publication Information available

Library of Congress Cataloging-in-Publication Data Is Available

ISBN: 978-1-5381-7675-7 (cloth : alk. paper)
ISBN: 978-1-5381-9892-6 (paper : alk. paper)
ISBN: 978-1-5381-7676-4 (electronic)

♾™ The paper used in this publication meets the minimum requirements of American National Standard for Information Sciences—Permanence of Paper for Printed Library Materials, ANSI/NISO Z39.48-1992.

Contents

ACKNOWLEDGMENTS

THE JOURNEY TOWARD COMPLETING THIS PROJECT WAS ANIMATED BY the belief that when great questions are asked, both the student and the teacher reap divine rewards. The capacity to ask substantive questions, to even inquire of something greater than oneself, is only possible from a place of profound love and support. I have been blessed with the most precious gifts of dedication, encouragement, and support from loving friends and family to enable this book to be written.

I want to acknowledge the excitement shared in my proposal expressed by Natalie Mandziuk, Senior Acquisitions Editor at Rowman & Littlefield Publishers. I am forever grateful to her for taking a chance on a first-time author like me. With her encouragement, I was introduced to Richard Brown, the Senior Executive Editor, Religion. Richard's sincerity, kindness, patient curiosity, and unflagging encouragement have enabled this project to become a reality. Thank you, Richard, for asking the right questions and sharing with me the best possible answers.

Jaylene Perez, Hannah Fisher, and the entire editorial team at Rowman & Littlefield are shining examples of what a publishing team can be. Each step of the process of preparing this work for publication has been authentically positive and glowingly responsive.

Special thanks to Rabbi Barry Schwartz, Stuart Maitlins, Ron Wolfson, Rafael Chaiken, and Rabbi Beth Lieberman for your counsel and insight into preparing this book for a proposal worthy of consideration.

While I have been consumed by the alluring mysteries the questions of the Torah reveal, the wisdom of the rabbinic tradition perpetually radiates the beauty in offering answers for the right occasion. I find great inspiration from their interpretations to humbly offer my own. We read:

> *Rabbi Jehudah said: When a person speaks with their companion, they hear the sound of a voice, but do not see any light with it; the Israelites heard the voice of the Holy One on Mount Sinai, and saw the voice going forth from the mouth of the Almighty in the lightning and the thunder, as it is said, "And all the people saw the thunderings and the lightnings."*[1]

Gleaning wisdom from my teachers is like hearing the sounds of the divine voice through shimmering light. I am grateful to the many teachers who helped me shape this project:

For twenty years, I held admiration for Rabbi J. B. Sacks from afar. He's a respected teacher, a kind soul, an energetic spirit, and a true scholar. When Rabbi Sacks offered to review the manuscript and offer helpful editorial suggestions, I was given a gift of faith. Rabbi Sacks's playful, encouraging, and critical eye sharpened the thoughts presented here. I am grateful for this and his helpful suggestions to frame the book with just the right amount of summary and commentary. Above all, the friendship forged in the process of this effort between us remains an enduring gift. Thank you.

The project of cataloging the questions in the Torah and ultimately crafting a commentary around them began in the summer of 2014 when I was a senior rabbinic fellow at the Shalom Hartman Institute in Jerusalem. My cohort and teachers there were the first ones to learn of this idea in its infancy and offered insight and helpful guidance that encouraged me to continue pursuing the project. I am most appreciative of my study partners, my *chevraya*, Rabbi Jacob Blumenthal and Rabbi Ari Sunshine, whose incisive thinking about everything from Talmud to Moses Maimonides sharpened my thinking and polished our friendship for a lifetime.

Rabbi Akiva says: If one studied Torah in his youth he should study more Torah in his old age; if he had students in his youth he should have additional students in his old age.[2]

The first eighteen years of my rabbinate were shaped by the experiences of leadership and learning with the Valley Beth Shalom community. Rabbi Harold Schulweis and Rabbi Ed Feinstein were inspiring partners in bringing authentic meaning to a community of seekers. With all the knowledge I acquired in rabbinical school, it was during these eighteen years that I discovered what knowledge needed to be shared with congregants, students, fellow members of the leadership, and the community at large. This book is in many ways a response to the questions posed by curious children in the schools, inquisitive adults in the Shabbat services, and the friends who saw the project of bringing a vibrant and relevant Judaism to the world as something that could only be discovered by asking the right questions.

I am excited to continue this journey of discovery and cultivating a dynamic Jewish identity in the world with the students, faculty, administration and leadership of the Academy for Jewish Religion California. AJRCA makes the audacious declaration that the world needs compassionate chaplains, innovative cantors, and rabbinic sages for 21st-century Jewish life. I am honored to journey along the path toward the beacon of light this institution emanates into the world.

And this is what Rabbi Ḥanina said: I have learned much from my teachers and even more from my friends, but from my students I have learned more than from all of them.[3]

For more than fifteen years I have had the privilege of teaching a group of dedicated learners, first through the auspices of the Florence Melton Adult School of Jewish Learning and now independently. Year after year my students invite me to create new curricula, pushing me to find exciting and relevant material to explore. More than a challenge to present the wisdom of the Jewish tradition meaningfully, this fine group of learners continues to teach me that the quest for knowledge never has to be fully satisfied. Even more, sharing the learning with fine souls is like dining at the most elegant feast.

I am grateful for the eternal friendship for the many dear friends and colleagues too numerous to list here who continually teach, amuse, and inspire me throughout my life. I am especially grateful to Rabbis Brian and Deborah Schuldrenfrei and their family for your open home and hearts.

To my beautiful children, Ethan, Arianna, and Elizabeth. You are the answers to our questions of why and how God is present in our lives. Each moment of your lives I'm privileged to witness is filled with marvel and awe. You continue to teach me how to model a world where the questions you ask are worth recording in a Torah.

To Becky, my most excellent partner in life and learning, my friend beyond compare who challenges me to be better in everything I do. This book is dedicated to you. You are my reason and my faith. You make my doubt holy.

To the Source of questions and the inspiration for answers. My quest to discover You unfolds in these pages and may they be worthy of drawing others near to your Truth.

Introduction: What Is a Question?

Commonly, questions are statements intended to evoke knowledge. The word "question" is Latin in origin and refers to the act of seeking. In the Hebrew language, to ask a question (לשאול) is also to seek out, or to inquire. The question frames an interest in discovering meaning and invites a response. As a basic human need, this curiosity can bring great purpose into our lives. The satisfaction of an answered question, or even the understanding of what the question seeks to answer, is inspiring, wondrous, even divine. In conversations and in teaching, questions are there to evoke a relationship. More than an opportunity to solicit and receive information, a question is posed to communicate a desire to connect to deeper truths and to discover sacred connections.

Questions do not have to be trivial—often we pose thoughts for which an explicit and simple answer is not intended to be readily found. These can be questions of identity, community or belonging, power and influence, and even hope. Indeed, these are the questions we are invited to ask not only of our sacred texts but also of ourselves in every time and generation.

The focus on a question can be playful too. It seems impossible to find our place in the world without some form of questing, of seeking out the truth that dwells around us. I believe this is the purpose of all the questions in the Torah: to cultivate relationships between people and ultimately to cultivate an authentic relationship toward eternal truth. Relationships are built by the courageous leap to connect. Questions can be a dramatization of that connection, bridges of the chasm between doubt and faith, between uncertainty and deep knowledge. And so, questions as important tools of language deserve attention.

What Is Interpretation?

The Psalmist asks, "Who is the one that desires life, loves long years discovering goodness?"[1] Answers to this question, or these questions, invite a kaleidoscope of responses. The good life may have some fundamental elements, but the impression one has of a good life shifts and deepens over time. More than the variety of responses a question like this offers, it is the structure of the question that introduces the moral equation. Questions beget more questions ever desirous of deepening our connections with one another. The concept that truth invites, even demands, interpretation is a great innovation of the Jewish project.

First readers of the Torah may scratch their heads at the peculiar dynamics of the text. Talking snakes and donkeys, dream-tellers, and prophets all seem extraordinary, let alone a text that asks questions of the characters, the readers, and even of itself! The interpretive tradition of Jewish mysticism, *Kabbalah*, captures this best.

> *Woe to the one who says that the Torah came to simply relate stories in an ordinary language, because if this is so, even in these times we could make a Torah from ordinary tales, and one even nicer than from those [ordinary tales]. If the Torah came to explain worldly subjects, even the rulers of the [present] world have books of even greater merit. If so, we could emulate what they [those stories] say and use them to compile some such Torah of our own. But really, of all that the Torah says, it holds supernal truths and sublime secrets.*[2]

Questions are the doorways to deeper wisdom. Interpretations are the prisms of meaning that emanate from individuals and communities seeking truth.

When Do Questions Appear in the Torah?

Questions are asked in many unique circumstances. The thesis of this book is that questions are posed in the search for certainty when doubt is present. More than a clarification of meaning or a resolution of uncertainty, the questions in the Torah validate the experience of doubt. They may even affirm the holiness of doubt by letting us know that asking questions is as sacred an endeavor as expressing absolute faith.

Throughout the Torah, the quantity and scope of the questions are highly dramatized to accentuate the uncertainty. Some questions can even be perceived as coy and instigating direct response when something more nuanced would be appropriate. For example, the questions posed to God by Abraham, by Moshe in response to the people's incessant complaints, or the litany of challenges expressed by Korach and his rebellious faction, are all in response to the dynamics of power and authority.[3] The questions help the reader understand the complexity of relationships and ultimately help us determine where God fits into our experience.

And still there are many questions that open the door to interpretations without any clear answers or resolutions. Consider the first questions of the Torah, "Where are you?" and "Am I my brother's keeper?"[4] Questions become theological constructions to better understand our relationship to God and even to ourselves.

While not the subject of this book, the book of Job details chapters of unanswered questions posed by God to Job to underscore the scope of uncertainty with which we contextualize our existence as human beings. Three entire chapters record some fifty questions to evoke a sense of awe and submission in the face of uncertainty! If faith is a commitment to a higher power without empirical proof, doubt is the recognition that questions unanswered can also inspire devotion and loyalty.

By asking questions, and even by listening to the questions others pose, we are given a sense of where we belong. It has indeed become an identifying marker of Jewish sensibility. The structure of a question and the variety of responses to that question become the foundation of who we are as a people. One of the most significant Jewish holidays, Passover (Pesah), for example, requires us to ask questions so we may better know who we are and what our life's purpose is.

The Limits of Questions

There may be limits to our questions even if they take generations to discover. Questions can inspire us when they plumb the depths of our potential. Questions can also be deflating and compel us to act from a place of convenience or simplicity. The Torah presents questions throughout its narrative to guide us toward the depths that inspire the soul, teaching us that defining the limits too narrowly or too expansively can alter our destiny prematurely.

The Talmud will grapple with the limits to questions when it imagines Moshe entering the study hall of Rabbi Akiva. As Moshe appears in the Beit Midrash, in Rabbi Akiva's classroom, he is dumbstruck by the content of the conversation. At one point in the confusion, a student asks Rabbi Akiva to explain the source of the teaching. Akiva attributes the learning to Moshe's teachings from Mount Sinai. While Moshe is relieved that the Torah will be in good hands so many generations later, he asks God to show him the reward of such loyalty to the Torah tradition. When Moshe sees the horrific execution of Rabbi Akiva, he cries, "Such Torah, and such reward?" "Be silent, for such is My decree," declares God in response.[5]

In the Talmudic example, Moshe seeks to justify his purpose as lawgiver and leader by witnessing the promulgation of his Torah many generations later. His satisfaction is undermined by his horror at Rabbi Akiva's demise. We don't see this as an end to the questions; indeed it only opens up an entirely different set of questions about the evil that exists in human experience. Without a good question, these deeper existential ideas would never be explored. Questions in the Torah encourage the search, knowing limits do exist.

THE FEELING OF QUESTIONS

One aspect of a question in relation to other forms of expression is the degree of emotion it implies. It is difficult, if not impossible, to express a curiosity, a desire for knowledge, or an invitation to a relationship without some emotive force. In some respects, well-placed and thoughtful questions are expressions of the soul. By "soul" here I mean the nexus of thought and emotion where intuition and instinct meet. This is perhaps one reason there are so many questions in this sacred book: to instruct us on the ways to grow our expressions of the soul.

ABOUT THIS BOOK

As a lifelong student of the Torah, each time I study the text I gain greater insight and inspiration as my own life experience grows and unfolds. I have since discovered that there are many more questions in the Torah that are spoken in the voice of God or by our biblical heroes themselves than I would have expected. God is curious and our heroes are ambivalent. That discovery invited a tremendous curiosity of my own and a sense of wonder about this book of sacred literature altogether. And given my training as a rabbi and teacher, the spirit of interpretation was ignited.

The Holiness of Doubt is a book about questions; specifically, about all the questions and their significance in the Torah. I continue to marvel that a book of sacred literature, a book that conveys truth, could be riddled with the uncertainties a question poses. I began to ask myself, "What does the Torah look like when you follow the path of verses with the questions as your guide? What new understanding is possible on such a journey?"

This book can be a helpful resource for reference, inquiry, and hopefully inspiration. Divided by the weekly Torah readings, the chapters of this book offer you an opportunity to read the questions as commentary. The study guide at the end of this book is a guideline for developing curricula and teaching the Torah through the lens of its questions.

The goal of this book is to explore how questions move the Torah narrative along. Studying the text in this way offers new insights for preserving the best and most elegant examples of creative interpretation recorded by students of the Torah throughout the generations. Indeed, there should be new categories of thinking in which to place these questions in the future after studying the text with its questions as your guide.

FINALLY . . . THE ANSWERS?

The questions in the Torah are more than literary devices to factual data points of an historical narrative. They do not merely punctuate the physical journeys of the people from Egypt to the Promised Land or exemplify how the family of Abraham sustained the covenant throughout the generations. There are meant to be answers to the questions. I hope you discover, as I have on my journey, the humbling nature of answering questions in the Torah. With great reverence, each question in this book was not posed lightly. Given the gravity each question holds in the grand narrative of the Jewish people, our answers should, even must, be as serious and sacred, intentional, and humble. Some of them are questions asked by God, after all. And students of the divine respond with the dignity of a humble servant, prompting each of us who seeks meaning from this ancient text to ask ourselves, "What questions will we ask?"

Part I

Introduction to Genesis

WE CAN IMAGINE THAT THE ORIGINS OF QUESTIONS IN THE TORAH evolve like the origins of the universe—statements to prompt clarity through the cosmic mess of creation. However, questions that highlight the grand designs to shape and form the nature of existence are noticeably absent. The definition of God as the primary force of creation emerges without any knowledge seeking. We presume God's eternality and do not question God's existence. While the first chapter of the Torah is designed to frame the origins of the universe, creation represents a small fraction of the entire book. And where the absence of questions might imply a tacit faith, the first questions reveal much deeper concerns of doubt and uncertainty in the human experience.

The idyllic Garden of Eden is more than a mythology to explain where the nascent Israelite nation was formed. The very nature of cultivating a garden is a theme that pervades the entire book. It is the foundation of our understanding of human experience. Leaving the tender support of the garden to cultivate meaning in the world becomes a primary goal of the Torah.

What comprises the human soul, its origins and its purpose, is introduced in the opening chapters of this book. The concept of nakedness also becomes a central concern for human beings. The need for protection transcends physicality. Protection has internal implications as well. The human being will be clothed in skin, garments, wisdom, and even covenants throughout the book. The dressing up of the human in the regal attire of a soulful being is the ultimate goal of the book and even the entire Torah. Questions are the pivotal moments that enable the human being to possess a soul worthy of divinity.

The questions in this book establish the relationship between God and humanity and between human beings themselves. They are, in Bloom's taxonomy of questions, analytical in nature. While the probing inquiry of the questions posed in the book builds relationships, they in turn create the definition of God that was initially absent in the opening chapter of the book. The questions of this book answer the curiosity of human existence and even more marvelous, the existence of God.

Genesis

B'REISHEET

3.1 "Did God really say: 'You shall not eat from any tree of the garden'?" (Snake to the woman)

3.9 "Where are you?" (God to man)

3.11 "Who told you that you were naked?" (God to man)

3.11 "Did you eat of that tree from which I had forbidden you to eat?" (God to man)

3.13 "What is this you have done?" (God to woman)

4.6 "Why are you distressed?" and "Why is your face fallen?" (God to Cain)

4.9 "Where is your brother Abel?" (God to Cain)

4.9 "Am I my brother's keeper?" (Cain to God)

4.10 "What have you done?" (God to Cain)

Beginning life in a garden powerfully demonstrates that our origins transcend our location. Walking among a menagerie of natural growth defines our identity distinctly from one shaped by a city or a cluster of tents. The garden is idyllic and replete with potential as is a flourishing possibility of identity. New life blossoms from the earth unbounded by rules of human cultivation; the fruit of a garden contains nutrients unseen by the naked eye.

And yet a garden, by definition, has boundaries, boundaries that can only come from the hands of the human or the Divine. Who defines those boundaries and how they become essential in the cultivation of the human being is the primary focus of the opening chapters of the book of Genesis.

This portion of the Torah and the questions it contains focus upon the relationship between God and humanity. From questions of authority and intention to questions of responsibility to the Divine Presence, the moments when a question is present are pivotal. Where does the responsibility for the relationship between God and humanity rest, in the guidance of God or in the will of the human being? The voice of accountability echoing in the encounters chronicled by the Torah emerges through the questions. Responses to the questions illuminate the development of human consciousness throughout the entire Bible.

The First Question?

3.1 "Did God really say: 'You shall not eat of any tree of the garden'?"

Upon first examination, the first question asked in the Torah is proffered neither by a human being nor by God. Instead the first question comes from the snake, who proposes to Eve that she eat the fruit from the tree of knowledge. It asks, **"Did God really say: 'You shall not eat of any tree of the garden'?"** The question is a delicious enticement, a seduction of curiosity, begging the interpretations of many as to the real intention of the snake's expression. First and foremost, we learn here that the act of questioning introduces a fundamental religious dilemma: doubt. We may not know what the voice of God in the Universe really intended by any instruction given to the human being. If we read the verse for its simple meaning here, God plainly instructed the human being not to eat the fruit. Human ambivalence toward rigid instruction is what prompts Eve's curiosity. Still it will be the deviousness of the snake's inquiry and human choice that set the tone for the remainder of the book.

The midrashic tradition even comes along to point out that the narrative of the serpent isn't even necessary in the development of the grand story of humanity outlined in the Bible. One could read the concluding verse of chapter 2, "And they were naked" (2:25) and resume the narrative in the middle of chapter 3, where it states, "And the man called his wife, Eve, and God made garments of skins for them" (3:20–21).[1] The entire episode is predicated on the interrogative as if to introduce the deceptive course questions can take upon us. Expulsion from Eden, then, is the consequence of nakedness. Perhaps this is the greatest challenge to the God of All. There is doubt with which we must contend. Doubt in the face of faith is like standing naked in an unfamiliar place.

I find that the introduction of this doubt is validated throughout the Torah. It is doubt that proves that our devotion and allegiance to God does not come from a correction or reconciliation or by denying the existence of uncertainty. Rather, we are taught through this example how we must carefully and properly address our doubting conscience. Perhaps questions expand our consciousness and help us become more divine ourselves? Or perhaps questions are deceptions of a truth originally intended for acceptance?

"Did God really say: 'You shall not eat of any tree of the garden'?" being the first question of the Torah, of the Bible, also suggests that the entire purpose of the book is to grapple with this question alone or at best the implication of this question. Even the construction of the question deviously undermines the statement that God does actually make: **"Of every tree in the garden you are free to eat, but as for the tree of knowledge of good and bad, you must not eat it; for as soon as you eat of it, you shall die."**[2]

Naked Is a State of Mind
3.9 "Where are you?"

God's first question to the human being in the Garden, **"Where are you?"** quickly moves beyond a clarification of location to an exploration of identity. We wonder what God is looking for, knowing that a divine being ought to have the capability of seeing and knowing all. We also learn from this question that divine inquiry implies a certain incomplete knowledge. Even if God knows the answer, the question guides the human being to participate in a response worthy of divinity.

We might infer that the question seeks to locate the essence of the human being, a remarkable quality we have in our capacity to reason and reflect on our existence. It is a feature that even God cannot see. What marvelous potential we possess—to see ourselves in perspective, to make definitions of role and purpose that extend beyond an objective measurement of existence. **"Where are you?"** implies a search for purpose—God desires the location where a human being is not ashamed of their objective perspective. It even appears through this search that the human has the ability to discover his or her capacity to reach the divine. God asks this question and is curious to learn any answer, for there really is no single or definitive answer. This may be an early indication that self-awareness is the essential precursor to self-transcendence.

And still, location precedes identity.

The human being's response here, a rare occasion with questions in the Torah, adds to our understanding of this question: **"I heard Your voice in the garden, and I was afraid, because I was naked so I hid."**[3] In itself, this is hardly a fulfilling response to the question. The human being identifies with his fear and not other virtues or vices. In many respects, the Torah's power in a question like this catalyzes a maturity from vice to virtue that human beings must undertake. In time the fear Adam feels here will be transformed into confidence and loyalty.

The nakedness of the human being is a shuddering awareness of inadequacy, not merely a sense of physical vulnerability. It is by implication that nakedness refers to the sensitivity of human beings around their bodies, but the question easily refers to a mental or spiritual nakedness as well. This question probes deeply into the human being's finitude, and God prompts a reaction from the human being himself. It is important to share that until this moment there is no awareness of a lack of human capacity. The word "naked" implies a lack of possession and does not determine the physical presence of the human being in the Garden.

The process of question and answer between God and humanity invites a level of cognition that human beings were either not expected to possess or not capable of possessing before this episode. But being able to respond to God's questions here implies that the human being can take responsibility for his actions and that his response is the outcome of thoughtful consideration. The question that follows confirms this: **"Did you eat of that tree?"**[4]

Rabbi Shlomo Yitzchaki (Rashi) translates this question as well and suggests that God is seeking the participation of understanding in the human being. God knows where we are but we do not. Rashi infers that the question is God's desire for us to discover the ability to translate our circumstances and respond.[5] The act of discernment is introduced here not only between good and evil but also in our relationship to God.

Nakedness is a state of mind that refers to the intention or lack of intention in the human being. Its opposite, being dressed, is an intentional act. To be clothed is to be intentional about one's physical and mental presence. Asking **"Where are you?"** at pivotal moments in life throughout the generations is to invite layers of perspective and interpretation as a question of identity and even purpose.

Who Invented Shame Anyway?

3.11 "Who told you that you were naked?"

3.11 "Did you eat of that tree from which I had forbidden you to eat?"

God asks, **"Who told you that you were naked? Did you eat of the tree from which I had forbidden you to eat?"** What makes these successive questions remarkable is that they remain unanswered in the text. The presumption is that God already knows the answers and that humans must intuitively respond to the deeper concern behind the interrogation. Or perhaps there is an oversight, even a negligence, in answering this question. The humans hear God but choose not to respond. In either interpretation, the human being is called out.

If one reads the questions without the penetrating force of God's judgment implied in them, the human being could simply answer, "No one told us we were naked" and "Yes, we did eat of the tree which you had forbidden." Their lack of reply here is stunning. Perhaps there is a breakdown in communication. Human beings don't understand God here. How did they know they were naked? What does it mean for something to be forbidden to a human being?

Or perhaps the more accurate response here is that it is human nature to greet judgment with silence. We feel something for the human beings here. We feel their shame.

Interpretations of this question inspire a level of intimacy with divinity that should not be quickly overlooked. The purpose of the question moves toward a level of knowing that God desires, possibly even needs. Once the appellation of **"very good"**[6] is added, the human being has now become embroiled in conflict, one from which God seeks accountability. **"Very good"** is becoming a relative term. There is no other creature that defies its nature as the human being does. Even the deceitful snake doesn't seem to betray its nature. It is the human being who reacts to the snake's natural inclination. The human being, on the other hand, is capable of self-deceit.

There is a sense that answering this particular question is shameful both for the humans and for God. God commands and the human disobeys. The human is commanded and is susceptible to distraction. Both limits of power define the experience of humanity and the human understanding of divinity clearly. The lesson of these questions is that the shame in disappointing God is too great to bear.

The Genesis of Accountability

3.13 "What is this you have done?"

Authentic friendships are defined in part by the moments where we discover new truths or delight in the surprise of living together. The questions we ask of each other are ways to invite a connection to those truths we may not have discovered on our own. In other words, friendships are built upon a shared experience of the truth. And real friendships grow from mutual responsibility.

Intimacy deepens when God asks the woman, **"What is this you have done?"** The idea that God wants to be involved in the decision-making of human beings is novel both for the Torah narrative and in the development of human conceptions of divinity. Whether or not God understands the potential depth of human reasoning and emotional response, the desire to be present in those moments is an elegant construct of religious doctrine. The religious seeker may ask, "Where am I welcoming God into my midst, and where is God asking me the question 'What is this you have done?'" In other words, conscience is self-accountability.

The focus on the human being's reaction to God's call for presence here is equally compelling. What unfolds is more than a catalog of events (Snake tempts woman; Woman eats fruit; Woman gives fruit to man; God discovers violation of the rule; God expels humans from the Garden). The interplay of dialogue here introduces this partnership and relationship between humanity and divinity in ways we might not have imagined. The text leaves us considering the consequences of disobedience and the invitation to relationship through inquiry. If God were merely a judge here, there would be no need for the question.

God wants a response to inspire human accountability, to promote the human being as more than a creature subject to its impulses, suggesting that somehow the human being can transcend his or her nature, that the human being can grow through failure and aspire to divinity through accountability. God wants to be Eve's friend.

This desire for accountability is grappled with throughout the Torah. No longer is there a question of whether or not human beings should be accountable for their behavior, because this question introduces the eternal question of to what degree the human being is capable and willing to take responsibility for his or her actions. Friendship demands this.

Accepting the Divine
4:6 "Why are you distressed?" and *"Why is your face fallen?"*

As much as the questions in the Torah reveal insight into the human condition, the questions God asks reveal so much more about God's purpose with humanity. One enduring question we ask in every generation is "What does God want from us?"

The Bible interprets God as much more than the supreme source of power in the universe. Chapter 1 of Genesis covers that. The rest of the Bible contends with the relationship God will have with humanity.

At first glance, God's role in the opening chapters of Genesis is like that of an intimate and concerned parent. The story of Abel and Cain is simple on the surface. God accepts one offering and not the other. Where we would expect the outcome to be as benevolent as the deity who made the choice, Cain's face falls. And so God expresses concern for Cain by asking, **"Why are you distressed?"** and **"Why is your face fallen?"**

When God accepted Abel's offering over Cain's, we were introduced to another powerful human experience, that of rejection. The feelings of rejection are incredibly powerful, so much so that they can prompt even murder—as we are about to learn.

What we can also learn here before the fateful actions Cain takes against his brother is that divine concern is more than an absolute power seeking to persuade human beings to understand their purpose. We've learned that God cannot control human choice, as evidenced in the Garden. Here we learn that God cannot control human feelings either. When reading these questions, we may see God as benevolent, but aloof. But there is perhaps a deeper and more sincere interpretation. God wants to help Cain grapple with his feelings of rejection by talking about his feelings with God. Instead there is palpable silence. We have an obscure hint of whom Cain does speak with in the following verse. It says, "Cain said to his brother Abel," and then the conversation is lost to the text.

What would have been different had Cain responded to God when God asked him to express his feelings? The sensitivity of the Torah recognizes the human instinct to handle the feelings of rejection alone—even if it is God who asks the human to share his feelings! The consequences of Cain's loneliness are painfully expressed in the murder of his brother.

We can also learn from God's follow up to Cain's silence in these questions. When Cain fails to respond to the questions, God fills the empty space with wisdom of the human condition: **"Surely, if you do right, there is uplift. But if you do not do right, sin crouches at the door; its urge is toward you. Yet you can be its master."**[7] We could ask the text, "What if God simply allowed the space to be filled with silent support and understanding?" Or we could interpret God's response as the compassionate understanding of suffering. When suffering occurs, seeing reasons for the suffering and a possible response to that suffering can be therapeutic, even inspiring.

Keeping Tabs
4:9 "Where is your brother Abel?"

The terse construction of the Cain-and-Abel narrative doesn't properly address its emotional impact. Where this story comes to define the quality of a relationship between siblings in particular, and between human beings in general, the sheer paucity of description is surprisingly short. Compare this episode to those that involve Abraham, Jacob, and even Joseph to place into context the significance of this episode in the grand narrative of the Torah.

We read in the span of two verses that Cain spoke to his brother Abel. Cain kills his brother. The next verse immediately prompts God's inquiry **"Where is your brother Abel?"** Cain's terse reply, **"I do not know,"** piques our curiosity. The exchange consists of twenty-seven words in all.

The possibility that the body of Abel is unaccounted for without any sense of knowledge on Cain's part seems far-fetched. After all, we just read that Cain killed Abel. We have to presume this is a lie. The first great lie of the Torah is intertwined with the first murder of the Torah.

Yet there are levels where Cain's ignorance could very well be honest. Cain does not know what happened to Abel after he killed him, either physically or spiritually. Since this is ostensibly the first death in the history of humanity, Cain may have had no idea what it meant to take his brother's life. Moreover there may be no understanding of the threshold between life and death. This moment then reveals yet another dimension of human accountability.

Despite their brevity, each step of this story deserves attention, including God's question to Cain. Like the moment the human beings discover their nakedness in the Garden and God asks, **"Where are you?"** the question **"Where is your brother Abel?"** simmers with a familiar tone of divine knowledge and the quest for human accountability.

Perhaps this is all a lead up to the powerful question **"Am I my brother's keeper?"**[8] This is the first question a human being asks God. It's a penetrating question we now explore.

Who Are You to Me?
4.9 "Am I my brother's keeper?"

"Am I my brother's keeper?" asked by the first child born to human parents, is one of those questions that continues to elicit a prism of interpretive meaning today. The context of the question is Cain's murder of his brother Abel in the wake of God's divine favor for Abel's offering. Once again this question points to God, who inquires into the behavior of the human being by seeking justification, location, or identity. The question itself prompts further inquiry: "Is it rhetorical or is it genuine curiosity?" And at the center of this question is the desire to understand exactly where the relationship between two people intersects.

A simple answer to the question of the text would be yes! This response transcends political realities and reaches deep into the recesses of existence. There is no definition of a human being as a completely autonomous, self-sufficient entity. The Torah is challenging us to determine if we are really our brothers' keepers. When we feel rejection, when our sense of self-worth is diminished by our own perception or the explicit actions of another, caring for another is a betrayal of our sense of dignity. How painful it must be to answer this question when our own ego is wounded and vulnerable! Perhaps Cain doesn't answer his own question because his emotional wounds are too deep.

There is a possible alternative answer. When the answer is no, then the relationship between individuals, and even those closest to us personally, remains broadly defined. This is to say that we can share a story, even a place of origin, but how our lives unfold and how we find meaning and purpose in the world is not dependent upon any other. Unlike this focus on brotherhood, the focus on keeping one's brother is indeterminate. When loyalty and responsibility intersect, when we feel most vulnerable, there is a sense that our own protection is more valuable than our commitment to others.

This narrative is a creative response to a human dilemma, one that grapples with subjective notions of loyalty, concern, and care. The framing of this question through Cain's perspective prompts us to ask ourselves how we might respond. How are we our brothers' keepers, and what would it be like if we were only solitary beings who met each other in moments of need?

We must ultimately remember that this is not a question for us but a question for God. In fact, God does not answer the question, a crucial indication that God is not accountable to humanity in the same way human beings are accountable to God or to each other. The very notion that Cain would pose this question of God also indicates that divine knowledge is not yet known to human beings and their progeny.

Responsibility Is a Way of Being

4.10 "What have you done?"

When do we say our behavior is innate and when do we ascribe it to experience? More succinctly, how do we learn to be responsible? It is likely that responsibility is as much taught as it is intuitive. The Torah takes a great interest in distinguishing between the two.

After Cain kills his brother Abel, God asks, **"What have you done?"** There are echoes of God's voice in the Garden when God asks Eve a similar question. More than an omniscient being patiently awaiting a response, with this question God is trying to evoke a sense of responsibility. In the Garden, Eve blames her behavior on the snake. Here Cain doesn't respond at all.

Shouldn't Cain have known that taking the life of his brother was forbidden? Didn't his father Adam confront the consequences of forbidden behavior, prompting his expulsion with Eve from the Garden? Adam must have felt compelled to explain to his children where they came from or what the rules of living are. It's plausible that the story of expulsion came up once at the dinner table.

Cain's reaction to his brother Abel's offering is a shining example of responsibility to the other. If Cain didn't care in some way, he wouldn't have done anything. God's inquiry of Cain, **"What have you done?"** is more than a search for the details of the crime committed. All the more so, Cain doesn't respond with a sense of innocence, as if to say, "What do you mean, what have I done? I haven't done anything!" Cain's tacit acknowledgement that his action has prompted God's inquiry exemplifies this pivotal step toward the cultivation of responsibility. God is not simply dictating the proper behavior expected of the human being. God seeks an awareness that can only come when responsibility to other human beings is present.

Either Cain should have known what was expected of him, especially since his mother was asked the same question, or Cain genuinely does not comprehend the consequences of his actions, of murder and unrestrained jealousy. The repetition of the question, an extremely rare occurrence in the entire *Tanach*, suggests that Cain's behavior may not have been premeditated or comprehended. God's question doesn't need to be repeated.

Responsibility cannot be expressed once and reckoned with our merits in perpetuity. It isn't a chance occurrence. It is a state of being in which an awareness of our actions and their consequences is expected in every situation. We fail most when we can or should be responsible and avoid our duty.

NOAH

The absence of questions in this portion is not surprising. There are many interpretations of the purpose of Noah and the Flood story in the Torah. Raising questions about the moral implications of God's universal condemnation of humanity shockingly isn't one of them. God's absolute certainty in the depravity of human beings that prompts the plan to repopulate the earth with the descendants of Noah is a cautionary tale to demonstrate the power and might of God. We'll also read the short narrative of the Tower of Babel in these chapters, where a desire to discover divinity prompts a scattering of humanity throughout the world and different languages. There is no doubt expressed in either of these narratives. God doesn't question humanity. Noah doesn't question God. The people do not question the Divine Presence before building a tower to find God themselves.

This text is also confirmation that divine curiosity has its limits. God's promise to Noah and the rest of humanity, **"Never again will I doom the Earth because of humanity . . . nor will I ever destroy every living being as I have done,"**[9] is a statement of certainty that does not emerge from some conflict or conversation in the narrative. The tower story resolves with **"Let us go down and confuse their speech there, so that they will not understand each other."**[10] We will not see God's decisive behavior without human engagement in the rest of the Torah. In fact, we will see that the resolution of conflict in every other episode in which the disobedience of humanity vexes God includes some form of the interrogative. A lack of questions here might even raise our concern for how authentic these historical moments truly are as well.

LECH LECHA

12.18 "What is this you have done to me?" (Pharaoh to Abram)

12:18 "Why did you not tell me she was your wife?" (Pharaoh to Abram)

12:19 "Why did you say, 'She is my sister' so that I took her to be my wife?" (Pharaoh to Abram)

15.2 "What can you give me seeing that I am childless?" (Abram to God)

15.8 "How shall I know that I am to possess it [the land]?" (Abram to God)

16:8 "Where have you come from and where are you going?" (Angel to Hagar)

17.17 "Can a child be born to a man one hundred years old or can Sarah bear a child at ninety?" (Abraham to God)

18.12 "Now that I am withered, am I to have enjoyment—with my husband so old?" (Sarah to herself or to God)

The questions in this portion begin to outline definitions of the self. In general we will read in the questions of Pharaoh and Abram and the question of the angel to Hagar attempts to locate the power of agency in the human being. The shift in focus from God to humanity in the family of Abram introduces questions about the self, the complex identity of an individual. Here we are invited to consider what role God plays in the life of a human being. Does God control the actions of Pharaoh? Can Hagar's rejection be softened by God's caring presence? What does it mean for Abram and his descendants to "be a blessing?"

The Jewish Self

12.18 "What is this you have done to me?"

12.18 "Why did you not tell me she was your wife?"

12.19 "Why did you say, 'She is my sister' so that I took her to be my wife?"

After chronicling the repopulation of the earth following the Deluge and then recording the generations of Noah that followed, the Torah moves rapidly forward to the story of Abram. By the time we meet him there are well-established civilizations throughout the world. Abram is literally the one who "passes over," the one who journeys from East to West. More than from Haran to Canaan then to Egypt and back to

Canaan, he represents the one who brings culture and identity between the civilizations. He's a journeyman, an educator, and a proselytizer, presumably roles the world has never yet seen.

We read that Abram must travel to Egypt to procure sufficient sustenance. He does not return to his homeland in Haran, or modern-day Turkey. There would have likely been enough there as well. He goes from a place of famine to a place of bounty, and there may be the implication that his newfound wealth is somehow the result of Pharaoh's misperceptions or Abram's trickery.

When Abram instructs his wife Sarai to identify herself as his sister and not his wife, Pharaoh suffers from a plague inflicted on him by God for taking Abram's wife inappropriately. When the ruse is discovered, Pharaoh asks, **"What is this you have done to me?"** and **"Why did you not tell me she was your wife?"** and **"Why did you say, 'She is my sister' so that I took her to be my wife?"**

This litany can be read in light of the questions God asks Eve and Cain, but there is a shimmering difference in the addition of **"to me?"** to Pharaoh's question. It is the first question of the Torah one human being asks another. This is the first time that an individual confronts his own power or authority other than that of God or a parent. Even the litany of questions in this moment indicates a distinction between questions asked by God or to God. They are selfish, and we learn that there are authorities with whom we must contend that are not God.

More than the machinations of power politics, there is an important discovery being made here. Abram is not like other people. He is treated like royalty without any pre-ordained human election. He bears no qualifications to confront Pharaoh and Pharaoh's power but for his relationship with Sarai. He will emerge from the encounter with great wealth—hardly an ethical model we envision for acceptable social behavior. And yet his purpose transcends this sleight of hand. Abram's destiny is to bring a message to the world, one that Egypt will not learn throughout the entire Torah narrative.

It would be enough that this one encounter defined Abram's emergent social ethic, but we'll meet this challenge in the following narrative of Abimelech and even that of Abram's Isaac a generation later. Where we could surmise that the manipulations are dubious, the fact that the Torah presents the conflict in the form of questions reveals that trajectories of greatness are neither perfect nor sublime. They are human and selfish. Abram wants to protect himself and his family. The pharaoh doesn't want to suffer from plagues. The Jewish self emerges not from deviousness but from the path to accountability. Abram must learn to take responsibility, a quality that he will grapple with throughout his journeys and one that God will patiently test.

And God Responds: The Genesis of Legacy

15.2 *"What can you give me seeing that I am childless?"*
15.8 *"How shall I know that I am to possess it [the land]?"*

What marvelous imaginations we possess, with which we believe we can predict the future! Yet with our imaginations we also narrow the scope of possibilities. We may imagine a future beyond any possible realities, but even that is a function of our limited expanse. We imagine futures that we hope might yet be but are left with an uncertainty that such possibilities may not be realized. Hence we have doubts. A question safely enables us to enter into a space of doubt without compromising the grandeur of a perfected reality as we envision it to be.

Abram cannot imagine God's promise without progeny. Abram asks, **"What can you give me seeing that I am childless?"** and **"How shall I know that I am to possess it [the land]?"** These questions introduce the elusive promise of a legacy. If God's blessings are things, there must be someone to inherit the stuff when Abram dies. No one ever asked God a question like this before!

God promises to make Abram's descendants into a great nation. Abram doesn't accept the promise as it is given nor can he see the logical consequence of such a promise because there are no children, no legitimate heirs to his legacy. Here is where faith and reason meet: when the answer to a question may exist beyond the circumstances of the moment.

Standing in the awesome presence of divinity could overwhelm us into silence. Abram's question of God here is precisely one of these moments in which the balance shifts, when God is not the only inquisitor of human behavior because the human being now seeks to better understand the rules of existence. Abram is equally curious as to how God will fulfill his promise as God is entrusting Abram with this duty.

This covenantal moment deepens the initial command from God. If God does not respond to Abram here, the journey narrative unravels into an aimless search for this promise. That is why God responds with the promise **"Look toward heaven and count the stars, if you are able to count them . . . so shall your offspring be."**[11] More than a quantity of infinite value, to be a blessing presumes a measure of self-exploration and discovery that God no longer provides. God's promise to Abram cannot be fulfilled without the covenantal agreement, and Abram's imagination is limitless.

God Speaks to the Heart

16.8 "Hagar, maidservant of Sarai, where have you come from and where are you going?"

This question isn't about directions. And what's being communicated isn't formed with speech and sound. This question highlights that God asks in a way that speaks to the heart. God wants to know how humans feel, not necessarily how humans behave. When God, in the voice of an angel, asks Hagar, **"Where have you come from and where are you going?"** the implication is not that she answers with a description of her step-by-step journey from Abram's camp to a desolate forsaken place in the desert. Hagar's response highlights the implication. **"I am running away from my mistress Sarai."** Perhaps her explicit response is not so direct after all. Perhaps her circumstances emerge from a response to terror or fear and not simply a description of unfolding events.

Our first impulse is to consider Hagar an outcast, someone who does not belong in the family, so to speak. She's a concubine to Abram, despised in the eyes of Sarai. This exchange is remarkable because it introduces how God speaks with someone other than a leading character. We are curious about the language Hagar uses to respond to the angel. Was she speaking in Hebrew like Abram, or Egyptian, the language of her homeland? Moreover, what is God looking for if not prompting a response of location?

We learn here that God already understands what running away implies. Our reading of the text implies an understanding we have too. The distance Hagar makes in the space between herself and the tents of Abram is for her and her unborn child's protection. There is also an existential awareness that destiny may be written for us by a pen and ink in the hands of others. God's decision to continue Abram's legacy through the child eventually born to Sarai, and not the child Hagar will give birth to, must have been unsettling.

Once Hagar communicates with the angel, a well—literally a well of revelation, *Be'er Le'hai Roee*[12]—is shown to her. More than God's loving attempt to assuage Hagar's fear both by providing a well of water to nourish her body and a promise of her child's blessing to nourish her soul, this question reveals to us an important lesson. We are not meant to wander the desert without a sense of direction. Our lives and our futures depend upon it.

Would You Tell God You Don't Believe?

17:17 "Can a child be born to a man a hundred years old, or can Sarah bear a child at ninety?"

18.12 "Now that I am withered, am I to have enjoyment—with my husband so old?"

The irony of nakedness in the opening chapters of Genesis is that there is no reference point to induce any embarrassment for one's vulnerability. Nakedness prompts the question: Is vulnerability innate or learned? Here two moments reveal a sense of nakedness, in the form of barrenness, that can only be satisfied with divine response. The vulnerability of barrenness has not been explored between God and humanity at this point. We simply know Sarai is barren and feels shame when her perception of Hagar's pregnancy lowers her in the esteem of her maidservant.

But do Abraham and Sarah feel ashamed here? Abraham asks God, **"Can a child be born to a man a hundred years old, or can Sarah bear a child at ninety?"** followed by Sarah's question **"Now that I am withered, am I to have enjoyment—with my husband so old?"** We first read these as expressions of corporeal concern. Even later when Sarah posits in disbelief, **"Who would have said to Abraham that Sarah would suckle children?!"**[13] the point of reference for this vulnerability is not God. Ironically, it's toward Abraham and Sarah.

Even so, tone can dramatically change the impact of these questions. Is the tone like that of Abraham who will confront God before the destruction of Sodom? Is this the tone of laughter, expressed in response to an idea that seems delightfully beyond human comprehension? Is the tone one of doubt and is their curiosity a hint of their disbelief?

These questions invite all three possibilities and offer meaningful understandings of the text that follows and the pending arrival of Isaac.

If we read the questions as confrontation, Abraham and Sarah embody a cautious faith, one that invites conversation with God, even argument with God, but does not see how the rules of biology and nature can be overcome by God's omnipotence.

If we read the questions as those with levity, the disbelief is one closer to self-doubt than God-doubt. Their laughter is as much a veil for their own uncertainties in their abilities as it is incomprehensible.

If we read the questions with a doubtful curiosity, we are still met with a layer of meaning not easily gleaned from the surface of the text: the expression of limitation. The awareness that physical ability becomes limited as one ages is also a novel subject for the Torah. Here it appears that the experience of embarrassment is also a dissolution of innocence.

Lack of belief isn't an affront to divinity. On the contrary, divine knowledge is the recognition that what was once a limitation has now become a possibility. Without authentic doubt, limitations arrest a relationship. Through doubt, by contrast, even the possibility of bearing a child in old age is powerful enough to overcome shame and confirm one's faith.

Vayera

18.9 "Where is your wife Sarah?" (Angels to Abraham)

18.12 "Now that I am withered, am I to have enjoyment—with my husband so old?" (Sarah to herself or to God)

18.13 "Why did Sarah laugh, saying, 'Shall I in truth bear a child, old as I am?'" (God to Abraham)

18.14 "Is anything too wondrous for the YHVH?" (God asking a rhetorical question)

18.17 "Shall I hide from Abraham what I am about to do, since Abraham is to become a great and populous nation and all the nations of the earth are to bless themselves by him?" (God to Godself)

18.23 "Will You sweep away the righteous along with the wicked?" (Abraham to God)

18:23 "What if there should be fifty innocent within the city;

18:23 "Will You then wipe out the place and not forgive it for the sake of the innocent fifty who are in it?" (Abraham to God)

18.25 "Shall not the judge of all the earth deal justly?" (Abraham to God)

18.28 "What if the fifty innocent should lack five?" (Abraham to God)

18:28 "Will you destroy the whole city for want of the five?" (Abraham to God)

18:29 "What if forty should be found there?" (Abraham to God)

18:30 "What if thirty should be found there?" (Abraham to God)

18:31 "What if twenty should be found there?" (Abraham to God)

18:32 "What if ten should be found there?" (Abraham to God)

19:5 "Where are the men who came to you tonight?" (Townspeople to Lot)

19:12 "Whom else have you here?" (Angels to Lot)

20:4 "O YHVH, will You slay people, even though innocent?" (Abimelech to God)

20:9 "What have you done to us?" (Abimelech to Abraham)

20:9 "What wrong have I done that you should bring so great a guilt upon me and my kingdom?" (Abimelech to Abraham)

20:10 "What, then," Abimelech demanded of Abraham, "was your purpose in doing this thing?"

21:7 "Who would have said to Abraham that Sarah would suckle children?!" (Sarah to herself)

21:17 "What troubles you Hagar?" (Angel to Hagar)

21:29 "What do these seven ewes which you have set apart mean?" (Abimelech to Abraham)

22:7 "Here are the firestone and the wood; but where is the sheep for the burnt offering?" (Isaac to Abraham)

In this portion, the questions reveal nuances in the relationships between people and assert that our connections are not merely transactions. Even God contemplates God's own actions in relation to Abraham through questions in this portion, something we have not read before. And because questions in the Torah are presented in the face of uncertainty, the reader is encouraged to contemplate the implications of each episode with a spirit of faith.

Comparatively this portion has the greatest number of questions, twenty-five in total! In the evolution of faith chronicled by the Torah, the moments when doubt is most evident provide an opportunity for understanding and depth not readily apparent by a reporting of events. We need God to contemplate destroying Sodom and Abraham to protest so we may discover our own voice for justice. We need Isaac to inquire about the journey he makes with his father so that we may also learn to question our circumstances. Each question cultivates a sense of holiness, even of divinity, in our own identity.

Doubting Out Loud

18.9 "Where is your wife Sarah?"

18.12 "Now that I am withered, am I to have enjoyment—with my husband so old?"

18.13 "Why did Sarah laugh, saying, 'Shall I in truth bear a child, old as I am?'"

18.14 "Is anything too wondrous for the YHVH?"

There was a time when the patterns of the seasons and the changes in climate were attributed to an act of divine will. Now the human being has come to understand that such changes are subject to the forces of nature. Where the composition of the universe was seen as the embodiment of God, we now see the presence of atoms and gravitational forces as fundamental building blocks of existence. These discoveries do not limit God but comprise our understanding of what divine knowledge can mean.

This entire episode is built on doubt and uncertainty. The angel's question of Abraham, **"Where is your wife Sarah?"** is asking for more than location. Sarah's question appears pragmatic: **"Now that I am withered, am I to have enjoyment—with my husband so old?"** Her concern even prompts God to ask Abraham, **"Why did Sarah laugh, saying, 'Shall I in truth bear a child, old as I am?'"** After the interchange, the reader is left asking, "Does God act beyond nature?" The Bible would have us believe so. And while thousands of years of discovery have uncovered the predictability of nature, we are still amazed by what exists and marvel in our discoveries of what had always existed before we discovered it.

It is not completely far-fetched to suppose that Sarah could give birth to a child. We have empirically proven examples of women physically capable of giving birth to healthy children well into their later years of life. Perhaps the question isn't a concern of natural phenomena. Rather, Sarah is amazed by the possibility. The limit was manifest in her mind and not her body. God exists in amazement as well as nature. The response, prompted by God's question for humanity, reminds us of this.

Philosophers posit that God is discovered in the space that intersects the limit of human understanding and infinite possibility. Even millennia after the discovery of God in the Bible, and as the limits of human understanding continue to expand, we wonder if there is ever a limit to God's possibility. The question **"Is anything too wondrous for the YHVH?"** stimulates this curiosity. The question, posed in a voice of unlimited possibility—of God—prompts further discovery of where those limits still exist. We are left to wonder even more so who is God trying to convince.

The dilemma of divine comprehension is responded to in the Book of Job. After God lists a litany of natural activities as descriptions of divine power, Job responds by saying, **"I know that You can do everything, that nothing you propose is impossible for You."**[14] This interplay of the divine question of authority and human responsibility is a deep thread through biblical philosophy, the idea that human beings, despite their creativity and capacity to expand their understanding, will be inevitably humbled by the overpowering forces of nature. Our search constantly resonates with the most divine question: **Is anything too wondrous for God?** When human ingenuity reaches its limit, the answer, even for the most skeptical, is "Maybe not."

Does God Suffer?

18.17 "Shall I hide from Abraham what I am about to do?"

It's in human nature to form thoughts and meditations before they are expressed. There is a significant amount of energy devoted to the practice of honing what we feel to ensure that what ultimately becomes an articulation of those thoughts is carefully considered. Presuming to know the thoughts of God is audacious enough, let alone recording God's inner thoughts before they are communicated to Abraham. The premise of divine authority is that every thought and action is carefully considered regardless of the time it takes to measure the consequences. Ultimately we want to believe that God's justice is true, even if we cannot see it as it appears to us.

The entire episode between Abraham and God that transpires just before the destruction of Sodom and Gomorrah reveals extraordinary insight into the mind of God. In fact, the question posed here, **"Shall I hide from Abraham what I am about to do?"** may prompt Abraham's challenge. It reveals that God is uncertain of the circumstances of the people of Sodom and seeks partnership with Abraham to confirm the judgment. The very hint of hiding knowledge is also an act of shame, which we learn from the opening chapters of the Torah when Adam and Eve hide from God out of embarrassment. What this question reveals even further is that there is a sense of suffering that God endures as a result of the judgment to destroy the towns. Suffering here is the belief that what is true is not fully understood. This too requires human meditation and reflection. The sense that God is grappling with the potential for goodness in the face of total wickedness is something humanity will struggle with and suffer from as well.

This question is an enticement to think like God. Perhaps the most audacious statement the Torah can make is that the mind of God is something human beings can understand. While philosophers will contend such efforts are illusory, questions like this and even questions presented in the voice of God teach us that the attempt to understand God has a measure of sacredness to it. We are given permission to ask questions of God and especially of each other because God models that behavior.

Difficult Conversations with God

18:23 "Will you sweep away the righteous along with the wicked?"

18:23 "What if there should be fifty innocent within the city;

18:23 "Will You then wipe out the place and not forgive it for the sake of the innocent fifty who are in it?" (Abraham to God)

18:25 "Shall not the judge of all the earth deal justly?"

18.28 "What if the fifty innocent should lack five?"

18:28 "Will you destroy the whole city for want of the five?"

18:29 "What if forty should be found there?"

18:30 "What if thirty should be found there?"

18:31 "What if twenty should be found there?"

18:32 "What if ten should be found there?"

In the Torah, the election of Abraham as progenitor of a new monotheism is not predicated on questioning. The powerful words of Genesis chapter 12 hearken to a message of obedience and destiny. The words **"Go to a land that I will show you . . . so that you may be a blessing"**[15] imply a sense of command. Unquestioning command. Our interpretative instinct may well conclude that such a pronouncement resulted from questions Abraham asked himself, as if to say that the appearance of divine voice resolves all doubt.

This is how the famous parable was brought to exemplify Abraham as the quintessential inquisitor. Abraham is like someone who sees an abandoned mansion engulfed in flames and cares enough to call out for its owner. So he asks, **"How can there be a palace aflame with no one to attend to it?"**[16] Abraham is the one who discovers God's world aflame with all its imperfections and complexities and discovers God through a question. Once God saw someone who cared enough to seek the source of everything, an everlasting partnership between God and humanity was forged. Here, all Abraham needed was a prompt.

Talking to God involves a tremendous amount of self-reflection and moderation. When the voice of divinity is audible, how we translate and understand what is expressed can be an elegant model for listening to other human beings. But what happens if after careful and measured consideration we hear something wrong or disagreeable?

Many interpretations have been shared surrounding the essential questions of the story unfolding in Sodom and Gomorrah. When Abraham learns of God's designs to destroy the cities of Sodom and Gomorrah, Abraham offers his challenge to God by asking, **"Will you sweep away the righteous along with the wicked?"** and **"Shall not the judge of all the earth deal justly?"** The seeker challenges the one who urged him to journey through foreign lands and prevail over uncertainties to quell the world aflame with licentiousness and the mendacity of spirit.[17] The classical reading of this verse challenges the unlimited potential for power in a deity who is actively involved in the life of human beings. Will this deity be more than a concerned neighbor or a benevolent, but judgmental, monarch? The simple reading is one of righteous indignation, even naive logic, using the mechanics of human behavior in the face of absolute power. Abraham's challenge heralds the human being into the divine court and presents him as a clever and unfazed arbiter of divine justice.

God doesn't have to answer the questions. Like a parent who holds back a response to enable the child to discover the truth on their own, the absence of a response will enable Abraham, the seeker of justice, the one who sees the world aflame, to craft the response he would expect God to say. Instead God answers directly, **"If I find within the city of Sodom fifty innocent ones, I will forgive the whole place for their sake."** And so the negotiation begins.

"What if the fifty innocent should lack five?" "Will you destroy the whole city for want of the five?" "What if forty should be found there?" "What if thirty should be found there?" "What if twenty should be found there?" "What if ten should be found there?"

Taken alone, this line of questioning struggles with divine justice and the potential for divine privilege. Not only does the first question invite a complete response on its own, it also establishes a fundamental integration of divine and human purpose. Humanity is given the knowledge of good and evil as it was discovered by Adam and Eve in the Garden. Whether or not God is acting with righteous intent here, the drama of God's justice is played out in the human realm. These questions introduce doubt in the existence of such perfect judgment. The echo of God's question preceding this encounter suggests divine ambivalence as well: **"Shall I tell Abraham what I'm about to do?"** The perfection of God is discounted by this line of inquiry. More than Abraham's desire to know the nature of God, this question challenges the very purpose of God. If the purpose of God is to forge sacred relationships, we learn here that even divine relationships are built on the sharing of uncertainties and vulnerabilities.

There is a deeper implication here too. God has deemed the people of Sodom and Gomorrah wicked. Abraham infers at the very least that his nephew and his nephew's family should not be counted among the wicked. This introduces a level of unforeseen trust that human beings are as they have always been. Abraham knew Lot before they parted ways. Would the tale end differently if Lot had actively participated in the wickedness of Sodom? Abraham presumes Lot has not done so. This is his risk. Abraham is betting everything on the his belief that Lot and his family are still devoted adherents to the Hebrew God. As the story unfolds, we should not undervalue that God is taking a risk too.

This question is as much about the identity of God—who judges all the earth—as it is about Abraham. God's answer to Abraham isn't a petty errand in the face of absolute power. The question unlocks the prism of God's justice in the world, one that does not easily refract through a human lens. And yet God entertains the possibility of change and is even willing to compromise on the fewest number of righteous beings to underscore the message. The cities will be destroyed because no one who lives there is worthy of divine presence. The story is in the narrative to remind us of God's presence in the spirit of Abraham.

Care for the Stranger?

19:5 "Where are the men who came to you tonight?"

After the Flood, God promises that the world will never again be destroyed for its wickedness, implying that willful disobedience of the divine laws of human dignity and respect for all creation are no longer subject to divine intervention. God will be involved in the unfolding drama of the human condition, but without a Torah, without a mutual understanding of human responsibility, God can only create and destroy the world. It's up to human beings to make it more humane. This episode is all the more perplexing in light of that divine promise from generations past.

Through the episode of Sodom and Gomorrah, we learn that questions in the Torah are not reserved for the righteous alone. The question asked by the nameless figures of Sodom reveals another facet of the Torah prism. Questions can be coercive, even forcibly influencing the behavior of another. It may be the danger in such unbridled animosity that prompts God to destroy the towns.

The interaction between Lot and the townspeople helps us refine and smooth out the arc of the moral universe. When Lot urges the travelers to rest in his home, the townspeople, perhaps suspicious of this unconventional accommodation, ask, **"Where are the men who came to you tonight?"** We presume that the townspeople are seeking knowledge and the potential to formally welcome these travelers to the community. Reading the narrative preceding this moment validates interpretations that suggest Lot was concerned for the travelers' safety, but the plain meaning of the verses is not so clear.

Many interpreters of this question read it euphemistically in that the men of Sodom wished to act perversely with the visitors, particularly in light of the immediate response that follows. In the minds of the residents, Lot has claimed the visitors for his own pleasure, leading them to respond sarcastically, **"The fellow came here as a foreigner and now he acts the ruler!"**

The ethic of caring for the stranger, first exemplified by Abraham leading up to this moment, is sublime. Lot's response to the question affirms his loyalty to this ethic. While modern readers bristle with his proposed replacement of the strangers with his daughters and even his willingness to stretch the truth about their virginity to maintain this loyalty, a crucial part of the narrative includes this test. When the strangers, now known to be angels of God, pull Lot back into the house to protect him and his family, we see that God's loyalty is the shimmering difference that can even be found in the darkest place on Earth.

The Question of Connection
19:12 "Whom else have you here?"

Welcoming the stranger is a cornerstone of Jewish ethics. There are many examples of this in command form after the Israelites emerge in freedom from their slavery in Egypt. But Abraham's story has become the foundational text for hospitality and openness. Abraham doesn't know the three strangers who make their way to his tent from the desert are emissaries of God. He simply welcomes them in and provides comfort for them on their journey. Then they promise his wife will give birth, and they will journey on to initiate the destruction of the cities of Sodom and Gomorrah.

We might only consider this generosity of spirit to rest in a few select individuals, people who embody a sense of kindness and dignity that isn't intuitive to everyone. But the journey from Abraham's tent to the city of Sodom demonstrates the world is not filled with God's justice yet. God's vision and Abraham's actions demonstrate that all of us are responsible for sharing this kindness. So when the angels ask Lot, **"Whom else have you here?"** the implication is they want more than a roll call of family members.

As we read the angels answering the question for themselves without any response from Lot, even going so far as to include **"anyone else that you have in the city,"**[18] they are seeking another form of identification. We could imagine that the condition of a relationship with Lot is by birth, or marriage, or tribal loyalty. Morality isn't genetic though. What the angels are potentially asking here is "Who among you will show kindness, even if it is detrimental to your comfort?" Lot has shown he understands this precept. The angels want to know if he taught it to others too. As the city crumbles from its wicked constitution, Lot and his family are rushed out of the city both in honor of Abraham's righteous arguments with God and in respect of the essential value of welcoming and caring for the stranger in our midst.

One Covenant for Everyone

20:4 "O YHVH, will You slay people, even though innocent?"

20:9 "What have you done to us?"

20:9 "What wrong have I done that you should bring so great a guilt upon me and my kingdom?"

20:10 "What, then,' Abimelech demanded of Abraham, 'was your purpose in doing this thing?'"

One goal of the Torah is to introduce the unique relationship humanity will have with God. As such, we will revel in our triumphant moments of covenantal responsibility. Noah represents the only human who is worthy of covenant—even divine instruction—in his generation. Abraham represents a model, a way of being that is accessible to all humanity in his generation. Meeting someone like Abimelech along the way of Abraham's journey reveals the human imperative toward divine justice regardless of biological or cultural connections.

Abraham's resistance to God in the episode of Sodom and Gomorrah is not the only example of righteous disobedience. Others must also voice concern for human dignity for Abraham's concern to be manifest. We do not read the story of God's vindication of evil in Sodom as emblematic of the entire human race. To be Jewish is not to profess an ideal completely separate from the experience of the rest of humanity. The Jew is effective when they reveal the deeper wisdom of living *within* the minds and hearts of others. The episode of Abimelech and the series of questions that motivate it is the recognition that human innocence can be reconciled with a God who expresses a particular will for one person while expressing concern for all humanity.

Abimelech, like Malki-Tzedek,[19] is one of those foreign voices of ethical responsibility. We read that Abraham returns to the land of Canaan after his journey to Egypt. Still fearful of reprisal from the local authorities and unsure of his potential power and influence, Abraham indicates that Sarah is his sister and not his wife. The strategy for success in Egypt will surely work here, or so the thinking goes. God visits plagues upon Abimelech and his people as a result.

Abimelech's question **"O YHVH, will You slay people, even though innocent?"** echoes Abraham's complaint to underscore a vital development in the nation of Israel. The world can act with righteousness too. Will the models of God's chosen people conspire with or against the truths of all people? God finds Abimelech in a dream to assure him and his family of continued prosperity while protecting his chosen prophet, Abraham, and the future of his family.

Abimelech demands a response from Abraham: **"'What, then,' Abimelech demanded of Abraham, 'was your purpose in doing this** thing?'" Because the challenge is to Abraham, we find him being tested once again, this time by another human being. Abraham's ethics are challenged. While the intimation of his and Sarah's status is uncertain, this episode comes to reveal a vital truth: God's justice is not in the hands of any one human being.

By comparison to the previous episode where Abraham and Sarah deceive others, there is a subtle but important distinction between Abimelech's outcry and Pharaoh's through the questions they ask. Pharaoh asks for himself, while Abimelech asks on behalf of his tribe, **"What have you done to us?"** and **"What wrong have I done that you should bring so great a guilt upon me and my kingdom?"** The shift from self to collective cannot be underestimated. The belief that one singular individual is subject to God's will limits the capacity of God. If God exacts punishment upon an individual, the reason or purpose of this act will only remain located in the self. Here the inquiry into God's justice shifts from the self to a collective consciousness to reveal the capacity of Abraham's God. Such an expansion is crucial to understanding the value one God for all will have alongside the birth of a unique nation of Abraham's children, a value based on compassion and human dignity.

Who Is Asking?

21:7 *"Who would have said to Abraham that Sarah would suckle children?!"*

In our experience, floods of thoughts constantly enter our consciousness and dissolve into memory rapidly and without coherence. Purpose in life can be defined, in part, by capturing a fleeting thought to glean a sense of meaning and significance from it. Where passing thoughts can dissolve as rapidly as they appear, the Torah captures one moment in the life of Sarah that changes her life forever.

Sarah asks, **"Who would have said to Abraham that Sarah would suckle children?!"** When we read Sarah's question here, we note that this is the first question of the Torah that is ostensibly spoken by someone to themselves. Although questions of this magnitude are not absent from the Torah narrative, only a few made it into the scrolls.

Sarah is not in conversation with Abraham or God though they will eventually become involved in her struggle. Sarah's self-reflective inquiry reveals a feature of human existence that appears naturally. She just doesn't have the body for childbearing. So what will it mean for her to raise a child?

This question may be focused on the act of child rearing, another original concept the Torah has yet to explore. While self-reflection becomes evident in the identities of our biblical heroes throughout the generations, the act of self-reflection when giving birth to a child is deliberately explored here. It's not simply that a child will be born, it is the act of raising the child that defines what our biblical heroes cannot fully comprehend.

The articulation of Sarah's interior life, though, is also a glimpse into the human spirit. Our awe and wonder in this awareness of limitation and the capacity to evolve beyond it is equally inspiring and at times beyond comprehension. A well-examined life is celebrated by accepting this wondrous capacity to be more than ourselves, to exist beyond our limits, to grow into our potential.

What Is Divine Concern? Why Does God Care?

21:17 "What troubles you Hagar?"

Hagar does not receive as much attention as she deserves. She is, after all, the mother of the first child of Abraham. She is a grandparent to the children of Esau, Isaac and Rebecca's first-born child. Once she is cast out of Abraham's tent, she might be fated to oblivion.

But God takes notice of her unlike any other character in the Bible.

A parent instinctively expresses concern for a child whether it is in response to the child's vulnerability or a self-driven need to protect the child. Regardless of the impulse to respond to a crisis, concern for others is something learned. God's concern for Hagar is not sudden. God even promises Abraham that Ishmael and Hagar will be protected and that a great nation will also grow from Ishmael's descendants.

Posing concern in the form of the question is intentional. God cannot help Hagar or Ishmael without her response. This presents another theological dilemma. If God knows that Hagar is suffering, why would

God ask for her confirmation? Here the question reveals a level of care that we may not have seen from God before this moment.

God's concern is exemplary here. We can even derive ethical models from the sincerity God's angel expresses for Hagar in her misery. Posing the concern in the form of a question not only elicits a response, it also establishes the potential for deeper connections with the inquisitor. We ask because we care.

While the Torah text does not explicitly describe future encounters between Abraham, Hagar, and Ishmael after her banishment, the interpretive tradition recovers the absence of her part in the drama. One midrash has Abraham visiting Hagar and Ishmael several times following their banishment. There is even a strong tradition that Abraham's second wife, Keturah, is really Hagar, taking a new name for her new status.[20] All these responses are amplified by God's concern. If God had not demonstrated a concern for Hagar's well-being, it is quite possible we would not care either. Where God shows concern, our responsibility is even greater.

Where Did You Get Your Name?

21:29 "What do these seven ewes which you have set apart mean?"

The naming of things by God in the creation story reveals much about the purpose of the narrative and in some respects the function of God. God names time, distinguishing between day and night. God fashions the cosmos and calls the heavens "Sky" and the land "Earth." While every other aspect of creation is already named, the particular focus on what God has explicitly named and what the human being names sheds light on the divine partnership that is yet to unfold. Just as important as it is to determine what God explicitly names and what has already been named by the time we encounter it in the Bible, the specific names the human being gives and for what reasons shape the narrative profoundly as well.

There are select occasions in the Bible when there is a focus on the naming of a place based on the actions and behavior of its people. One such occasion arises in the question posed by Abimelech when he and Abraham strike a pact in the desert for the space where Abraham will eventually dwell. In response to Abraham's curious ritual of lamb separation, Abimelech asks, **"What do these seven ewes which you have** set apart mean?" Abraham replies specifically, **"You are to accept these seven ewes as proof that I dug this well,"** and the text comes in to clarify, **"Hence that place was called Be'er Sheva, for there the two of them swore an oath."**[21] There is also an explicit play on the word *Sheva*, which can mean "oath" and "seven" here, thus poetically enhancing the naming ceremony. Neither Abimelech nor Abraham name the place Be'er Sheva. It is a point of reference from another source, suggesting that naming of a place becomes relevant when its orientation is identified by someone who has little or no role in the act of naming.

The formation of this encounter as a question deliberately encourages us to seek out the meaning behind the names of other places too. There is power in the act of naming that should not be overlooked. The pact between Abraham and Abimelech is so significant that future visitors to and dwellers in the place will henceforth refer to the place by that name. But the name of the place does not describe its function. People in the Bible didn't go to Be'er Sheva to make oaths and certainly not in the present day. But the spirit of collaboration and common understanding shared in the place can inspire visitors to discover sacred connections as well.

One of the gifts of the Jewish imagination has been the power of interpretation and the permission to seek out and define names as fundamental to our understanding of our world. Places do matter. If Be'er Sheva, a modern-day city in the foothills of the desert in Israel, has an illustrious history, then every place identified with the presence of God and the oaths of God's servants is worthy of recognition too.

Questions Invite Connection

22:7 "Here are the firestone and the wood; but where is the sheep for the burnt offering?"

Can we fully share our personal spiritual drama with others? Or is our experience of transcendence a solitary journey in which our loved ones and fellows at best are passive participants? In Abraham's journey up the mountain to offer his son Isaac, God tests this balance between the realities of different human beings in the quest for divine connection.

Abraham's quest is toward the altar. What is Isaac's quest here?

Isaac's question to his father is remarkably simple. He asks, **"Here are the firestone and the wood; but where is the sheep for the burnt offering?"** If the journey is to connect with God, what is required to fulfill such a task? In those days, it was logical to kill an animal and offer it as a sacrifice to God. The pause between the question and response here fosters a chasm of interpretation. Whether or not Isaac inferred that he would be the sacrifice to God, the inquiry is presented to us as a dramatic unfolding of the relationship between parent and child. Where Abraham reveals and withholds information is among the most dramatic elements of the Akedah narrative (presumably with God as well). We assume Abraham doesn't want to disclose the nature of their hike prematurely and knows that his task is fraught with uncertainty. Abraham's response also confirms the vague sense of purpose he is to share with his son, as if to say that the goal is to follow God's instructions as they are given even if Isaac did not hear them being commanded.

To read this question as a deep exploration of Abraham's individual spiritual quest is to recognize that there is also a limit to his shared experience. Building a religious doctrine upon collective understanding, by contrast, requires an openness to share intention and purpose even when those goals are not yet completely formed. When collective understanding and openness are absent, we walk toward the altar uncertain we possess all the necessary gifts to make offerings to God. Isaac may be asking about a sheep, or Isaac may even be asking about himself. Or Isaac is seeking the most essential element of the religious experience, that of authentic connection. His father provides an extraordinary answer here: **"God will see to the sheep for His burnt offering, my son."** The next line is poignant: **"And the two of them walked on together."**[22]

CHAYEI SARAH

23:15 "My lord, what's 400 shekel between me and you for this land?" (Ephron to Abraham)

24:5 "What if the woman does not consent to follow me to this land, shall I then take your son back to the land from which you came?" (Eliezer to Abraham)

24:23 "Whose daughter are you?" (Eliezer to Rebecca)

24:23 "Is there room in your father's house for us to spend the night?" (Eliezer to Rebecca)

24:31 "Why do you stand outside when I have made room in the house [for you] and a place for the camels?" (Laban to Eliezer)

24:39 "What if the woman does not follow me?" (Eliezer explaining his dialogue with Abraham)

24:47 "Whose daughter are you?" (Eliezer to Betuel)

24:58 "Will you go with this man?" (Betuel, the mother, and Laban to Rebecca)

24:65 "Who is this man that walks from the field to come meet us?" (Rebecca to Eliezer)

Until this part of the Torah narrative, the primary concerns of life and death have been merely recorded as facts (**"These are the generations of . . . "**). These chapters will confront the end of Sarah's life, the procurement for Isaac's bride (Rebecca), and Abraham's later years and ultimate demise—all moments that embrace the sensitivity and complexity in the transitions of life. They have become a part of the narrative to deepen the psychological and sociological development of Abraham's family and legacy, concepts that can only be reflected upon when one's needs are fully met. In essence, Abraham is almost a complete person in these final verses that chronicle his epic journey. The comfort he has to contemplate his legacy is quite different from his acceptance of God's promises of his youth. The questions explored here are expressed with great uncertainty that the future will be even more secure than the present. One great lesson from this portion is that what begins with uncertainty concludes in love.

Defining Friendship through Questions

23:15 "My lord, what's 400 shekel between me and you for this land?"

We often meet in times of need people with whom we eventually develop meaningful relationships. These moments, when we are open and vulnerable, become opportunities for others to see reflections of our authentic selves. More than a revelation of ourselves to others, we can also see the truth of others in moments of uncertainty. At some point, the question "Who is this person to me?" comes into focus and comes to define who becomes our friend and who is an associate, a helper, or a stranger along the way.

Abraham's purchase of Ephron the Hittite's property is not simply a transaction to confirm ownership. There is a potential relationship emerging between the two that the verses of the Torah capture. This potential is revealed when Ephron asks, **"My lord, what's 400 shekel between me and you for this land?"** Rather than the record of a transaction, Ephron's question reveals a desire for a relationship, particularly since the question details **"between me and you."**

Classical commentary will pick up on this sensitive reading as well. Rabbi Shlomo Yitzchaki or Rashi the great Torah commentator, outlines the statement as one of friendship. Rashi writes, "Between two such friends as we are, of what importance is that? Nothing at all! Leave business alone and bury your dead!"[23] A few generations later, Ovadiah Sforno, another great Torah commentator, depicts this exchange as a minor transaction, stating, "It is so insignificant a matter that the acquisition can be made by a mere declaration without being recorded in a document."[24]

In both comments, the sense that the financial exchange is trivial compared to the magnitude of need reveals a social construct that is meant to build relationships. When matters of life and death come into focus, the mechanics of connections with others are less concerned with the transactional nature of relationships and more concerned with the integrity or dignity of being human. The focus on friendship, or in later episodes of this portion familial connections, is as important as our duty to care for ourselves and the people whom we define as of immediate concern.

With Perfect Faith

24:5 *"What if the woman does not consent to follow me to this land, shall I then take your son back to the land from which you came?"*

24:39 *"What if the woman does not follow me?"*

When defining perfection, without fail we quickly go to the absence of flaws or the fulfillment of a duty. An object or an action that is pristine may be perfect in construction, but perfection is a relative concept. The subjectivity of perfection is all the more evident in faith because faith is an inner experience measured by the way it is expressed. Perfect faith, should it exist, is when inner beliefs are consistent with external practice.

The story of Abraham helps us understand this best. Classical Jewish commentary focuses on Abraham's journeys as ten trials he must endure to validate his devotion to the God of All.[25] From heeding the call to travel to the land of Canaan to bringing his son to the altar, there are ten distinct moments when Abraham's faith is tested. We will even read that Abraham is **"blessed in everything."**[26] And yet Abraham's story doesn't conclude when the knife is lowered and he and his son return home from the mountain following the tenth test. We might presume that his success in achieving perfect faith enables him to enjoy the rest of his days without any tests. Abraham's blissful retirement should be a reward for his tremendous, and somewhat audacious, struggle to bring God into the world. God's promise to perpetuate Abraham's lineage through Isaac isn't complete, however, and Abraham's life isn't perfect yet.

So Abraham asks his servant Eliezer to return to Haran so that Eliezer may find a suitable wife for Isaac. Abraham is explicit in telling him, **"You will not take a wife for my son from the daughters of the Canaanites among whom I dwell, but will go to the land of my birth and get a wife for my son Isaac."**[27] Eliezer challenges Abraham's conditions by asking, **"What if the woman does not consent to follow me to this land, shall I then take your son back to the land from which you came?"** The question is quite logical. Eliezer can certainly find a wife for him, but the chances that she will leave her parents' home to journey to a distant land for a husband she has never met seems quite far-fetched. He will even repeat the question to Rebecca's father and brother: **"What if the woman does not follow me?"** affirming his concern for Abraham's apparently unrealistic expectations.

Abraham's condition that Isaac's future wife must return reveals a dimension of faith that we haven't grappled with yet. While Abraham's insistence implies his faith is immutable, it is the success of Eliezer's mission that reveals what perfect faith looks like. Abraham says, **"And if the woman does not consent to follow you, you shall then be clear of this oath to me; but do not take my son back there."**[28]

Abraham's sense of purpose is truly tied to God's promise. There is no compromise from Abraham here even though Isaac could have easily lived in Haran. Perfect faith is not necessarily the unflinching belief that our expectations will become reality. Abraham's perfect faith is that even if Eliezer cannot fulfill his command, there will be another way to fulfill God's promise.

Certainly Gracious

24:31 "Why do you stand outside when I have made room in the house [for you] and a place for the camels?"

One of the underlying themes of the book of Genesis is the abiding concept of hospitality and generosity: Abraham welcomes strangers into his tent; Abraham's nephew, Lot, brings strangers into his home and protects them from the menacing neighbors; Joseph hosts his brothers in the palace.[29] The attention to these moments at the entrances and exits are more than dramatic storytelling. There is an ethic of kindness here that becomes a hallmark of identity for the children of Abraham.

Rebecca's brother Laban is a great example of this generous spirit that has grown famous from Abraham's journeys so far. This is evidenced by Laban's greeting to Eliezer when Eliezer meets Rebecca and wants her to return to Canaan and marry Isaac. Laban first invites Eliezer into the home using the name of YHVH, **"Come in, O blessed of YHVH."**[30] He follows this greeting with a question: **"Why do you stand outside when I have made room in the house [for you] and a place for the camels?"** This moment could have easily been reflected as a statement of hospitality as if to say, "Come inside! And here's a place for your camels too." Rather, the exchange is recorded in the form of the interrogative to reveal deeper concerns in the act of hospitality.

"Why do you stand outside?" is an awkward construction for an invitation. On the surface, we might assume Laban's question is a playful attempt to put the guest, here Eliezer, at ease. One implication could be "You thought you were just a servant, but you are the trusted emissary of my uncle, the great Abraham, whose fame and influence have reached us here in Haran. Come on in!" There is also a tension in Laban's question. A sensitive reading may lead us to see some uncertainty in Laban's authority and role. Laban doesn't know who Eliezer really is. The Torah takes an interest in Laban's recognition of the gifts given to Rebecca by Eliezer, prompting his own greeting and gracious hospitality. An official of a monarch would not be challenged with a question to enter. We may also read this question as a gesture of opportunity. If Eliezer was generous with the gifts to his sister, perhaps there is more to share?

Through all of this, this concept of hospitality is a cornerstone ethic of the Jewish people, here reflected by figures adjacent to Abraham's destiny. Whether it is an expression of honor in the presence of dignitaries or the invitations of wayfarers and servants, creating a space for the other in the home is a practiced value the Torah wants us to recognize and emulate. While we may not pose questions to our guests upon welcoming them into our home, we can celebrate a value that transcends the individual and becomes an essential feature of a culture. Where we welcome guests, we welcome the presence of God.

To Know and Be Known
24:23 "Whose daughter are you?"
24:23 "Is there room in your father's house for us to spend the night?"
24:47 "Whose daughter are you?"

Great characters of epic tales are introduced to us either through a dramatic conflict or by heroic revelation. The Torah as a grand narrative will also identify the next hero, Rebecca, from a place of curiosity. Eliezer could have ostensibly found anyone along his journey to Haran to be a suitable match for Isaac, but Rebecca's kindness and attention will become the foundation of Eliezer's qualifications to bring home the right partner for his master's son.

Eliezer's acknowledgement of Rebecca in the questions of this section are proffered as more than the search for the convenient arrangement of a mate. When Eliezer first meets Rebecca, he asks, **"Whose daughter are you? Is there room in your father's house for us to spend the night?"** and later **"Whose daughter are you?"** The immediate succession of questions in the first instance implies that what Eliezer seeks isn't simply the satisfaction of demands for a wayward traveler looking for respite from his journey. Knowing that Rebecca's responses are going to change her life and the future of the Jewish story, we recognize that the manner in which Eliezer takes note of her is revealing. Eliezer wants to know how to relate to her. He's even going to reiterate his desire to relate to her when he recounts his journey to her father Betuel and brother Laban.[31] By seeing her, he is also noting that she is a member of a family, a branch of continuity that is going to bind Abraham's fate to the fate of the extended family. Indeed, the language of God is used by Laban to acknowledge the privilege of Eliezer and his mission.[32] Word of Abraham's magnificent wealth, the discovery of the God of All, and his mission to be a blessing to the nations of the world around him have reached the home front of Haran.

Seeing the face of the other is a bridge between darkness and light, between night and day, between us and them, even between stranger and kin. Eliezer finds in Rebecca's kindness (Heb. *chesed*) the conditions for his interest. His question also reminds us that kindness is focused and connected to the sacred bonds of family. The future family of Abraham's progeny and the discovery of God in all people depends upon values that are expressed for everyone.

Choosing God
24:58 "Will you go with this man?"

The evolution of human thinking recorded in the Torah celebrates the power in individual decision-making. Where collective will has brought harm to civilizations before (the generation of the Flood; the Tower of Babel; Sodom and Gomorrah), an emphasis on personal choice in the narrative is a God-given gift to be used wisely by the human being. The sway of parents, communal leaders, even society fade in the glow of individuality. Ultimately it appears that the Torah celebrates this power to choose.

As the tension between self-determination and collective responsibility tightens in the unfolding stories of the Torah, the choice of Rebecca and her future is an object of interest and concern. Rebecca's mother (unnamed) and her brother (presumably Laban) prompt Rebecca to choose by asking, **"Will you go with this man?"** Rebecca will be the one who bravely elects to leave her homeland to meet a man she has never seen to grow a family of her own. She is like her cousin, Abraham, who heeded the call of God to go from his land of birth to a place shown to him. Invited by Abraham's ambassador Eliezer, she trusts in his mission to guide her toward a brighter destiny. What courage she must have possessed to say yes!

The act of choosing may even have passed on to the expressions during the wedding vows. The act of partnership codified by the rabbis, called *kinyan*, is an innovation borne from the biblical tradition. The gesture of the groom turning to the bride and expressing his commitment to her is well known: *Haray At Mekudeshet Li*, "You are made holy to me." It is the central affirmation recited during a wedding ceremony. In modernity, women have been taking the same words and reciting them in response, *Haray Atah Mekudash Li*, to signify equivalence in the partnership.

As readers, we are certain Rebecca's decision will bring a bounty of blessing and prosperity though we know the consequences of her choice will be fraught with conflict and intrigue along the way. Rebecca's will cannot be certain without her own sense of faith. It's a different faith from that of our spiritual founder, Abraham. Like Abraham, she believes that her future will be a profound fulfillment of the divine destiny of humanity even if she is uncertain of the people and forces that will shape her journey. But uniquely, this is the fate of a life of self-determination. The Torah will continue to wrestle with this idea, like the wrestling that takes place in Rebecca's womb as a symbol of this struggle within all of us.

Love at First Sight?

24:65 "Who is this man that walks from the field to come meet us?"

Is there such a thing as love at first sight? Or is it the stuff of dreams and fantasies? We speak of it through stories of relationships that have blossomed over time. What defines "first sight," and is it even possible to identify love as it happens?

The first time the word *ahavah* (love) is used in the Torah unfolds here during the tale of Rebecca and Isaac's first meeting. Rebecca's question to Eliezer at the conclusion of their journey from Haran to Canaan, **"Who is this man that walks from the field to come meet us?"** prompts us to consider what she saw. Her tone can reveal so much more if we're able to listen carefully!

More than an opportunity for the Torah to show us the ways of courtship in ancient Israel, the text is revealing the sensitivity of human encounter. This is best seen in Rebecca's response. As she wraps herself in her veil to display modesty, we are invited to experience for a moment what love at first sight might be like. It's why the Jewish tradition focuses on this moment and likens it to every bride and groom who are about to meet before the wedding canopy. The bride veils herself in the moments leading up to the wedding canopy to separate herself from the attention of others and to focus her attention on the **"one in whom [her] soul delights."**[33] It's a gesture we express when the person we encounter is someone worthy of respect and deference. If there is such a thing as love at first sight, it is the act of covering oneself to see the other that this gesture models for us.

This question itself is definitional. It illustrates the kind of relationship Rebecca and Isaac will enjoy together. She does not simply follow Eliezer's lead to meet her groom. Her question affirms that the man she is destined to marry is one whom she relates to first. As we turn the page and learn the ways their journey is fraught with struggle, barrenness, jealousy, and favoritism, we won't forget this first great act. Rebecca's question for our text is more than an inquiry of identity (*Who is he to me?*); it has become a question of perpetual seeking.

Love at first sight happens when love is present in every sight.

TOLEDOT

25:22 "If this is my condition, why am I so?" (Rebecca to God?)

26:9 "How could you say 'She is my sister'?" (Abimelech to Isaac)

26:27 "Why did you come to me, seeing that you have been hostile to me and have sent me away from you?" (Isaac to Abimelech, Ahuzzat, and Phicol)

27:12 "Perhaps he will feel me and I will seem to him as a trickster and I will bring a curse upon me and not a blessing?" (Isaac to Rebecca)

27:18 "Who are you, my son?" (Isaac to Jacob or Esau)

27:20 "How is it that you found it [the meat] so quickly, my son?" (Isaac to Jacob or Esau)

27:24 "Are you really my son Esau?" (Isaac to Jacob)

27:32 "Who are you?" (Isaac to Jacob)

27:33 "Who [is it] that brought me hunted meat and came to me and I blessed him?" (Isaac to Esau)

27:36 "Was he then named Jacob that he might supplant me these two times?" (Esau to Isaac)

27:36 "Did you not reserve a blessing for me?" (Esau to Isaac)

27:37 "What can I do, my son?" (Isaac to Esau)

27:38 "Have you but one blessing, Father?" (Esau to Isaac)

27:46 "What good would life be to me?" (Rebecca to Isaac?)

The focus on the individual becomes acute in the chapters that chronicle the lives of Isaac and his family. It is remarkable to note that almost all of the questions found here include some form of the first person pronoun. This inward turn and outward articulation of experience becomes a consistent subject of interest in the Torah. How we identify our experiences in relation to the world around us comes to define our identity as members of a family and even as one in relationship with divinity. The fractals of interpretation emerge from these personal experiences and will help to identify the unique character and identity of the Jewish people.

Do We Doubt God or Ourselves?

25:22 "If this is my condition, why am I so?"

27:46 "What good would life be to me?"

Rebecca, the second matriarch in the family of Abraham, furthers the question of identity as she carries her twin children, Jacob and Esau, in her womb. She struggles with the difficulty of her pregnancy and she asks, presumably of God, **"If this is my condition, why am I so?"** The process of inquiry Rebecca expresses here is more than a question of temporary condition. She is reaching deeply into her very essence as a human being in the midst of her travail. Such a struggle should not be overlooked as the narrative of her family unfolds.

On one level, her question is logical: If our purpose is to perpetuate and multiply human life on Earth, is there a limit to the emotional and physical pain one must endure through the process of childbirth?

In other words, Rebecca seems to be asking what the definition of her purpose as a human being is. God's response, **"Two nations are in your womb,"**[34] may or may not offer comfort to her existential complaint. It is remarkable, however, that the response here is not just that she is having twins but that the children she is yet to bear are two distinct and separate nations. The answer to her question is that her purpose is more than her own devising. Indeed, the purpose of posing her question here is to produce an answer that she could not determine through her own reasoning. I imagine Rebecca would have been deeply concerned yet profoundly honored to fulfill such a role, to be the mother of two nations. Since we do not have a record of her ongoing conversation with God after she asks her question, we invite the kaleidoscopes of interpretation to offer meaning in her response.

On one level, the question emerges from anxiety carried over from her barrenness. If the purpose of the human being is "to be fruitful and multiply," then what could possibly be the purpose of an individual who cannot bear children or one who understands her covenantal responsibility but her biological condition prevents her from fulfilling it? The question is borne from uncertainty here.

This perspective is consistent with another question Rebecca asks, after Jacob flees from home: **"What good would life be to me?"**[35] This question is expressed as an elusive apology for sending Jacob to Haran to find a wife from her homeland. The intention and thrust of the question reveal as much about Rebecca's doubting conscience as they do the human element of self-preservation through our children's identities.

Who Are We to Tell Stories of Our Ancestors' Lies?

26:9 "How could you say, 'She is my sister'?"

Abraham's manipulation of Pharaoh[36] and Abimelech of Gerar[37] with regard to Sarah's relationship to him is often glossed over in the classical commentaries because it is morally dubious. Rather than challenge the premise, we read elegant rationalizations for his actions that prioritize fear of death over the ethic of responsibility. If the Torah teaches us anything here, it is that the act of lying has enduring consequences.

45

We meet Abimelech once again when Isaac is digging his father's wells in the desert around Be'er Sheva. Abimelech can either be the same man Isaac's father encountered through his journey in the land of Canaan or he is a typology, a chief of tribes representing a world tangential to the Abrahamic covenant and heroic encounters with the universal God. When Isaac dwells in Gerar and meets Abimelech, he first repeats the same trope his father rehearsed regarding his mother a generation earlier by indicating his wife, Rebecca, is his sister. When Abimelech himself discovers Isaac consorting, literally, "playing," with Rebecca in the camp, Abimelech confronts him and endeavors to understand the blatant lie. When Abimelech asks, **"How could you say, 'She is my sister'?"** the demand for understanding isn't simply interpersonal, indicated by the interrogative "how." Here Abimelech wants an explanation for Isaac's choices. If he is the same person, he surely must have remembered the same experience with Abraham just years before! Isaac's response for fear of his life isn't a sufficient answer to this either.

More than the intimation of deception that is implied in the patriarchs' journeys to holy encounters with God, it is the recognition by others that there is a truth the children of Abraham must be accountable to. Abraham used the rationale of a half-truth to justify his deception. Isaac will explain clearly to Abimelech his own reason was fear. For us, we have to recognize the capacity to lie exists within us. In both circumstances, it will be God who promises Abimelech will be protected as the whistle-blower of their deceit. How Abraham and Isaac become accountable to God for this remains a curiosity for interpretations to explore.

Purposeful Complaint

26:27 "Why did you come to me, seeing that you have been hostile to me and have sent me away from you?"

If the Torah only narrated the triumphs of heroes, the vast experience of life would be relegated to the shadows of being where truth and doubt lurk, ever fearful of validation. Instead the text reveals the evolution of the human spirit through characters who struggle in life. Isaac's and Rebecca's lives are anything but idyllic though they are biblical heroes. They are powerfully real.

Some of Isaac's struggles are revealed through his encounters with Abimelech. When regional struggles over water rights appear to be the focus of concern for Abraham's son and the fulfillment of the promise to be a **"blessing unto the nations,"** Abimelech seeks a common understanding with Isaac as he did with Abraham. Yet Isaac's suspicion of Abimelech reveals much about the challenges we confront among strangers when he asks, **"Why did you come to me, seeing that you have been hostile to me and have sent me away from you?"** Directed to Abimelech and his chiefs, Isaac is first reacting to the perception of territorial dispute. Posing this question, Isaac seems to want an answer he has already surmised on his own. His interpretation of their hostility prompted him to distance himself from his neighbors, and their visit to him seems unnecessary if not an act of provocation.

Abimelech's invocation of Isaac's God in response to the question is more than political theater.[38] He's communicating a shared language of responsibility. Abimelech doesn't answer Isaac's question with a rationale for the herdsman of his clan. Rather, by invoking God's name he hopes to strike a pact. And as a result, they reach an agreement and share a meal.

Isaac's concern here validates the faithful expression of conflict and resolution. This is a question of turning a stranger into a friend. Where Isaac's suspicion is prompted by Abimelech's herdsman's actions, Abimelech's focus on the God of Abraham demonstrates that trust can be built upon the common goals of responsibility and equality. The episode is included in the Torah precisely to teach us that trust located in the God of Abraham and Isaac can establish common understanding and even mutual economic and social benefit. If our complicated biblical heroes can reach such conclusions to build confidence among strangers, we might be able to as well.

Trust Your Instincts

27:18 *"Who are you, my son?"*
27:20 *"How is it that you found it [the meat] so quickly, my son?"*
27:24 *"Are you really my son Esau?"*

Didn't Isaac know Jacob brought him the meat for the blessing? Even with all his disabilities and Rebecca's clever costume design, the very nature of Isaac's questions here imply a measure of doubt based on his suspicion of the truth. When questions are framed by doubt, they are often a confirmation of what is already known.

We may even read the question more deeply, seeing **"Who are you, my son?"** as a question of identity. Isaac doubts that Jacob is Esau and asks with profound depth about his son's character: "Who are you, Jacob, to deceive your father and steal a blessing from me?" And Jacob responds with an outright lie. **"I am Esau, your firstborn."**

The power of this series of questions transcends the dramatic episode they are situated in. One core message of this story is the identification and confidence we place in the heroes of the Torah to discover the truth and the harrowing realization that such truth can be disguised, here in a furry coat of sheepskin. The Torah of these questions is that the truth is not always as it appears. How we respond to the truth that is revealed to us, even with our doubts, defines our character. This episode isn't merely recorded to teach us about the conflicts between Isaac, Rebecca, Esau, or Jacob alone. There is a deeper message here of trust and truth. There is a sense that truth can exist where you trust it to exist. Isaac's blessing of Jacob may be more connected to his trust that Jacob will do the right thing with the blessing than his mistrust in Jacob's deception.

Naturally this provokes a dilemma in the mind of the reader. In whom do we trust? Even in the moment when God's divine blessing is to be evoked, we cannot rely upon God for confirmation. This becomes a watershed moment in the life of the family of Abraham as well as in our own development as responsible people in our day. Even with the proximate intimacy of our ancestors with the God of Israel, we are learning that the experience of trust and truth transcend divine intervention. God's will is for humanity to choose and act in accordance with the laws of dignity for all of creation. In this story, Jacob's lie and Isaac's willful blessing despite his doubt validates human agency. The fact that God does not intervene is a profound realization that God's beloved children will make choices without a guiding hand.

Despite all this, the moment leaves us grappling with the dilemma of a future built upon deception. We will contend with it until Jacob wrestles a blessing from the angel a lifetime later. Then the blessing of the future will rest.

Blessing Wrestlers

27:32 *"Who are you?"*

27:33 *"Who [is it] that brought me hunted meat and came to me and I blessed him?"*

The repetition of the question, **"Who are you?"** this time asked of Esau, underscores Isaac's piercing inquiry into his children's identities. The sensitive reader might wonder why Isaac would need to pose this question, especially if he believed the past visitor was Esau. Even if we surmise the question is framed by surprise because the voice is Esau's and he thought Esau was there earlier, what prompted him to ask the question at all?

Isaac wants to know where his blessings will end up.

Behind any question framed as **"Who are you?"** is the prepositional phrase "to me" that is implied. One cannot ask for identity without some correlation. Frequently there is some fear latent in the request, as if to ascertain whether the object of concern, the "you," is a threat or an ally. How terribly disturbing it is that a father poses the question to both of his children, separately and potentially in succession borne from a sense of threat?

Interpretations cast Isaac as a simple-minded, traumatized, self-centered soul near death, easily manipulated by those around him whom he should trust. **"Who are you?"** is not a question of trust. It's another example of Isaac's traumatized spirit. The young man nearly sacrificed by his father in the name of God is now responsible for conveying the blessing of this God to his child, and he's mortified by what that implies. Will his children ascend the mountain to kill each other? Their progeny? Him?

Perhaps Isaac's intentions can be read differently. It is possible that Isaac fully understands the power and significance of God's blessing based on his own experience with the divine in his life. He intentionally reserved the innermost blessing for Esau because it is associated with strength and terror (or fear and trembling). That's why he'll reassert his curiosity by asking, **"Who [is it] that brought me hunted meat and came**

to me and I blessed him?" The question may be asked with a trepidation unrecorded by the text.

Jacob, the more delicate child, was being sheltered by Isaac's preference. The very nature of Jacob's wrestled blessing reveals a deeper truth of the emerging psyche of the Israelite. Blessings are given through the overcoming of obstacles—of confronting the challenge and seeking a path of human and divine partnership. We may even come to celebrate Jacob's actions because it is through his tenacity and resolve in confronting the perceived terror and awesome power of God that he is capable of wrestling the innermost blessing of divine partnership and unconditional love.

What About Me?

27:36 *"Was he then named Jacob that he might supplant me these two times?"*

27:36 *"Did you not reserve a blessing for me?"*

The episode of Isaac's blessing for Jacob emphasizes the painful consequences of election, all the more so when the prize is God's benevolence. More than the collateral damage Jacob's actions will shape for future generations, the intensity of Isaac and Esau's discovery of the stolen blessing is poured out onto the scroll as a pinnacle of emotional trauma.

The successive questions posed by Esau here evoke a sense of conflict with the entire nature of blessing and destiny. Esau will cry out, **"Was he then named Jacob that he might supplant me these two times?"** and even more succinctly, **"Did you not reserve a blessing for me?"** to capture his father's attention. In this moment, our glimpse into Esau's pain is a psychosomatic tug on our own hearts. Esau's need to be loved reflects our need to be recognized and loved as well. Jacob's subsequent escape from any confrontation with Esau amplifies the silence that bloats the absence of blessing—the sting of rejection. We can sympathize with Esau's pain even though the force of the narrative will ultimately flow in Jacob's favor.

The story of Jacob is more than an epic tale of election and legacy. Indeed, one primary reason we learn from the pivotal moments in his life is to inspire our own capacity to change. Jacob is the one who capitalizes on his brother's hunger, deceives his father for a blessing, discovers God in unlikely places, and grows a family brimming with conflict, manipulation, and loss. The Jewish people are called the Children of Jacob not simply because his father bestowed God's blessing on him and the biological links between his children and ours endure but because we are the descendants of a complex struggle with divinity and autonomy that is constantly tested throughout our lives. Through Jacob's journey, we are constantly prompted to ask ourselves, "Can we change too?" For Esau, and perhaps his parents who found his choice in life partners disappointing,[39] the lack of change in the face of a moral imperative is crucial to the blessings bestowed by God and parents to the children of Abraham.

Our legacy, then, is the recognition that destiny is not history—that the past is not the future. Only change confirms this.

There's Always More Than One Blessing

27:37 "What can I do, my son?"

27:38 "Have you but one blessing, Father?"

Unlike other biblical characters, Isaac's identity reflects the quiet resignation with which he confronts his life. We meet him outside his mother's tent as his father's servant brings his wife to him. We watch him wander in the desert digging his father's wells and surviving on the benefits of others. He summons his son to bring him meat so that he may bestow a blessing upon him. It should not surprise us when he raises his hands in response to his beloved son's pleas and asks, **"What can I do, my son?"** There is only one divine blessing, or so he understands. And yet his acquiescence makes our conscience shudder.

We can read this episode with compassion for the son who was almost sacrificed on the altar of absolute faith. Destiny seems to have been written for Isaac. He is not the author of his life or his legacy. Yet there is a deeper human quality of responsibility that we can glimpse in our own psyches. It is the nagging suspicion that we are not in control despite our most creative selves. And still we resonate with the defiant spirit within us that compels our faith that our actions do matter. We want to take hold of Isaac and remind him *there are more than enough blessings for everyone!*

It is why Esau's powerful supplication to Isaac leaves us all the more unsettled. **"Have you but one blessing, Father?"** is not only a question for the faithful who plead for divine favor knowing their fate has been sealed, it is also a referendum on the notion that one God elects only one person to be blessed. Moreover, Esau does receive a blessing from his father but is left dissatisfied with the gesture, perhaps because his brother is implicated there too.[40]

Jacob's journey may ultimately become the courageous decoupling from the misguided perception of a singular blessing from God. In fact, the answer to Esau's question in our minds is a resounding no! And still the biblical narrative will continue to unfold and reveal that God's election grows from an individual to a nation and ultimately to the entire family of humanity.

VAYETZE

29:4 "My brothers, where are you from?" (Jacob to the sheepherders)

29:5 "Do you know Laban, son of Nachor?" (Jacob to sheepherders)

29:6 "Is he well?" (Jacob to sheepherders)

29:15 "Just because you are a kinsman, should you serve me for nothing?" (Laban to Jacob)

29:15 "What is your wage need?" (Laban to Jacob)

29:25 "What is this you have done to me?" (Jacob to Laban)

29:25 "Didn't I work for you for Rachel?" (Jacob to Laban)

29:25 "Why did you deceive me?" (Jacob to Laban)

30:2 "Can I take the place of God, who has denied you the fruit of the womb?" (Jacob to Rachel)

30:15 "Was it not enough for you to take away my husband, that you would also take my son's mandrakes?" (Leah to Rachel)

30:30 "When will I provide for my own house too?" (Jacob to Laban)

30:31 "What can I give you?" (Laban to Jacob)

31:14 "Will we still have a portion of our father's inheritance?" (Leah and Rachel to Jacob)

31:26 "What did you mean by keeping me in the dark and carrying off my daughters like captives of a sword?" (Laban to Jacob)

31:27–8 "Why did you flee in secrecy and stole from me and did not tell me?" (Laban to Jacob)

31:30 "Why did you steal my god[s]?" (Laban to Jacob)

31:36 "What is my transgression, what is my sin that you pursued after me?" (Jacob to Laban)

31:37 "You rummaged through my possessions, where have you found all of your possessions?" (Jacob to Laban)

31:43 "What can I do for my daughters today, or the children they have borne?" (Laban to Jacob)

The pivotal shift in the chapters of this portion is found in the way the story is being told. The focus on Jacob's journey has expanded beyond the singular narrative of the family of Abraham where even the occasional side narrative of pharaohs, tribal leaders, or nephews is in relation to Abraham's experience. We learn as much if not more about Jacob's father-in-law, Laban, and his wives, Leah and Rachel, in these chapters and even more in the questions they ask. As Jacob grows prosperous, questions of sufficiency and loyalty to all that he has acquired are reflected by others' actions and reactions to Jacob's evolving soul as well.

What is most remarkable is that the conversations between humanity and divinity are no longer direct but are manifested only in dreams. There is no actual dialogue between any of the characters and God in these chapters. As the voice of God recedes, or transforms, into the interior voice of humanity, the questions posed here reveal just how much conflict and uncertainty can exist between people and ultimately with one's relationship with God.

Where Are You From?

29:4 "My brothers, where are you from?"

Jacob sets out to return to his ancestral home in search of a mate, in search of Rachel. When he heads toward the land of Haran, the childhood home of Abraham and his mother, Rebecca, he meets a group of sheepherders by the mouth of a well. Jacob asks them, **"Where are you from?"** Their response, while geographical in description, is also designed to cultivate a relationship. The question is not merely placed in the text for Jacob to ask for directions. Rather the purpose of the question is to confirm his expectation that he has approached the land of his ancestors. Here Jacob is attempting to identify the place where his people originate, and he is also trying to determine who his people are. By asking for Laban, Rachel's father and his uncle, he is beginning to identify his place among this family. The concept of distant cousins is a novelty. The suggestion that family extends beyond a geographic boundary opens up a possibility to learn about shared values and to distinguish the varieties of familial connections. This simple question will set the stage for the moment when Rachel and Leah travel to Canaan with their father's idols. But there is much to explore and discover before that part of the journey is revealed.

Jacob has fled his father's home. He was sent by his mother, Rebecca, to return to her native land, to the native land of Jacob's ancestors. Like them, Jacob must in some way connect his root identity with a place, a specific location that will define some parameters of his personality and his potential. The Torah is quite clear that the journeys of our patriarchs must in some way pass through the ancient homeland of Haran. More than a pilgrimage to his past, Jacob's journey to Haran is to try and fulfill what his father and grandfather had not yet achieved, that of a fully confederated tribe. The return to Haran is a test for the patriarch. Can the identity of this new family exist among the families of the world? It will be through Jacob that a *people* is born. His own growth and development as an individual will become a cornerstone of values for a people, for a nation.

When Jacob asks this question, we are invited to explore its subtleties too. He might have asked "Where is my family?" or "Where will I find the family of Abraham or Rebecca?" These are questions that imply a predetermined connection. By asking **"Where are *you* from?"** Jacob is searching for his own location through their identity. It's helpful to add here that the determination of family or tribe is necessarily built in relation to others—in whom we are most like.

The narrative unfolds with Jacob's connection to his ancestral family and the eventual separation from them. Laban's joyous proclamation

"You are truly my bone and flesh"[41] is an affirmation that Jacob belongs to him, the family, and the tribe. And yet Jacob's own family will become ardent monotheists, rejecting the idols of his father-in-law to separate from him and to return to the land of Canaan. Becoming a people, then, is as much about self-determination as it is about distinguishing a group from its neighbors. Indeed, this is a core feature of Jewish identity: we are constantly striving toward who we might yet be.

Family in More Than Name
29:5 *"Do you know Laban, son of Nachor?"*
29:6 *"Is he well?"*

The beginning of Jacob's life in Paddan-aram, or Haran, represents another dramatic shift from the previous stories told of our ancestors. The stylistic change transcends documentary hypotheses or even scribal flourish. The goal of the story from this point forward, and potentially in the remaining chapters of the book, is to expand the depth of Jacob's worldview. The other biblical characters blend into the background of Jacob's life. (Perhaps this is the gift of a blessing from God in becoming the central character in the story of our lives.)

When Jacob arrives in the area of Haran, he needs to locate himself while the readers need to locate themselves in Jacob's drama. The questions posed by Jacob reveal the mundane experiences of living, but they also elucidate the crucial significance of what is unfolding.

Jacob's relationship with the sheepherders is illuminating. First we learn that Jacob is unafraid of seeking help to accomplish his goal. He could have easily observed the behavior of the sheepherders and accumulated sufficient information to determine this was the place he needed to be. Instead these innocuous interrogatives are intended to build a relationship with Jacob's extended family. When Jacob asks, **"Do you know Laban son of Nachor?"** and **"Is he well?"** he is demonstrating a level of concern that typifies the children of Abraham. Indeed, Jacob's expressed concern reveals that, though he was once seen as a manipulative, self-centered, and petulant twin, he is now showing some signs of empathy, some recognition that the world does not revolve around him and his own concerns. While not the subject of this study, the fact Jacob seeks

Laban as a child of Nachor, his grandfather, and not Betuel, his father, may also expand Jacob's sphere of concern when trying to make a connection with the sheepherders. Nachor's reputation is multi-generational, something Jacob may not have seen as a value before.

This is why the story shifts in tone. Jacob goes from a tent dweller to a wanderer when God suddenly appears to him, to this moment when he seeks to locate himself in relation to others. Jacob will become the patriarch and the model of human becoming by his recognition that he needs the world as much as it needs him. We learn from these questions as well so that we may more fully become a part of Jacob's drama. It isn't simply that Jacob asks questions that we would ask. It is that Jacob's questions and the unfolding definition of his identity that we will read in the following verses give us permission to see that Jacob's growth will inspire us to grow as well.

Biblical Occupations

29:14 "Just because you are a kinsman, should you serve me for nothing?"
29:14 "What is your wage need?"

The subjects of work and compensation are a crucial part of the Torah's legal and historical record. The concept of slavery dominates the narrative of identity and becomes a core theme that defines the nation of Israel. The treatment of the worker will be prominently interspersed throughout the codes of law that follow. While archaeological and historical data are replete with arrangements between master and servant, boss and employee, Laban's question to Jacob here introduces a social expectation of working relationships that should not be readily overlooked. The question **"Just because you are a kinsman, should you serve me for nothing?"** immediately followed by **"What is your wage need?"** introduces a dimension of negotiation not only inherent in the characters involved in the narrative but also featuring a cultural expectation that becomes a hallmark of Laban's worldview.

"Just because you are a kinsman, should you serve me for nothing?" This statement is laden with assumptions about the relationships families maintain. Moreover, Laban is comfortably shattering those assumptions to invite Jacob's participation in his family dynamic. The invitation is so open that Jacob's intentions for Rachel become a fait accompli. The dramatic turn of events when Jacob discovers that he's married Leah and not Rachel first also looms in the background. Even if the reader encounters this dialogue without the knowledge of what is yet to come, the very implication that the standard is being tested is evident.

It isn't like Jacob will be working at a local fast-food restaurant for his uncle! These questions, like the ones surrounding Jacob's growing identity that precede them, are posed not as questions of clarification. These questions instruct us to cultivate a relationship with both Laban and Jacob that transcends the transactional nature of the words themselves. We must ask how Laban's questions help move the Torah narrative along. Laban is one of the most underrated characters of the Torah, not only for his manipulations of Jacob's spirit but also for his profound lack of trust. His role in the Torah is nonetheless essential, for without him and the invitations posed in these questions, Jacob would never become the patriarch promised through his blessings from God. Laban is an agent of redemption, and the negotiation for Rachel's hand is an impetus for Jacob to serve his uncle for something greater than himself. Indeed, Jacob's journey to living with his soul begins when he requests Rachel's hand in marriage and her father agrees.

Cleverness and Kindness
29:25 "What is this you have done to me?"
29:25 "Didn't I work for you for Rachel?"
29:25 "Why did you deceive me?"

In the late twentieth century, Rabbi Abraham Joshua Heschel was famously quoted as saying, "When I was young, I admired clever people. Now that I am old, I admire kind people." We're quick to focus on the qualities of kindness and what makes them worthy of admiration and to view clever behavior as an immaturity to overcome. While this has a certain truth to it, the innate human quality of deception, particularly to gain some advantage, is something the Torah brings into focus. The drama of Jacob's narrative is that the deception that surrounded the blessing by God from his father, Isaac, is counterbalanced by the deception he experiences from his uncle, Laban, when he learns that he has married

Leah in place of Rachel. After all, Laban proclaims upon meeting Jacob and hearing of his story that brought him to Haran, **"You are truly my bone and flesh."**[42]

Jacob's past experience should have prepared him for Laban's potential switch. Jacob knows what it means to be clever and what it means to withhold complete information for his own benefit. Jacob persuaded his brother to sell his birthright. The level of cunning and forethought needed to even propose such a scheme reveals the inherent nature of human beings to strive for self-preservation even at the expense of those closest to them, here a twin brother.

But Jacob does not see this one coming. What happened?

Perhaps the journey to Haran by way of Beth El changed Jacob. Jacob is beginning to bring trust into his world. God's presence with him inspires his confidence. When Jacob asks Laban in succession, **"What is this you have done to me?"** and **"Didn't I work for you for Rachel?"** and **"Why did you deceive me?"** the thrust of his concern isn't merely a factual response. Laban certainly provides a logic for his decision. Jacob is asking a deeper question that implies "I have lived a life of deception but I am changing. As I see the world filled with kindness and with God's blessing, why would you deceive me?" Perhaps even further, "Why isn't my kindness enough to prevent you from deceiving me?"

Jacob's growing awareness isn't merely a recompense for his past behavior. If it were, then he would have easily resumed the posture of the tricking self of his former life. Instead, Jacob's growing awareness teaches us to cultivate the personality trait that sees past cleverness to the face of kindness. Some may even call this humility.

Divine Limitation

30:2 "Can I take the place of God, who has denied you the fruit of the womb?"

What does it take to reach the limit of one's potential? For some the threshold is often low, set upon by the paralyzing experiences of fear, lack of confidence, and uncertainty. Others may simply say, "The sky is the limit," believing there are no shackles or impediments in the quest to achieve the fullness of their potential. Heroes are those who meet and exceed limits wherever they are found.

For all that our patriarchs learn from their blessed relationship with God, the recognition that divine limits in nature are beyond their control is not surprising. Jacob will rhetorically ask Rachel, in response to her concern for childbearing, **"Can I take the place of God, who has denied you the fruit of the womb?"** However, when Jacob frames his response to Rachel's protest of her barrenness this way, there is something quite unsettling here. Jacob has tested the limits his entire life so far. This is the same Jacob who conceived of the birthright exchange from his twin brother. He was the one willing to don a coat of sheep's fur to ensure his father's blessing. He was the one willing to work for his uncle for fourteen years to secure the hands of his two wives. He will be the man who confronts an angel to wrestle a new blessing from God. Why wouldn't he conjure some of that potential for his beloved wife now?

The Torah's concerns for the biological limitations of the human being are moral in their consequence. Disobedience in the Garden was punished with mortality. The resonance of Rebecca's plaintive cry **"If [the severity of childbirth] is so, why do I exist?"**[43] are heard in this exchange, as if Rachel has behaved in some way worthy of punishment. The power of the narrative here is that Rachel is blameless. Even more so, Rachel will be the one to test her limits and expand her potential as she seeks out the mandrakes from Leah to help her conceive a child of her own.[44]

The phrase **"take the place of God"** is new here. It will be revisited later with Joseph and his brothers.[45] It is a significant evolution of the human being as a partner with divinity. In particular, it further defines Jacob as a soul who recognizes his own limitations. It is appropriate to interpret his question to Rachel here not from a place of indignance but from the place where Jacob's limitations introduce the possibility of divine influence in the drama of his life, indeed in the lives of his progeny and legacy.

It seems easier to share that God's participation in the life of a child is evident after the successful birth. But to recognize there is an element of divine influence in the conception of a child invites a deeper sense of human limitation. It introduces a sense of wonder into the experience of life; that a growing soul, no matter how intelligent and industrious they may be, will always perceive the surprise of living as a gift from the realm of the potential, the world where possibilities are limitless. Jacob saw this in Rebecca's turmoil and perhaps the preciousness of their children together will be framed by their limitless love.

Sharing Is Caring

30:15 "Was it not enough for you to take away my husband, that you would also take my son's mandrakes?"

We don't really know much about the relationship between Rachel and Leah. Their relationship must have been quite a story! It is remarkable that after we learn they share the same husband, the dynamic of their relationship is largely relegated to the interpretive tradition. There we will hear echoes of Rachel's whispers to Leah on her wedding night to Jacob[46] to help us imagine how they were able to contend with this extraordinary arrangement. In the Torah text, however, Rachel even goes so far as to name her son Naphtali, inspired by her tense relationship with Leah.[47] But the moments we actually hear Rachel and Leah speaking to each other through the text are few. And their exchange will give us a definition of the eternal value of their role as matriarchs of the Jewish heritage.

In the narrative that outlines the birth of Jacob's children, Rachel's request for her nephew Reuven's mandrakes seems simple enough on the surface. We are meant to understand the powers of fertility the mandrakes contain and Rachel's legitimate desire for them so she may be blessed with children by Jacob. However, Leah's response in the form of a question probes deeply into the implied antipathy the sisters share between each other.

When Leah asks, **"Was it not enough for you to take away my husband, that you would also take my son's mandrakes?"** we are thrust into an implied tension between Leah and Rachel as they share the same man. But we also discover a sensibility here exemplified by Leah's response. The sophistication of her emotional composure sheds light on their relationship and the perceived imbalance of power in their relationships with Jacob and roles in the family. Despite Leah's fecundity and prosperity, Jacob's love for Rachel is unbearable to her.

Rachel knows this. And so they strike a bargain. Mandrakes for more children. Leah grows more powerful, and Rachel will eventually give birth to children of her own. The number of children born to Rachel are fewer than half born to Leah. And yet Leah's value in bearing more children transcends the relative value of Jacob's love for her. Despite Leah's coarsened rejection, she accepts Rachel's request for the mandrakes in exchange for more children.

In a sense, Leah's question is answered by Rachel's bargain. It simply wasn't enough that Rachel had Jacob's affection. Rachel's determination is inspirational because she employs the tools of negotiation to change her fate. Perhaps in response to Jacob, who asks, **"Am I in the place of God?"**[48] Rachel understands that human intervention in the divine role of childbearing is vital. This exchange affirms that in human partnership, divine legacies are born.

Defining "Enough"

30:30 "When will I provide for my own house too?"

The spiritual path is sturdily paved by definitions of "enough." When one's material needs are satisfied, it is possible to focus attention upon a concern for others, even a concern for God. This is the path that will lead Abraham to Egypt in a time of famine, and it will prompt Esau to cry out to his father, **"Have you but one blessing?"**[49] The Torah constantly grapples with this throughout the journeys of the Israelites and throughout the generations recorded in the Bible.

Some will attribute Jacob's spiritual transformation during his encounter with the angel by the river Jabbok[50] as his ultimate definition of "enough." The wrestling moment is an awakening to new responsibility borne from the divine struggle. Indeed, the moment the angel asks to be released and in return Jacob wrestles from the angel a blessing, a powerful and deeply spiritual truth transpires. Jacob's story teaches us that this type of spiritual transformation can take a lifetime to occur. By the time he meets the angel, Jacob is ready for change. The moment when he prepares for his departure from Laban's house is one of those steps toward change.

When we hear Jacob ask Laban, **"When will I provide for my own house too?"** our first reaction might be to revert to our original perception of Jacob as the conniving, self-centered individual who turns a narrative toward his own needs, eclipsing the well-being and betterment of others, even his family, around him. And yet we detect a shift in tone here. Jacob's question is rooted in the context of his service to Laban. He is measuring his value in relation to another. We can read this question as a limit to his service to Laban so that he may better serve the divine.

The Torah comes to teach us the purpose of the human being is to be in service to God. While the nobility of divine service is indeed worthy of lifelong pursuit, without a sense of material security and the potential for flourishing, service to God is at best a secondary concern. Jacob's request here is legitimate. He identifies a need that can no longer be satisfied by his father-in-law's generosity. His purpose to fulfill his role as servant of God demands an amount of material prosperity he has never quite known until now. . . . He needs enough.

Questions with Strings Attached
30:31 "What can I give you?"

In contrast to Jacob's question to Laban from the previous verse, the tone of this question is roiled with deceit. Laban, as a biblical character, typifies actions based on half-truths and self-serving motivations. He becomes a central figure in the Bible precisely because his manipulations compel Jacob to change his own behavior. Laban isn't someone who will evolve after all the years of Jacob's dutiful service to him. Laban's calculations even prompt his daughters to retaliate as they leave his home by taking his household gods with them. There is no trust in the home they now ask to leave.

When Laban asks, **"What can I give you?"** we are compelled to grapple with the conflict of trust and mistrust within us. We feel for Jacob, the one who worked for Laban for many years to win the hand of his beloved daughter, Rachel. We also feel for Jacob, the one who manipulated his brother and misled his father into giving him blessings. Our heart is once again wavering between the generosity of spirit that Laban embodies in this moment and the mistrust we feel from the sting of his earlier trickery.

Jacob has certainly earned his blessings from Laban. He has had a successful career, a family with many children, and enough of his own prosperity to return to his homeland, much like his grandfather, a self-made titan of nomadic culture. Jacob doesn't need anything more from Laban. But we sense what Jacob senses. Laban wants to pay Jacob to commit him to work for another fourteen years, maybe more. Jacob can no longer tolerate that arrangement.

We will learn that trust and understanding form the bedrock of modern commerce. Laban and Jacob's story in the Bible is recorded to educate future generations that even family members will have questionable intent when the subject of prosperity and success is involved. The message remains that Jacob, once complicit in his own deceitful behavior, can evolve to become a man of integrity, something God has commanded from his partners in creation since the beginning. Jacob can no longer remain with his uncle. His integrity is calling him home.

The Question of Leaving Home

31:14 "Will we still have a portion of our father's inheritance?"

As Jacob informs his wives that they will be making the journey back to Canaan with all their amassed wealth and prosperity, their questions reveal a greater concern for security than the material bounty they currently possess. The question **"Will we still have a portion of our father's inheritance?"** a rare occasion in which both sisters speak in unison, expresses the concern for a value system that exists regardless of material wealth.

On the surface, we are reading the underlying political forces of tribal associations. Jacob is kin to Laban's tribal family and therefore is subject to his benefactor's influence. Similarly, Laban cultivates some antipathy toward Jacob because Jacob's success surpasses his own. As we have discussed before, what prompts this separation is that Jacob has evolved. His story is the quintessential journey of the human soul. Leah and Rachel's question is a reflection that their fate is cast with his. Have they grown as well?

One possible reading of the question is as an expression of resignation. Their father's inheritance isn't exclusively material. This reading appears plausible with the statement that follows: **"We are perceived as strangers to him, now that he has sold us and used up our purchase price [dowry]."** They are concerned that a lack of attention, either substantively or subjectively, is the consequence of their alliance with their husband. Jacob changes over the years with Laban. We can sensitively read into Rachel and Leah's legacy that they have also grown. This is perhaps confirmed by their admission that God has blessed them with children and abundance, and their recognition that the women they have become are no longer dependent upon their father's influence. Their characters have developed in the story as well.

Once again the questioners here appear to be self-motivated, and the possible answers they seek would be to quantify and validate their needs. We may also infer that the purpose of these questions emerges from their own growth and development as matriarchs. Their understanding that their fate is now cast with their husband and not their father is a sign that the entire family project is evolving as well. Jacob's family as a tribe is born.

Letting Go

31:26 "What did you mean by keeping me in the dark and carrying off my daughters like captives of the sword?"

31:27 "Why did you flee in secrecy and stole from me and did not tell me?"

31:30 "Why did you steal my god[s]?"

Complicated family relationships are among the central motifs of the book of Genesis. By learning about the nuanced connections between family members, we may be able to better interpret the relationships we have with strangers and the world around us. Indeed, knowing the points of connection between the people closest to us, we may even begin to interpret our relationship with God. The relationship between Laban, his daughters, and his son-in-law Jacob is no exception, though the divine message may be more difficult to discern.

Laban's emotional response to Jacob's surreptitious departure glimmers with sincerity. After all, he is a father who has raised and cared for his daughters and to notice their absence so abruptly reveals a level of concern beyond the transactional nature of any daughters-for-prosperity exchange.[51] Moreover, Laban asks outright, **"What did you mean by keeping me in the dark and carrying off my daughters like captives of the sword?"** The metaphorical consideration implies that Laban may actually have feelings for his daughters. Yet his appearance with an indeterminate number of kinsmen to overtake Jacob's family, now a full three days' journey away from him, leaves us suspicious of his true intentions.

One dimension of Laban's paternal concern for his daughters is their safety and well-being. We've seen this side of him before: Laban brought Jacob into the tribe and protected him. He even married off his daughters to Jacob as kinsman and worthy spouse. As we will see, though, this episode is as much about Rachel and Leah as it is about Laban. They will eschew his protection and resolve that his failures are a consequence of his devotion to local deities and not the God of Jacob. They will take his father's possessions in secret and hide them from him, seemingly justified for their actions in the face of God's all-encompassing power and beneficence to them. On the surface, Laban's concern is genuine, but his daughters and son-in-law do not receive his reactions here with any sincerity.

When Laban presses Jacob further and asks, **"Why did you flee in secrecy and stole from me and did not tell me?"** we begin to sense the threat Laban is experiencing now that part of his family is leaving him. Indeed, what the text may be implying here is that Laban's uncertainty is more a result of his lack of faith in the God of Jacob than it is a concern for lost revenue in the business. We just read that God appears to Laban in a dream to caution him not to harm Jacob. Yet his question implies that the slight he feels is undeterred, even by God.

Laban seems to make his feelings explicit with his next question in this episode, **"Why did you steal my god[s]?"** The language of theft here amplifies the tension between Laban and Jacob. Jacob's general response, here read with a tone of authenticity, **"I was afraid because I thought you would take your daughters from me by force,"** raises our concern for God's protection. What does Jacob have to fear?

The Torah captures this moment and the questions that move it forward to reveal a deeper truth about the complicated nature of our relationships. When uncertainty compels us to hold on tightly to our truths from narrow places (the word "stolen" is mentioned several times in the narrative), faith in divine influence provides a sense of gratitude and appreciation for what has been gained. Jacob will ultimately remind Laban in response to Laban's direct questions of the prosperity they have both amassed over the years. Maybe Laban could take a lesson in letting go here as well.

A Moral Accounting

31:36 "What is my transgression, what is my sin that you pursued after me?"

31:37 "You rummaged through my possessions, where have you found all of your possessions?"

When the early commentators were curious how God was revealed to Abraham, they imagined him as a youthful apprentice working in his father's idol-making workshop.[52] As customers came in to purchase the idols, Abraham would employ clever logic to undermine their beliefs in objects that only represented a finite power of natural and divine force. Early interpretations of the Torah understood that there has always been the contention of one true force of creation with multiple forces. The moments in the Torah that recognize there are other deities are dramatic, whether they are epic battles between Egypt and Israel or emotional accusations like those Laban hurls at Jacob as they return home to Canaan.

When Laban overtakes Jacob and his family as they return to Canaan, Laban presumes Jacob stole his household idols. The irony of the moment is that Jacob has never professed loyalty to any other deity than the God of his fathers. The conversation turns much deeper to Laban's true concern, which is what remains in his possession after he has given away his daughters and his prosperity to Jacob. In other words, if the clay objects were so valuable to him, couldn't he simply have replaced them when he noticed they were missing? Laban's obsession is less with the objects as it is focused on control of his daughters and his son-in-law.

Jacob's response is powerful in that it reveals a sense of moral certitude he was not able to wield until now. Jacob was the deceiving, manipulative son, refusing to accept responsibility for his actions, even fleeing his homeland to escape the threat of sibling and filial judgment.

After a long journey of self-discovery and accountability, Jacob is ready to return home and is angered by Laban's accusations. When he asks, **"What is my transgression, what is my sin that you pursued after me?"** and **"You rummaged through my possessions, where have you found all of your possessions?"** the implication of Jacob is that he stands before Laban blameless. He is in fact blameless despite his wives' own manipulations to actually take their father's idols with them.

Here a new truth emerges about the discovery of the God of Israel as well. Jacob's evolution into a man of integrity, an *Eesh Tamim*, allows him to defend himself against Laban's accusations. Moreover, the recognition that Jacob would not have any use for Laban's idols and that Rachel and Leah take them as retribution for their father's manipulations reveals that gods other than the one true God of Israel are susceptible to deceit. This episode affirms that YHVH is not a deity of form but of spirit. Here the spirit is one of integrity.

What Is Divine Acceptance?

31:43 "What can I do for my daughters today, or the children they have borne?"

A parent's pride is realized when their child can express their independence. More than a sense of prosperity, the knowledge that their child can thrive in the world on their own is one of the greatest joys a parent can experience. After all the conflict and the dramatic turns of Laban's relationship with his daughters and son-in-law, the question Laban poses here should not simply be read as a sign of defeat. When he asks, **"What can I do for my daughters today, or the children they have borne?"** this expression is a full measure of pride. He has nothing more to offer, and he's fulfilled his duty as a parent.

The preamble to this moment is misleading as well. Laban makes a proclamation that all he sees belongs to him but then seems to evaluate his possessions and ask what more he could provide for his daughters. This intensely human moment reveals the power of the parent and the influence of divinity. The parent wants to verify all that has been provided to his children, and now he recognizes that what his children need is their own space. It's tough to let go, since a parent devotes a significant portion of their lifetime to ensuring the health and prosperity of their child. But it is the letting go that enables the child to affirm that health and prosperity and pave the future paths they take.

This narrative becomes a part of the Torah to enlighten the human dimension of divine acceptance. The divine influence of this moment is that both Jacob and Laban realize their prosperity has emerged from their letting go—Jacob in letting go of his indentured servitude, and Laban in letting go of his claim on his children's lives. What makes letting go so challenging is that the very definition of divine influence, the privilege of creating and cultivating life in a child, is analogous to the creation of the entire universe. We must recognize that with all our very best efforts to create and sustain a universe in which our children will thrive, the discovery of God's universe is meant to be made alone. Letting go of loved ones to empower them to seek the presence of God in the world is difficult. And yet it is precisely that capacity to seek the presence of God that stirs a sense of pride in the parent.

This is affirmed by the pact Jacob and Laban make following Laban's acknowledgment. They make a pact ensuring that Jacob will continue to provide for Leah and Rachel's well-being. Then Jacob makes an offering to the God of Israel, and they partake of a meal. The celebration of this moment is that parent and children have separated well. It may also be why Jacob will eventually call the space *Makhanyim* (God's Camp).

We have echoes of this epic moment in our days too. The wedding celebration is the culmination of preparations for the child to create the world anew with a loving partner. The parents have the privilege of letting go of their children, however difficult, and the blessing of that union is a promise of divine acceptance by all.

VAYISHLACH

32:18 "Who are you, and where are you going, and who are these before you?" (Jacob to his servants, anticipating the questions Esau will ask them)

32:28 "What is your name?" (Angel to Jacob)

32:30 "What is your name?" (Jacob to angel)

32:30 "Why did you ask for my name?" (Angel to Jacob)

33:5 "Who are these to you?" (Esau to Jacob)

33:8 "Who is this whole camp that I am meeting [in relation] to you?" (Esau to Jacob)

33:15 "Why is this, have I found favor in my lord's eye?" (Esau to Jacob)

34:31 "Should one deal with our sister as with a harlot?" (Shimon and Levi to Jacob)

The transformation of Jacob, the reunion with his twin brother Esau, and the resettlement of his family in the land of Canaan prompt many questions about relationships with oneself, with family members, and with the world around us. In the chapters of this portion, we see how Jacob ultimately comes to terms with his own soul as he wrestles with and prevails over an angel in the middle of the night. He also has to define the relationship of his family to his brother as they reunite in the land of Canaan. The question of the relationship between Jacob's family and the neighboring tribe of Shechem is brought into focus as well, where even the physical mark of loyalty, circumcision, is not a sufficient definition of moral character for Abraham's family. The conflicts borne from fraternal strife will continue with the sons of Jacob in the following chapters, but the questions of familial loyalty are resolved as Jacob and Esau join together when they bury their father Isaac.

Anticipating Questions

32:18 "Who are you, and where are you going, and who are these before you?"

Anticipating questions is one way we try to act like God. Not only does it suggest that the one who preempts the question possesses a certain divine quality, a capacity to read into the mind of another and determine their motivations, it also implies that the questioner can be understood in some way other than in their explicit behavior.

Jacob's very nature of forecasting the thinking of another is stunning. His grandfather Abraham did this when he and Sarah went to Pharaoh's court. His father Isaac did this when he met Abimelech in the desert. As an archetype of this divine quality, Jacob's sensibility regarding the intentions of others is evident throughout his life. In particular, we saw him ask his mother Rebecca to consider his response should his father discover his clever disguise as Esau to obtain the blessing. We see this sensibility emerge again here, this time when he prompts his servants to respond to a series of questions he believes Esau will ask: **"Who are you, and where are you going, and who are these [animals] before you?"**

After all these years, how could Jacob possibly know what his brother would be truly thinking? Jacob could take into consideration that his brother's attitude has changed just as he changed himself. Moreover, had Jacob inferred that his brother might not actually seek his life as recompense for the stolen blessing, the wrestling moment, which leaves Jacob lame, might not have been necessary. But he sends gifts ahead with the hope that the answer to his questions is a peace offering.

The Torah's interest in the human spirit is driven both by external behavior and by the internal thinking that animates decisions, feelings, and desires. The rabbis of the tradition will pick up this theme when they teach, "God desires the heart."[53] Jacob's concern at the moment he returns to the land of Canaan reveals as much about Jacob's actions as it does about his intentions. By thinking strategically and preparing for his brother's angry reception on his return home, Jacob is also showing a level of concern that transcends any apparent concern for his life and the well-being of his family. Jacob cares about what his brother thinks. The response that he prompts his men to share with Esau, should Esau ask such questions, is to be transparent and clear. Jacob's plan represents an attempt to encourage feelings of favor in his brother and assuage Esau's vengeful pledge years ago to kill him.

The encounter between Esau and Jacob underlines the divine quality of anticipating questions. When Esau rejects Jacob's offer of livestock as a gift to curry his favor and rather responds, "I have enough,"[54] Jacob presses Esau to accept the gift and adds, **"To see your face is like seeing the face of God."**[55]

There is a deeper sense of spiritual discipline in the wise anticipation of another's questions. Jacob is teaching us to see the needs of another. When carefully crafted, this can indeed bring the favorable result of **"seeing the face of God."**

Knowing the Other

32:28 "What is your name?"
32:30 "What is your name?"
32:30 "Why did you ask for my name?"

Of all the possible human activities to describe in a book of sacred truth, the Torah pays particular attention to the act of naming. In people, places, and relationships, a name signifies purpose and connection. In the Garden of Eden, the first human being names all the animals but does not find his partner, his helpmate, until God creates her. The act of naming is not simply an exercise of knowledge. Identifying the other by name builds a relationship, a connection that can potentially transcend hierarchies, authorities, and dominion. The absence of a name, a circumstance that also occurs in the book on occasion, typifies a different kind of relationship—perhaps to elevate the purpose of names and relationships.

It would be easier to read the wrestling encounter between Jacob and the angel without the activity of naming. Jacob wrestles with a divine being and prevails. He's a hero. Within a short, two-verse span, three questions are posed, **"What is your name?"** the angel asks Jacob. **"What is/Tell me your name?"** Jacob says to the angel. **"Why did you ask for my name?"** the angel queries in response.

The one short verse between these questioning moments reveals the deeper truth. Jacob's name will change to become *Israel*, the eponymous moniker of the Jewish people in perpetuity. It is given as a blessing.

This exchange through questions offers us some deeper insight into the purpose of inquiry. Questions help us navigate a world of mystery. When we don't know who or what is before us, a name helps us give shape to the unknown, to resolve the uncertainty in some way. When the divine being asks for Jacob's name and blesses him with a new name, it is at that moment that the divine being sees Jacob as someone who has changed, who has grown, who has become a soul. "Israel" may have symbolic value for what quality it represents, but the depth of the blessing here is that the divine being resolves an uncertainty in Jacob by giving him a new name.

Jacob will also seek the name of the angel to identify his relationship to it. In fact, when the divine being responds, **"You must not ask my** name!" Jacob cannot contend with something so profound occurring without a name to attach to it, so he proceeds to name the place where the struggle occurred. He calls the place *Peniel* (face of God) and explains, **"I have seen a divine being face to face, yet my life has been preserved."**[56]

When Jacob bestows a name upon the place and not the being with whom he wrestled, we also learn how names can transcend the identity of the other. He calls the place Peniel because he'll remember he saw divinity there. He did this before when he encountered divine beings on his journey to Haran. For Jacob, the places he names will have God's name attached to them. Here we learn that Jacob's name will also have God's name attached to it. This is how we know that Jacob is finally worthy of God's truest blessings: knowing and being known.

To Whom Do We Belong?

33:5 "Who are these to you?"

33:8 "Who is this whole camp that I am meeting [in relation] to you?"

The appellation that signifies what we are called among our people is more than a name on a birth certificate. Not only are we called by our parents' names as a way of identifying ourselves to the community (like *Jacob ben Isaac* in Hebrew), but there are also Jewish customs of naming children in loving memory of ancestors who have passed on. In the Jewish tradition, naming our children after our ancestors defines our identity by their most noble qualities in hope that their legacies become, in the words of Rabbi Harold M. Schulweis, "the immortality of influence."[57] When the Bible asks for names or the relationships of people to each other, we should not gloss over the deeper purpose of the question.

When Esau meets Jacob's family, we sense a loving embrace of Jacob's maids, children, and wives when he asks, **"Who are these to you?"** Esau and Jacob have just been reconciled in a moment of intimacy we have not yet seen between any two siblings. Esau first sees Jacob and then sees his family. Although in these circumstances it would seem fairly obvious that the people Jacob has surrounding him are family, Esau's question truly touches a deeper nerve, that of the relation of the people to Jacob. **"To you"** implies that Esau's interest is not in the connection he may have with this group of people alone. The implication behind the second question, **"Who is [to you] this whole camp that I am meeting?"** indicates that the people we surround ourselves with aren't merely accessories. The Torah's sensitivity in describing Esau's crowd as "four hundred men" and Jacob's gesture of gifting his prosperity to his brother signal the shift in their thinking as brothers altogether. Jacob's people mean to him that he cares about something, here someone, more than himself. Jacob is unafraid to share his bounty with his brother. Esau's offer to escort the family into the land signifies that Esau has grown as well.

Perhaps this new perception is best expressed by Jacob when he insists on Esau's acceptance of his gift by saying, **"To see your face is like seeing the face of God."** Jacob sees divinity in his family and shares them with Esau—perhaps as recognition of the blessing he received from his father. But here Jacob also sees divinity in his brother Esau. This statement is most poignant after the long and arduous journey Jacob has taken to return home. Seeing the face of his twin brother is like seeing the face of God.

Aww, You Shouldn't Have!
33:15 "Why is this, have I found favor in my lord's eye?"

The experience of gifts in the Bible is almost always tied to some payment or reconciliation of responsibility. Abram receives gifts from Pharaoh to compensate for his favor of Sarai in Egypt. Abimelech receives gifts in return for protection and safety for the vulnerable nomadic families of Abraham and Isaac. Here Jacob is offered the gift of safe escort into the land of Canaan from his twin brother Esau, but Jacob kindly refuses. When Jacob asks, **"Why is this, have I found favor in my lord's eyes?"** the question of reconciliation between the brothers is subtly addressed.

Just moments earlier, Jacob had offered gifts from the prosperity of his years in Haran to Esau, which Esau respectfully denied. Now Esau is extending a gesture of kindness and Jacob responds with a question, a question that leaves the reader curious as to the intention of the gift-giving. It's easy for the interpreter to read Esau's offer of protection as a safeguard against his brother's attempts to take more of his own belongings, as if the escorts are to ensure Jacob doesn't take anything that doesn't belong to him along the way. But we can also read this as an affirmation of Jacob's changed behavior. He truly has become a self-sufficient person through his journey, and even the kind gesture of protection by his brother Esau is unnecessary.

Feigning humility is a fairly common response to awkward situations. The imbalance of relationships often prompts expressions of smallness or humility, particularly in the face of a kind gesture. But the core expression here is gratitude. Being thankful for a gesture or a kindness that you receive opens up a world of certainty. Their gifts to each other help the brothers understand their intentions. Here the intentions are layered with kindness.

There is another dimension of gratitude here. Until this moment, Jacob has been perceived as a foil to Esau's intentions (**"Was he then named Jacob that he might supplant me these two times?"**).[58] Now Jacob reacts to Esau's generosity with a bit of surprise. Although his recognition of his own prosperity enables him to decline Esau's offer, Jacob is also acknowledging that he has found favor in his brother's eyes! This beautiful and powerful moment of reconciliation enables them to join in caring for their father when he dies—together. If gratitude is the recognition that our blessings are more than we deserve, this moment is the great realization for Jacob and Esau that their reunion is a form of healing and hope, an abundance of blessings they both understand are more than they deserve.

Human Retribution Is Not Divine
34:31 "Should one deal with our sister as with a harlot?"

We are uncomfortable speaking about sexuality, especially in light of a book of divine truth. Layers of shame and discomfort around the body are reflected in the Torah's attitude toward the body. But there is also a dimension of ignorance that discomfort in even speaking about sex will perpetuate. Where the Torah could illuminate the healthy and joyful elements of physical and emotional intimacy without any graphic details to titillate the senses, we are often only left grappling with the terror and trauma of physical closeness gone awry.

And so the brief episode of Jacob's daughter Dinah and her encounters with the men of Shechem is a painful awareness of unrestrained sexual force. The brothers attack the people of Shechem in response to one of their son's lustful connection to Dinah when we read she was taken **"by force."**[59] In striving to build a connection and relationship with B'nai Yisrael, there is a troubling disruption in the sense of family or tribal purity. Jacob's sons Shimon and Levi lead a stealth mission into the camp of Shechem to wipe out the male inhabitants, and the rest of the brothers enter the town to plunder riches in retaliation for Dinah's defilement.

Jacob is concerned for his reputation among the other tribes in the land of Canaan, prompting the response by Shimon and Levi in the form of a question. They respond to Jacob's horror in learning they slaughtered the citizens of Shechem by asking, **"Should one deal with our sister as with a harlot?"**

Once again we are unsettled by a question that has rhetorical undertones, especially since it marks the end of the narrative. We do not know the response from Jacob here, as the text promptly moves in another direction. Behind the thrust of the question itself, once again, is this search for identity as a family and as a people. Shimon and Levi are simultaneously responding to the moral indignity Shechem casts upon the family of Jacob and the role and reputation they will maintain in the comity of tribes in Canaan.

The power of this moment framed in a question is the moral judgment it places upon us. Does their question resolve their discomfort? Is it even possible to agree with their actions without a degree of unbidden vengeance? As readers we know that Jacob's disapproval will culminate in his indictment of Shimon and Levi in his final blessings. And yet there is no retribution, human or divine, that results from this act. Where is the God of Abraham to stand in their way, to exert some moral force and compel the sons of Jacob to bring the people of Shechem to God's justice? Grappling with these uncertainties makes this narrative vital to the Torah narrative, and it will sustain a powerful attitude toward power and sexuality that endures even today.

VAYESHEV

37:8 "Do you mean to reign over us?" (The brothers to Joseph)
37:8 "Do you wish to rule over us?" (The brothers to Joseph)
37:10 "What is this dream you have dreamt?" (Jacob to Joseph)

37:10 "Are we to come, I and your mother and your brothers, and bow to the earth before you?" (Jacob to Joseph)

37:15 "What do you seek?" (Man to Joseph)

37:16 "I am looking for my brothers. Could you tell me where they are pasturing?" (Joseph to man)

37:26 "What profit is there if we kill our brother and cover his blood?" (Yehuda to his brothers)

37:30 "The boy is gone, and where will I go?" (Reuben to his brothers or Reuben to himself)

42:26 "Did I not tell you, do no wrong to the boy?" (Reuben to his brothers. This is a question posed in later chapters, but its message is best addressed here.)

38:16 "What will you give me if you sleep with me?" (Tamar to Judah)

38:18 "What will I give you as a pledge?" (Judah to Tamar)

38:21 "Where is the harlot, that was at Eynayim along the way?" (Judah to the men)

39:9 "How then could I do this most wicked thing, and sin before God?" (Joseph to Potiphar's wife)

40:7 "Why are your faces down [evil] today?" (Joseph to the guards)

The epic tale of Joseph begins in these chapters and this particular portion is focused on the circumstances and events that bring about Joseph's rise to influence in Pharaoh's court. Knowing the arc of Joseph's story as one riddled with fate and fortune, we reflect upon the profoundly human questions found here and the glaring absence of God. As we learn, the reference to God as the source of divine authority is frequently expressed by Joseph in a manner unlike that of his father and grandfathers before him. There is some connection to fortune and divine authority that Joseph senses. It is through Joseph's experiences that we explore moral complexities without reliance upon divine intervention. In God's absence, we discover heroic models of self-reliance and ingenuity.

Questioning Authority
37:8 "Do you mean to reign over us?"
37:8 "Do you wish to rule over us?"

When lines of authority are tested, whether by a hero or an antagonist, our faith ripples with concern. We sometimes delight when authority is undermined with a sense of justice and retribution, and we may also express consternation when the challenges to authority topple the social order for what seem to be self-motives.

Long before the Ten Commandments codified honoring parents as an essential responsibility ordained by God, the very notion of children usurping parents' authority or of a subordinate using manipulation to gain advantage over a superior seemed unnatural. All through nature we witness the constant testing and alignment of authority based on strength, guile, and a little luck. At its core, the story of Joseph wrestles with this tension. Why is it that we bristle at the notion of challenged authority, here expressed between brothers? When Joseph's brothers respond to his dreams by asking, **"Do you mean to reign over us? Do you wish to rule over us?"** there is a deeper sense of challenge to the nature of sibling relationships than the moment might have intended.

The Torah doesn't spare details in describing Joseph's favored position in the family and his youthful arrogance. When Joseph brings the recollection of his dreams to his brothers, he doesn't offer any explanation. As a result, the brothers and later his father infer Joseph's ulterior motives. Perhaps their feeling of threat is implicit in their own understanding of the natural order. Jacob's youth is also bound up in a manipulation of this order. We presume the brothers have already learned their role, possibly as a result of their life experience. Joseph is just a boy, after all. Their questions when he brings them his dream are, therefore, reasonable.

We bristle at challenges to authority because they can be insatiable. Hence there is a sense of doubt implicit in a challenge. These questions seek to resolve the uncertainty. Is he challenging them or not? While the possibility of mistrust is unsettling to us, it is probably the most authentic reading of this moment. The brothers' concern here isn't some failure of their imagination. It is a test of their trust, one that will only be realized many years later. It is this moment that reminds us to question authority judiciously. When we learn to trust deeply, our trust inevitably returns to God, the source of trust in the universe.

Questioning Authority, Continued

37:10 "What is this dream you have dreamt? Are we to come, I and your mother and your brothers, and bow to the earth before you?"

Here the question structure parallels that of the previous questions that grapple with authority and power and the test of trust. Jacob asks Joseph, **"What is this dream you have dreamt? Are we to come, I and your mother and your brothers, and bow to the earth before you?"** The implication is direct here. Jacob interprets the meaning of Joseph's perceived braggadocio and prompts his son to confirm his suspicion. It is as if he blatantly asks, "Did you mean what I think you meant to say?" This is not a question of clarification. Jacob bristles at his son's flaunting of his talents and intends to correct him with a clarification of certainty. All these questions can be implied in the resolution of the moment, when the text notes in the next verse, **"And his father kept the matter in mind."**

Joseph will come to demonstrate a mastery of unraveling mysteries, and yet we are not given his response here. There is a concern for the power dynamics of a family and where authority rests, and we are meant to wrestle with situations where that power is upturned, where the power of the younger overtakes that of the elder to reveal divine truths about the nature of power itself. Joseph is empowered in spite of his brothers and father and beyond the elegant turning of his circumstances from enslavement to leadership. How Joseph will ultimately respond to his new position is of great interest to the text. It is not simply his story we follow and how a talented young man travels from the pit to a seat of greatness. We are encouraged to reflect on the notion of power altogether and what one must possess to be worthy of the privilege of power.

Stranger Directions

37:15 "What do you seek?"

37:16 "I am looking for my brothers. Could you tell me where they are pasturing?"

There are rare occasions in the Bible when we meet a nameless person whose presence influences the journeys of our heroes. In the book of Genesis, when the social fabric of the Jewish people is still being woven, there is one instance of a man without any indication of his function or purpose who discovers Joseph wandering in a field seeking out his brothers, who are likely pasturing nearby. Their encounter will influence the children of Jacob forever.

When Joseph meets the man, he doesn't ask the man for directions; rather, the man asks Joseph what he is seeking. More than a stranger who is a part of the backdrop of Joseph's life, this man takes an active interest in Joseph. Perhaps the man is like the angels who visit Abraham and Sarah. This man appears simply to move fate along. When the man asks, **"What do you seek?"** the exchange reveals something vital in the encounter of strangers. The man must have perceived Joseph's wandering as a concern to be addressed. Strangers are no longer strangers when a question is introduced.

The stranger's question prompts a response. Joseph chooses to respond to the man with a request for help. When Joseph says, **"I am looking for my brothers. Could you tell me where they are pasturing?"** we remember that Joseph, the dreamer, is not prescient in everything. Joseph may intuit the quality of the relationships he has with his family from his dreams, but the details that will prompt his fate remain unknown to him. It takes a stranger to point him in that direction. It is reasonable to assume that the stranger's role here is significant for Joseph even though the encounter is seemingly banal. The Torah's introduction of a stranger into this heroic journey through a question reveals the dynamic ability of the individual to choose his own path and receive the guiding hand of divine intervention through uncertainty.

Surely the stranger could not have known the intentions of the brothers. The only detail that is certain in this entire narrative is the name of the location toward which the stranger saw the brothers' caravan traveling: Dothan. Since all the other details are general, Joseph's encounter with the stranger can be readily forgotten. However, we should not overlook the interchange of these two and the question that brings them together. The stranger asks Joseph what he is seeking, and Joseph responds. Location may have been the response, but as the narrative quickly continues, Joseph may very well be seeking the peace of his brothers, *"Et Shalom Acheecha."*[60] It will take many years before *shalom* will return to them all.

On Second Thought

37:26 "What profit is there if we kill our brother and cover his blood?"

Heroism is celebrated because it involves deliberate action at the right time. Foolishness, acting without forethought, is perhaps a temporary flaw of the hero and only to be overcome with greater awareness and knowledge. As a heroic tale, the Torah rarely invites us to reflect upon the uncertainties of our heroes. We witness the characters' actions and not their inner conflicts, prepared to accept the consequences of their actions. Clearly this text is more than a hero's journey. The episode of Joseph and his brothers magnifies the differences between heroes and fools.

The moment when Judah asks a question of his brothers as they conspire to kill Joseph exemplifies the power of second thoughts, and the capacity to think again that changes the destiny of the entire family. Judah asks his brothers, **"What profit is there if we kill our brother and cover his blood?"** At first we consider this question a measure of careful calculation. There is a moral balance between the satisfaction of silencing his brother's incessant dreams of power and authority with the messiness of his murder, the rationale the brothers would have to conjure in the face of their father's grief, and the burden their consciences would have to carry.

There is also another purpose to the question, one that interpreters of the Torah have grappled with before. Is Judah's intention to dissuade his brothers from causing irreparable harm or is Judah looking to profit from his brother's demise?[61] The former perspective is supported by the following verse, which states, **"Come, let us sell him to the Ishmaelites, but let us not do away with him ourselves. After all, he is our brother, our own flesh."**[62]

Telling the hero's story of the Jewish people guides us to read Judah's proposed response as a way to assuage the vengeful thoughts of his brothers. By softening their decree and persuading them to sell Joseph to the passing caravan, Judah is effectively saving his brother's life and propelling into motion the long journey to Egypt and enslavement that God pronounced to their great-grandfather Abraham generations ago.

Seeing Judah as a cold and calculating profiteer not only disturbs our perception of the hero, it denies the very purpose of the question, which is to introduce the power of consideration. Second thoughts may yield more desirable results should we choose to entertain them. In this light,

Judah's capacity for reflection is a heroic model for the nascent Jewish people despite the unseemly circumstances that prompt his query.

Unanswerable Questions

37:30 "The boy is gone, and where will I go?"

42:26 "Did I not tell you, do no wrong to the boy?" (This is a question posed in later chapters, but its message is best addressed here.)

There are moments when expressions of despair, frustration, disappointment, or even joy take form in a question. **"Why does this always happen to me?"**[63] and **"How can I repay God for the blessings given to me?"**[64] are two examples of questions in the Bible that express emotion greater than any answer can provide. Rather than seeking a rationale that will never completely satisfy a sense of loss or overflowing emotion, these kinds of questions are an opportunity to meet God deeply. The use of a question to express a sense of total uncertainty is more than an interrogative. We express ourselves through these kinds of questions because our experience needs to be shared and we don't know how best to convey our feelings.

When Joseph is sold by his brothers to a caravan of Midianites traveling to Egypt and his brothers conspire to inform their father he was killed by a wild beast, Reuben expresses a certain existential terror. Reuben persuaded the others not to kill Joseph and inspired them to throw him in a pit instead. When he discovers that Joseph is missing when he goes to the pit, he exclaims, **"The boy is gone, and where will I go?"**[65] We presume his anxiety is related to the unbearable responsibility of notifying his father of the tragic news.

We may also read the question more deeply to learn more of Reuben's burden. His despair is more than a cry for a better plan. There is some awareness in this moment of his limit, one that he may not have acknowledged before. He could not persuade his brothers to leave Joseph alone and his initial plan to **"save him from them and restore him to his father"**[66] failed. There is no specific consequence for Reuben's failure, but the lingering angst behind his question here is whether or not he could have done anything to change their minds. This also reveals the thin lines of connection between the twelve siblings. Questions of loyalty to the clan, even loyalty to a sibling of the same father, are thrust into the light with this question, and Joseph's apparent demise reveals Reuben's despair for family unity.

In fact, Reuben's failure to persuade his brothers is going to resurface when they meet Joseph in Egypt. Joseph asks Benjamin to return with the brothers while Joseph holds Shimon as pledge for them to return. Reuben then pleads with his brothers and asks, **"Did I not tell you, do no wrong to the boy?"** While the brothers later become an amalgam of identity, Reuben's unique role as the great convener of the siblings dissolves through his despair.

The total uncertainty in Reuben's expressions introduces a human quality we may prefer to overlook. Our lack of control in difficult situations can test our faith in God and in ourselves. We can feel like the circumstances are so overwhelming that we will be cast into oblivion by our failure. Reuben's life and legacy remind us that the journey to the Promised Land is long. Our success, maybe even our failures, is celebrated by questions along the way.

Confusing Family and Futures

38:16 *"What will you give me if you sleep with me?"*
38:18 *"What will I give you as a pledge?"*
38:21 *"Where is the harlot, that was at Eynayim along the way?"*

A family is not only defined biologically. A family can also be defined by a shared common destiny. We learn this from the book of Genesis, where concern for the lineage of Abraham and his descendants is punctuated by narratives that exemplify qualities of character as conditions for family connections. These stories inspire us to explore who we are meant to become. Knowing that Judah is a significant figure among the families of B'nai Yisrael, what is shared about his life in the chapters of this epic narrative are not merely stories passed through time. The confusing and somewhat painful episode of Judah and Tamar exemplifies this commitment to the continuity and character of our biblical heroes.

Judah tends his sheep near Timna, where the widow of his two deceased sons, Tamar, lived while awaiting her marriage to Judah's third son, Shelah. Upon hearing of his arrival, Tamar positions herself as consort for Judah on his way into Timna. Tamar asks, **"What will you give me if you come into me?"** a seemingly innocuous request given her theatrical occupation as a harlot. In the negotiation of such an encounter, one that prompts a pledge to fulfill his promise to pay her for their intimacy, Judah asks, **"What will I give you as a pledge?"** Tamar asks for his staff and cord. Underneath the words are Tamar's concern for redemption and restoration to the family as a daughter of Judah and an inheritor of the family estate. Judah's obliviousness is an indication of his mental state (he did just lose his wife). His cavalier response in the moment typifies a sense of physical urge over logic and reason. Even a moment's forethought might have prompted his concern for Tamar's complicated request.

While the knowledge of a daughter-in-law's body is certainly not something expected of a father-in-law, it also seems that there could have been at least some awareness of who Tamar was by the time she consented for him to lay with her. Judah's lack of awareness is the focal point of the story when he sends his friend to bring his commitment to her and then must ask around, **"Where is the harlot, that was at Eynayim along the way?"** The impersonal nature of the transaction hardly seems worth recording in a biblical accounting. However, it prompts us to plumb the depths of our concern for others in new ways.

This Torah narrative reveals a valuable lesson. More than the redemption of a daughter-in-law and the assurance that Judah's lineage will continue through a child he conceived with Tamar, Judah's acknowledgement of neglect for Tamar paints a picture of moral rectitude entirely consistent with Abraham—that of righteous behavior (*tzedakah*). Judah sees Tamar's actions as a correction of his negligence. The Torah is not only concerned with the moral behavior of its heroes on a first impression. If this narrative teaches us anything, it is that an opportunity to right the wrongs of the world is not only possible but necessary.

Maybe this is why the lineage of David and the future identity of Judaism are born from this encounter.

Fatal Questions
39:9 "How then could I do this most wicked thing, and sin before God?"

Unanswered questions can be dangerous, even fatal. When a question encourages us to change our perspective by seeing a situation differently, we are liberated by the discovered truths a well-placed question reveals. By contrast, unheeded questions have the potential to set future courses toward consequences beyond repair. The narrative events surrounding Joseph and Potiphar's wife illuminate this failure of questions to resolve a crucial search for understanding.

On the surface, Joseph's question to Potiphar's wife, **"How then could I do this most wicked thing, and sin before God?"** seems futile. The very act of Joseph's faithful request in the form of a question is being posed to someone with an unquenched desire. Joseph pleads for logic. Her propositions for physical intimacy are **"wicked,"** and the consequence of such behavior would be a **"sin before God."** Desire can be so disorienting that even questions that caution against divine disobedience can be overlooked.

We may also consider that neither Joseph nor Potiphar's wife fully understand the nature of wickedness and divine sin. We can assume that there was some cultural influence from the moments like Cain's banishment to wander the world after taking his brother's life, or the generation of the Flood who were utterly irredeemable from their sinful behavior. Adulterous behavior is a new concept for the Torah: there is no command prohibiting the behavior yet, and Joseph has already condemned it!

Potiphar's wife may also not have understood the problem with her extramarital dalliances. She intuits that his protests are a rejection of her and proceeds to condemn him. Presuming Joseph would share his chaste rebuff of her advances, she proceeds to accuse Joseph of attempted rape. Her desire and her actions are consistent with her impulses. There is no measure of reason or context to change her mind.

Like all the events that fatally move Joseph through his adult life, the moment is critical in his ability to ultimately receive an audience with Pharaoh and ascend to become the second-most-powerful person in Egypt of his time. In this sense, his protest is ultimately fortuitous.

When a question is ignored or overlooked, the consequences are left to fate. Our awe for Joseph is that he will time and again rise above his harrowing circumstances and emerge stronger and more powerful than before. Our interest is heightened when we consider that questions like these can alter the destinies of our heroes. We too may also have the power to influence our destinies when our well-placed questions are heard and heeded.

A Wonderful Religion

40:7 *"Why are your faces downcast [evil] today?"*

Joseph's story as a magnificent dream interpreter shapes the final chapters of the book of Genesis. Like other great epic narratives, there are turning points when the potential success of the hero is in jeopardy. The excitement is revealed when the hero overcomes adversity and emerges even stronger than before. When Joseph lands in jail after being accused of sleeping with his master's wife, we think all is lost, until the cupbearer and baker become his cellmates.

Joseph senses their distress after they experience simultaneous dreams. Once he is in their presence, the questions ensue when Joseph asks Pharaoh's courtiers the cupbearer and the baker, who were with him, **"Why are your faces downcast [evil] today?"** This pivotal moment describes two essential qualities we are invited to emulate. The first is that we should not be afraid to take note of the suffering of others. Surely Joseph could have witnessed the distress of his prison mates and turned a careless shoulder to them. More than a caring response, Joseph has a special skill to share here, one that invites dream interpretations brimming with potential. But we should not overlook the essential act: Joseph cares.

A second quality is revealed in the statement that follows the exchange between Joseph, the cupbearer, and the baker. When Joseph responds to their uncertainty with a statement of certainty, **"Are not interpretations/solutions [to dreams] from God!"** he reveals something that will take the remaining chapters of this book to demonstrate. Joseph recognizes that his gift, his potential, is not something he acquired through his own efforts alone. He identifies his capacity to interpret dreams as a gift from God. It is Joseph's ability to receive wisdom from God and share it even when the message might be detrimental to his life. He must have remembered that his brothers sought to kill him when they learned of their subservience from his dreams. Even with this negative association, his gift of interpretation coming from God may be the only certainty he possesses.

This is where the message of faith is instructive to the reader. Joseph, the hero of the story, is thrown into jail and left to die. Without any demonstrable hope for salvation, Joseph is able to use his gift and his faith to redeem himself from the bleak circumstances of his existence. If Joseph can see through the darkness of his captivity to embrace his godly gifts, we may be inspired to discover our own gifts as well.

MIKETZ

41:38 "Is there one like this, a man who has the spirit of God?" (Pharaoh to his servants)

42:1 "Why do you keep looking [at each other]?" (Jacob to his sons)

42:7 "From where did you come?" (Joseph to his brothers)

42:26 "Did I not tell you, do no wrong to the boy?" (Reuben to his brothers; for discussion of this question, see 37:30 above.)

42:28 "What is this that God has done to us?" (The brothers to each other)

43:6 "Why did you do evil to me and tell the man there is another brother?" (Jacob to his sons)

43:7 "He [Joseph] asked us and our descendants directly, 'Is your father alive? Do you have a brother?'" (The brothers to Jacob)

43:7 "How were we to know that he would say, 'Bring your brother here'?"

43:27 "Is the father you spoke of well? Is he still living?" (Joseph to his brothers)

43:29 "Is this the young brother you spoke of to me?" (Joseph to his brothers)

44:4 "Why have you paid for good with evil?" (Joseph to his steward to ask the brothers when he overtakes them)

44:5 "Is this not the cup from which my master drinks, and he uses to practice divinity?" (Joseph's steward to the brothers)

44:7 "Why do you speak these words?" (The brothers to the steward)

44:8 "How could we steal from your master's house silver or gold?" (The brothers to the steward)

44:15 "What is this deed that you have done?" (Joseph to his brothers)

44:15 "Did you not know conjuring divinity is something for a man such as me?" (Joseph to his brothers)

44:16 "What can we tell [ask] to my lord, what can we say, and how can we clear ourselves?" (Yehuda to Joseph)

While the surface of this portion deals exclusively with the story of Joseph, his experiences in Egypt, and his reunion with his brothers, the questions posed and explored in these chapters confront the deeper levels of uncertainty and doubt in human relationships. The contrived relationship Joseph creates between himself and his brothers attempts to define and sharpen the moral code of the children of Jacob. Joseph's questions to his brothers engender doubt among them so that they will ultimately have to become accountable for their actions—especially the actions many years before that propelled Joseph to his position of power.

One in a Million

41:38 "Is there another one like this, a man who has the spirit of God?"

Living in a world population surpassing 7.5 billion people today, the concept of one in a million seems shallow. The notion that the world produces singular individuals capable of superhuman qualities is muted when we consider how improbable the uniqueness of one person can be. And yet our instinct is to constantly look for the outlier, the one whose actions defy the norms. Perhaps we hope that we have the capacity to exceed our own limits. Perhaps we hope that there is something greater than ourselves.

In the ancient Middle East when the world population was significantly smaller, a Pharaoh was considered a god. He possessed superhuman qualities, and the Pharaoh's administrative skills were only surpassed by his ability to divine truth better than anyone else. When Pharaoh asks, **"Is there another one like this, a man who has the spirit of God?"** our sensitive reading may first scrutinize the tone of this question. Pharoah seems to be asking whether the kingdom can be managed by anyone else besides the Hebrew slave. When there is no direct response to his question, Pharaoh continues by pronouncing, **"Since God has made all this known to you, there is none so discerning and wise as you."** This is quite a generous adulation considering Joseph is a foreigner who recently spent years in prison, who interpreted the dream of another describing that man's impending doom, and who conveniently suggested Pharaoh should appoint someone discerning and wise.

And yet there is a sense that Pharaoh does indeed believe no one could fulfill the role of chief economic advisor better than Joseph. Dream-telling and executive leadership are synonymous in the mind of Pharaoh. This is why the question here is more than an interrogative of clarification. This question is meant to reveal a core assumption we have in social organization that there are those who can fulfill roles and responsibilities better than others, even better than the Pharaoh. Empowering Joseph is an affirmation of the unique destiny of Abraham and his descendants. At the same time, the power is ephemeral, for we know that the story will take a fatal turn when there is a new Pharaoh **"who did not know Joseph."**[67] In other words, there is no one wiser and more discerning than another. Joseph's entire life story once again hinges on a fateful twist of events that plays to his favor.

Had Pharaoh answered his own question differently, Joseph's fate would have been sealed and the family might have never considered traveling to Egypt during the years of famine because there would not have been a qualified advisor to ration the bountiful yields. Perhaps a deeper message can be found in Pharaoh's prerequisite, **"a man who has the spirit of God."** Given this description, Joseph's unique status is most assuredly necessary. In fact it is his faith and humility that sustain him for the remainder of his life and sustain the family of Jacob in Egypt for another generation.

Get Up and Go!
42:1 "Why do you keep looking [at each other]?"

It is a common problem, generally left unspoken, that we often fail to stop before making a situation worse than it already is. Scientists call this an "escalation of commitment," or as some term it, a "commitment bias." The concern is that when we learn a decision might be detrimental, our instinct is to redouble our efforts in the hope that pouring more effort and time into a losing proposition will somehow stem the tide and make it turn out for the better. More often than not, our misguided efforts result in total failure.

The Torah takes an interest in this through the characters of the book of Genesis. We've seen individual remorse expressed by the patriarchs and matriarchs, and we see it clearly in the children of Jacob. But the act of changing our behavior before catastrophe? The heroic journey seems to relish the inability of the hero to see the consequences of his actions.

We are left to wonder what the brothers must have thought of their choice to sell Joseph to the Midianites. They knew their brother wasn't killed by a wild beast, and we presume they must have had a nagging sense that he was still living somewhere. The dreams of Joseph's youth, in which the brothers were subservient to him, might still become reality.

We may even wonder more when Jacob turns to his sons and asks, **"Why do you keep looking [at each other]?"** He wishes to know what the brothers really knew at the time. It is also entirely plausible that this particular moment reveals the brothers know more than they are able or willing to share. In other words, they fall prey to an escalation of commitment at this moment, knowing that to tell their father Joseph rose to power in Egypt would be to admit they willingly chose to sell him out of the family.

The Hebrew grammar here may also reveal an insight that we might readily overlook. Jacob "sees" the bounty in Egypt compared to the famine in Canaan. He asks the brothers what they "see" or what it is they are "looking at." The action implies a certain internal process. The sight Jacob compels his sons to consider is the sight of their inaction, even if it is simply seeing through the shame of asking for food from a neighboring ruler.

Jacob has grown a soul in ways that can only be expressed in a heroic journey of failure and recovery. It is also entirely plausible to suspect that Jacob "saw" the potential for the brothers to accept responsibility and grow their own souls. This question is perhaps the pivotal moment in which the brothers, blinded by their commitment to a failed proposition of erasing their brother's memory from their lives, are now compelled to confront their mistake and seek true forgiveness.

Authenticity
42:7 *"From where did you come?"*

A well-formed question as much reveals the character of the questioner as it highlights the depth and maturity of the one who answers. Questions in the Torah enable us to glimpse the world through new prisms, and they reveal deeper truths that were not evident before as we focus on the people who ask them. We have seen a question of location asked several times before. This time the questioner already knows the answer and awaits the response to confirm his suspicions.

The concluding episodes of the book of Genesis inspire the kinds of interpretation that explore the sophistication of the identities of the characters described in the stories. Joseph's story isn't merely entertainment. When he first sees his brothers and remembers **"the dreams that he had dreamed about them,"**[68] his question is more than a playful game of cat and mouse to trap his brothers in their vulnerability. Joseph asks his brothers, **"From where did you come?"** Here the brothers have the opportunity to describe the journey of their family from Abraham's roots, or the toil of their family as they settled in Canaan, or perhaps even the trauma of their experience of selling their brother to a caravan of traders. The operative word throughout the entire episode is about recognition (*hakarah*). *Hakarah* is also a word used to describe a stranger, a foreigner, or a *Nochri*. How Joseph recognizes his brothers and how they come to recognize him is the dominant motif of the entire narrative.

The dual meaning of *hakarah* carries through this moment and invites varieties of interpretation of who recognizes whom. To Joseph, these men are not foreigners at all. But to the brothers, Joseph is a total foreigner. His clothes are different, his features have matured, and certainly his position is unlikely considering where they last left him. Joseph's question to the brothers is as much a reflection of them and their awareness as it is of Joseph's journey.

When the brothers respond, **"From the land Canaan, to procure food,"**[69] Joseph has a better idea of whom he is facing. These are not the recalcitrant brothers who heartlessly threw him into the pit nor are they truly penitent brothers who express their remorse in the brokenness of their family. Joseph sees an opening here, an opportunity to correct the injustices of the past and to set a course of healing for the family. Asking someone from whence they came is never simply about location. It is always an invitation to tell the story of that journey. Joseph sees this and provides his brothers with an opportunity to describe more of themselves. When they choose not to offer more than their location, Joseph begins to call them spies. It will take quite a bit of coercion for them to speak the truth of their journey before Joseph can authentically and wholeheartedly reveal himself to them.

Faith and Fate

42:28 "What is this that God has done to us?"

The Torah is a chronicle of origins, of the foundations of a society, of definitions of power and political structures, and it is ultimately a document of faith. More than believing in the veracity of the stories it contains, the faithful believe in its eternal messages of humanity in light of the quest for holiness. Moments when faith is absent or challenged are also crucial to the narrative. They are presented not to undermine the ultimate premise of faith in the Holy One but to acknowledge the dimensions of disbelief and the consequences of avoiding or ignoring one's doubt.

This could not be more understated or profound than in the story of Jacob's sons. Jacob's journey to an everlasting faith in God is the basis of the faith for his children and the generations that follow. It is somewhat surprising to discover that Jacob's children, except Joseph, refer to God only twice throughout the entire narrative of their lives. By contrast, Joseph has always referred to God, of being God-fearing, of ascribing his abilities to the blessing God has bestowed upon him. The glaring absence of the brothers' faith throughout the chapters of their lives speaks volumes about their individual characters and also elucidates our understanding of how Jacob's children could fall into slavery just a few generations later.

The first time the sons of Jacob mention God is when they stand dumbfounded by the bounty given to them by the vizier of Egypt, or Joseph. They ask, **"What is this that God has done to us?"** Our first impression is that the brothers are expressing fear for the punishment they are to receive from this mysterious authority figure.

The Torah does not specify which brother asks the question either. The text simply states, **"They turned to one another."** On the one hand, the anonymity of this question is deeply meaningful. It doesn't matter who asks a question pointing to God's presence. Whenever God can be a part of the story, God is welcomed. On the other hand, this question comes at a time of crisis. It is a response to the fear that this Egyptian leader will imprison them or even sentence them to death. The question, then, is an expression of desperation, an attempt to grasp at meaning in a moment of great uncertainty. God isn't a part of the conversation at all. In this sense, God is the excuse.

There is a hint of faith in the brothers' question here. They recognize that there are other forces somehow intervening in their very human quest for sustenance. Their faithful path resumes when they continue to move forward, accepting responsibility for their fate despite its gravely uncertain consequences. In the end, the brothers' acceptance is precisely what melts Joseph's heart to embrace them once again.

Real Intelligence

43:6 *"Why did you do evil to me and tell the man there is another brother?"*

43:7 *"He [Joseph] asked us and our descendants directly, 'Is your father alive? Do you have a brother?'"*

43:8 *"How were we to know that he would say, 'Bring your brother here'?"*

A vital sign of intelligence is demonstrated by our capacity to anticipate the needs of another. More than the clever projections that are often used by an intelligent person to gain some personal advantage, the truly intelligent being understands and anticipates another's needs as being both strategic and mutually beneficial. Determining when to consider the needs of another, however, is deeply situational and demands another form of intelligence, that of emotional intelligence.

Sensing the blindness or inability of another to see what is necessary is equally challenging. The Torah identifies this concern in the episode of Joseph and his brothers when their limited knowledge prompts a vexing perplexity in their father Jacob. When Jacob asks his sons, **"Why did you do evil to me and tell the man there is another brother?"** we may initially sense Jacob's disappointment in his sons' willingness to share the unnecessary information of Benjamin's existence in the midst of their transaction with the vizier of Egypt for food.

The episode is somewhat peculiar in that the sons are making decisions for their father in another land, and while they are speaking on his behalf, the father becomes irate. The sons respond to Jacob's inquiry by rationalizing the persistent inquiries of the vizier: **"He asked us and our descendants directly, 'Is your father alive? Do you have a brother?' And we answered him accordingly. How were we to know that he would say, 'Bring your brother here'?"**

On the one hand, the responses of Reuben and Judah, who prepare to take all responsibility for Benjamin through their return to Egypt, reveals the level of care about their brother that seems so crucial in Joseph's story. For Joseph, to see their care of Benjamin is redemptive especially because they did not care about him.

On the other hand, the questions reveal a deeper problem. The brothers, who are calculating enough to tell their father one of his sons was killed by a wild beast, cannot outsmart the vizier of Egypt. Their emotional intelligence here is immature. Jacob's frustration may also be that his sons are not using their intelligence to navigate this complicated situation.

Joseph could have easily exacted revenge upon his brothers and no one have would have known! But when Joseph says he is a man who fears God, what he is saying is that revenge is not godly. Joseph wants to be restored to his family after all these years and is using his emotional intelligence to anticipate the moment when the brothers will be most capable of recognizing the favor of their circumstances. Hence the probing inquiries into the remaining family in Canaan.

There is one more facet of the narrative that is not fully resolved. Shimon is held back in Egypt as collateral for the brothers to return with Benjamin. Jacob recognizes the horror of the situation when they return to him from Egypt. And then the text states that they remained while consuming the rations given to them. The Torah is not specific about the amount of time the brothers remain in Canaan after receiving both the food rations and the return of their money they were supposed to use to acquire food! We may comfortably assume that there was more time than necessary, even if they were starving to the point of death, before they even considered returning to Egypt.[70] Didn't they care about their brother Shimon? Wouldn't they have wanted to resolve the conflict as quickly as possible? Moreover, we no longer hear of Shimon in the narrative other than that he is eventually returned to his brothers.[71] Their perceived carelessness here is what inflames Jacob and even compels them to be open to ultimately receiving Joseph once again into the family.

Trust, but Verify

43:27 "Is the father you spoke of well? Is he still living?"
43:29 "Is this the young brother you spoke of to me?"

In the later books of the Torah, there are going to be many laws pertaining to oath swearing, the circumstances for nullifying a promise, and the consequences for breaking an oath. Making commitments on future outcomes was an essential thread in the social fabric of ancient Israel and is so even in contemporary society. The foundations of trust that must exist within a family and even within a community are sacrosanct, hence the Torah's concern with proper commitments. The test of those promises becomes the subject of the hero's drama and comes into focus in the story of Joseph and his brothers.

Joseph knows his brothers have not been faithful in the past, so their promise to return to Egypt with their younger brother remains uncertain in his mind. More than exchanging polite greetings when the brothers do indeed return to Egypt, Joseph asks, **"Is the father you spoke of well? Is he still living?"** and **"Is this the young brother you spoke of to me?"** He is verifying that the brothers are honoring their pledge. In his capacity as vizier, it seems a bit excessive to require the pledge of a brother in return for the presence of another. Joseph keeps his commitment and unceremoniously returns Shimon to them.

For the reader, though, there is a transparency here that the brothers cannot yet see. Joseph has been totally honest with them all along. His concern for his father and his brother Benjamin is amplified by their absence when the brothers first appear in Egypt. Joseph's insistence on Benjamin's presence is both a verification of his concern for the brothers' commitment and a reflection of his ulterior goal: reunion with his family.

Joseph's line of questioning establishes an important condition of trust: the verification of commitment. The demonstration of trusting behavior, particularly in a distrusting environment, by hearing from the brothers in response to his questions is the prerequisite of an authentic relationship. It seems Judah is becoming aware of this when he pledges to protect Benjamin with his own life.[72] Joseph isn't uncertain about his desire to reveal himself to his brothers. The verifications of their commitment will confirm his trust.

Ordering Questions and Questioning Orders

44:4 "Why have you paid for good with evil?"

44:5 "Is this not the cup from which my master drinks, and he uses to practice divinity?"

44:7 "Why do you speak these words?"

44:8 "How could we steal from your master's house silver or gold?"

The pinnacle of intrigue and deception in the Joseph story occurs when he deliberately orders his silver goblet to be placed in Benjamin's bag of rations. As the brothers return home to Canaan, Joseph orders his steward to overtake the brothers and ask the following questions upon discovering the goblet: **"Why have you paid for good with evil?"** and **"Is this not the cup from which my master drinks, and he uses to practice divinity?"** The text explains that the steward poses the questions just as he has been ordered to do.

There is something so deflating about this narrative. Despite Joseph's power and authority, his overt manipulation of the steward and his brothers is antithetical to the entire project of the Torah. Joseph has been honest and transparent with his brothers until now, and he considers himself a God-fearing man. Yet this deceptive act seems to imply that morality is not a divine imperative but a human invention to employ for one's personal gain and influence. Joseph, the man who says his gifts come from God, is now instructing his servant to entrap others. Even if we suggest that Joseph needed to create this tension so that the brothers would experience a change of heart, the implication that libelous accusations can be used at all is unsettling. We might imagine what the steward must have been thinking when Joseph set up this ruse and then how he felt when he fulfilled his master's command to execute it. This is hardly the exemplary behavior of a heroic figure.

And yet this deception will precipitate one of the most emotionally charged moments in the entire book of Genesis. When the brothers first challenge the accusation by asking, **"Why do you speak these words?"** and **"How could we steal from your master's house silver or gold?"** we begin to see the veneer of their family as a unit cracking. They cannot protect their younger brother from the accusations of the leader in Egypt, and they cannot return home to their father with yet more devastating news of his beloved child's captivity. Their protest is a statement of absolute loyalty, one that we ought to have expected when Joseph found them herding sheep in the fields many years ago. Their journey to family and tribal responsibility is truly revealed at this moment.

Perhaps Joseph's actions were in anticipation of this discovery. Maybe Joseph understood that only when the brothers had so much to lose would they ultimately take responsibility for each other. The following questions and Joseph's declaration to his brothers can be redemptive. Joseph's questions will restore order to the family, just as he dreamed as a child.

Checkmate

44:15 "What is this deed that you have done?"

44:15 "Did you not know conjuring divinity is something for a man such as me?"

44:16 "What can we tell [ask] to my lord, what can we say, and how can we clear ourselves?"

There are times when we direct a conversation to a conclusion with only one option. These checkmate moments are the culmination of many possible outcomes in which the next action seems inevitable. The drama of the story of Joseph and his brothers is amplified by the potential for multiple outcomes of their conflict. The brothers' deliberate choice to sell Joseph to the traders, and Joseph's willful choice to at first hide his identity from them in Egypt and create a unique story, is at best an elaborate myth to describe how *B'nai Yisrael* ended up enslaved in Egypt.

Joseph's last attempt to compel his brothers to accept responsibility for their misdeeds unfolds through a series of questions. Unlike the questions he has posed to them before this moment, he still wants confirmation of their honesty. They have been, after all, caught red-handed with a silver goblet he has accused them of stealing. When Joseph asks, **"What is this deed that you have done?"** he presents the brothers with another set of choices. Like the first question Joseph asks his brothers, **"From where do you come?"**[73] Joseph wants them to tell their story, to explain their purpose in such a way that includes their negligence and carelessness. They can certainly choose to deflect their responsibility, but that would either prolong the story or propel it to a tragic conclusion.

There is even the sense that Joseph's question to his brothers at this moment is self-reflective. This is confirmed as Joseph immediately follows his first question by asking, **"Did you not know conjuring divinity is something for a man such as me?"** Why does Joseph turn the inquiry to himself at this point? To instill fear and doubt in the minds of his brothers? While these curiosities may be evoked by the surface meaning of the questions, Joseph is essentially asking himself, **"What is this deed you have done?!"**

This is the point when no other options are possible, when all questions that follow will reach the same conclusion. Judah recognizes this. Perhaps his experience with Tamar has taught him well.[74] When Yehuda asks, **"What can we tell [ask] to my lord, what can we say, and how can we clear ourselves?"** at that moment, Joseph and his brothers move toward the powerful reconciliation that highlights the entire book of Genesis and cements the loyalty of the families of Jacob for time immemorial.

VAYIGASH

44:19 "My lord asked us, 'Have you a father or a brother?'" (Yehuda to Joseph)

44:34 "How can I go up to my father, and the child [Benjamin] is not with us?" (Yehuda to Joseph)

45:3 "Is my father still living?" (Joseph to his brothers)

46:33 "What is your occupation?" (Joseph explaining the question Pharaoh will ask the brothers)

47:3 "What is your occupation?" (Pharaoh to the brothers)
47:8 "How many are the years of your life?" (Pharaoh to Jacob)

In the climactic moments of Joseph's story, indeed of the entire book of Genesis, the questions posed seemingly create a shift in our thinking and experience of divinity. There are no questions that even allude to the existence or presence of God here, and yet each question offers an interpretive frame to understand where God dwells in the human experience of being. From questions of heritage and legacy to questions of identity and purpose, the role of doubt in these chapters is one of curiosity and hope. Learning to pose questions like this in the Torah helps us shape our own sense of the divine presence in our lives when we ask seemingly factual questions of relationships, occupations, and even age and accept the invitation to respond with God in mind.

The Object Becomes the Subject

44:19 "My lord asked us, 'Have you a father or a brother?'"
44:34 "How can I go up to my father, and the child [Benjamin] is not with us?"
45:3 "Is my father still living?"

At the moment when the brothers are most vulnerable, Judah boldly shifts the narrative. Joseph's ploy to force the brothers into submission is all but certain, yet Judah compels Joseph to respond to his questions. This remarkable shift in tone has been the subject of much interpretation simply understood from the surface of the text. We may wonder when Judah did indeed know that Joseph was their brother. Judah's questions simmer with this compelling revelation of identity.

Judah asks the pointed question **"My lord asked us, 'Have you a father or a brother?'"** both as a recapitulation of the events that precipitated this tense encounter and to pierce the veil of Joseph's deception. Judah wants to know if Joseph is really compassionate and as God-fearing as he claimed when they first met. Judah's questions, while somewhat cavalier given the superficial balance of the relationship between Joseph and his brothers, are essential questions to verify Joseph's true intentions.

Judah's recapitulation of the episode from the first encounter between Joseph and the brothers is precisely what Joseph has longed for all these years. Judah recounts the connection of Benjamin to Jacob and Jacob's grief in losing both his sons. Joseph must understand from this that he is part of the story even if he does not know how they framed his absence as part of that story. Judah appeals to Joseph's sensibilities even further when he asks, **"How can I go up to my father, and the child [Benjamin] is not with us?"** Judah has come to understand something profound in the dynamic that is unfolding between them. Not only has he asked Joseph to account for his persistent inquiries about their father and brother, he has now invited him to commiserate with his conflict in his father's well-being. With this question, Judah is now testing Joseph.

Joseph's revelation and question in response teach us a lesson about authentic relationships. First, if Joseph has listened to Judah's story, he will know that Jacob is still alive. In fact, he has already asked about his father several times before, implying the factual answer to the question is presumably known. Yet when Joseph asks, **"Is my father still living?"** feelings of reunion are palpable, a deep connection gushing from the words. Not only is Joseph's reference point significant in saying **"my father,"** the desire for Joseph to continue writing his story with his brothers is what changes the tone of the rest of the book. In fact, this identification of family is what propels the children of Jacob to settle in the land of Egypt and to prosper immensely.

Are You What You Do?

46:33 "What is your occupation?"

47:3 "What is your occupation?"

The Torah's command to instruct your children to ask questions about the story of slavery and redemption in Egypt is an essential feature of the Jewish religion. Indeed, the Passover seder and the experience of questioning our history are among the most significant contributions the Jewish people have shared with the world. It is through the exchange of questions and answers that we not only better understand our roots but also project our purpose into the future. The Torah reminds us that defining our identity by our personal and collective histories is not completely determinative. The entire premise of Abraham's discovery of God and the covenant confirms that our history is not our destiny.

Histories and destinies begin to unfold after Joseph is reunited with his family in Egypt. The exchange between Pharoah, Jacob, and Jacob's children affirms how our histories become our destinies with a little creative storytelling. This imitation of identity appears in the exchange between Joseph and his brothers in advance of their introduction to Pharaoh. Joseph guides the brothers by urging, **"So, when Pharaoh summons you and asks, 'What is your occupation?' you shall answer him, 'Your servants have always been breeders of livestock.'"** Joseph is helping the brothers appeal to the sensibilities of Pharaoh. We'll learn that **"all shepherds are abhorrent to the Egyptians."**[75] Joseph wants his family to live freely in Egypt, and he knows just what they must say to persuade Pharaoh to welcome them.

The prompt of the question is quite innovative but something we've seen from Joseph before.[76] Joseph's coaching is a tool of social engineering that seems to undermine the family's autonomy. When we accept Joseph's direction as that of an advocate planning to appeal to a superior on behalf of a supplicant, it's not difficult to see the manipulative quality of this approach.

It is perhaps even more insightful when Pharaoh does indeed ask the question **"What is your occupation?"** and the brothers' response is not word for word as Joseph guides. Pharaoh asks the question exactly as Joseph predicted, but the brothers omit the rationale that qualifies their relevance and value to Pharaoh.[77]

Whether we interpret this response to reflect the character of the brothers as a monolithic group and one reticent to be identified narrowly, or read into this that the brothers are indeed following Joseph's guidance and direction it should not be underestimated to what degree the brothers adopt the identity they have professed. While the ensuing chapters will transform these nomads into slaves to Pharaonic domination, their peaceful and prosperous sojourn in Egypt is built upon a contrived identity, one Joseph has designated for them. In the span of a few verses, this family brimming with potential to become God's chosen people has become narrowly defined as a subgroup of an Egyptian dynasty.

The concluding stories of Genesis set for us the stage of a powerful revolution in identity. Our histories are not our destinies. What we do is not who we are. When what we do is who we are, enslavement is but one generation away.

Number Your Years

47:8 "How many are the years of your life?"

Abraham's journey continues far beyond the span of his lifetime. Abraham's legacy is the wandering from birthplace to birthright and the obstacles and tests along the way that prove his worth in every generation. The enigmatic visit to Egypt when we first take interest in his life quest reveals that the great hero is also subject to the forces and authorities of the day. When Pharaoh sent him away with great riches so that he might settle in the land of Canaan and prosper, it seemed inconceivable that his progeny would return and be regarded as equals, elders of the land, worthy of respect and dignity.

At the end of the book of Genesis, the pharaoh of Joseph's generation treats Abraham's grandson Jacob with an uncommon respect either borne from his regard for Joseph or because the name of Abraham is still remembered in the halls of Pharaoh's palace. When Jacob eventually dies, Pharaoh is even going to escort him to his burial!

Pharaoh's question to Jacob here is not simply curiosity about chronology. When Pharaoh greets Jacob and asks, **"How many are the years of your life?"** we are initially moved by his interest. Why should Pharaoh care? Yet when Jacob responds by saying, **"The years of my sojourn are 130. Few and hard have been the years of my life, nor do they come up to the life spans of my fathers during their sojourns,"** he is signaling that the epic journey of his ancestors has been fraught with struggle and sacrifice. By framing the response to the question with an appraisal of his own life, Jacob's response to Pharaoh is that the quality of years are far more worthy of respect than the number of years one walks upon the earth.

This exchange is quite terse relative to the concluding chapters of the book of Genesis. On the one hand, its brevity elucidates the interest and care of this pharaoh for the well-being of Jacob and maybe even his children. On the other hand, this brief episode underscores the dramatic change that will occur under the pharaoh of the future who **"does not know Joseph."**[78] The pharaoh of future generations will have no concern for the sons of Jacob or the legacies of Abraham and Isaac.

Whenever we ask a person their age, we are seeking some relationship with them. Whether it is the elder looking to commiserate with the experiences of youth or a youth seeking the wisdom that an elder can offer, the request is always a reflection of some desire to know the other better. Pharaoh's question is prompted by Jacob's blessing![79] Jacob has a long and complicated relationship with blessings. He hasn't even blessed his children at this point.

Jacob's number of years reflects the growth and depth of his soul. More than the struggles that he compares to those of his ancestors, it is Jacob's capacity to bless the other that makes Abraham's journey endure.

VAYECHI

48:8 "Who are these?" (Jacob to Joseph, referring to his grandchildren)
50:19 "Am I in the place of God?" (Joseph to his brothers)

The final chapters of the book of Genesis are more than a culmination of one family's journey into Egypt. The blessings uttered by Jacob in the final moments of his life look forward to the evolving narrative of his children and grandchildren to become the foundations of their identity as a nation. They are no longer a confederation of tribes. They are a family with a destiny; their fate will be universal throughout their experience in Egypt and throughout the generations to follow. The two short questions posed here are affirmations of a divine role in the lives of Jacob's children without the authoritative or commanding voice of God. We meet the conclusion of the book of Genesis with trepidation. The echoes of God's voice, while inspiring Jacob to bless and Joseph to act justly, leave us wondering if the God of All will be recognized by anyone but the family.

To Know Is To Feel

48:8 "Who are these?"

At the end of the book of Genesis, we witness the tremendous capacity of the human being to sense the world around him, to anticipate and understand the needs of others, and to recognize the lasting power of God's presence. The drama of Jacob's death and the promise of continuity through his children and grandchildren is not contingent upon God's intervention. Their faith will endure despite the absence of words and gestures confirming God's existence. As we will read in the final chapters of the book, there is a tremendous amount of faith in what will become of the children of Jacob.

One episode in particular reveals this sensitive touch to find God in others around us. Jacob promises that Joseph's two sons Ephraim and Menashe will be blessed by God. Before he even places his hands upon their heads and conveys words as his father did for him, Jacob has already determined who these children will be. That is why the question he asks when they enter his presence is peculiar. **"Who are these?"** is a question that portrays Jacob as an aged grandfather incapable of discerning the presence of others before him, just like his own enfeebled father. The text even goes so far as to make this explicit, **"Now Israel's eyes were dim with age; he could not see."**[80] We are beginning to learn here that to know is to feel—much as Isaac felt his son's hairy frame, but on an even deeper level.

As we have seen,[81] questions like this are not concerned with proximal identity. We may wonder if Jacob senses the difference in the upbringing of these two children given the privileges of their father's position and their experience in a royal court. They have not been raised among a confederation of tents in the expanse of the desert. Jacob isn't asking what kinds of people his grandchildren are, though. He must also sense that Joseph, the man Jacob's other sons could not recognize, may be a different child than the one he thought was killed in the fields near Dotan. And so he asks, **"Who are these?"** intentionally. The question is ultimately directed to Joseph.

Joseph is the one who exemplifies a change most similar to the transformation Jacob undergoes. When Jacob asks about the children, he is really attempting to discern how much of his beloved child endures in the man who is now his benefactor and the family savior. It is as if his question invites Joseph to proclaim Ephraim and Manashe are children of Israel even though their upbringing has been completely in Egyptian culture. It is why we feel the sense of comfort that Jacob expresses when he says, **"I never expected to see you again, and here God has let me see your children as well."**[82]

Jacob's final moments of life are filled with faith. It's inspiring to read and feel that faithful touch endures in his children and grandchildren. A question like this also confirms our relationships with those close to us and can sustain us in every generation.

It's Bigger Than You Thought
50:19 "Am I in the place of God?"

We are often too comfortable in our understanding of the world around us, depending upon reliability and certainty to provide a salve for our anxious thoughts. When we encounter information or circumstances that challenge our comfort, we are pressed to make a choice. Do we embrace the new reality as it is presenting itself to us, or do we twist and bend new understandings to fit neatly into our existing worldviews? While both approaches have their merits and values in the right places and times, the very act of choosing in light of new information can be daunting, even stultifying. The last question in the book of Genesis brings this quest for new certainty to light.

When Joseph's brothers fling themselves upon his mercy and prepare to be enslaved by him, Joseph asks, **"Am I in the place of God?"** Joseph's response to his brothers' fear of reprisal extends beyond their momentary concern as an expression of confidence. Joseph is summarizing his life and theirs by expanding the narrow concern for fraternal revenge and framing their present and future in epic proportions.

This question **"Am I in the place of God?"** pierces the realms of eternal seeking. In God's absence, Joseph's question is liberating. Abraham walks with God, and Joseph walks in God's shadow. God is eminently present with the first human beings in the Garden, yet God is profoundly removed in the stories of Joseph and his siblings in Egypt. If the beginning of the book is God seeking the human being (*Ayeka?* [**Where are**

you?]) the end of the book is the human being confidently locating himself in deference to the One. Human beings now have their own distinct identity, and through Jacob and Joseph we learn that our relationship with the divine is in partnership.

Who asks a question like this? In it are the echoes of Jacob's literal question to Rachel amidst the struggles with her barrenness.[83] The implication of Joseph's faith in response to the brothers' submission, which foreshadows their eventual enslavement, is empowering. Because it is the last question of the book, we are invited to answer the question ourselves, formally recognizing our potential in relationship to the divine source of life.

CONCLUSION

Genesis begins with the sublime tapestry of creation to convey the spirit of completion in existence. We read, **"And God blessed the seventh day and declared it holy—having ceased on it from all the work of creation that God had done."**[84] Where the eternal nature of God's presence in the world ends and begins anew, the human experience of creation develops precariously in between. Human nature does not instinctively experience completion, and as such we experience uncertainty and doubt. The joy of rest and reflection, the satisfaction that what one has is enough, the transcendent quality of simply being are learned behaviors. Thus families are born, relationships forged, communities developed, and ultimately nations are established perhaps in part to resolve the incompleteness of creation. From the beginning of Genesis to its conclusion, we witness the evolution of the singular human being into the complexities of a national family. It's quite extraordinary in perspective!

The book teaches us to grapple with the paradoxical nature of being: that there is an eternal quest for wholeness and that creation is not quite whole at all. The sacred text of the Torah introduces questions to mediate the experience of existing between the two. Without these questions as a part of the text, these qualities would be coarsened by some determinate value (e.g., human beings always sin; we are never allowed to challenge God's justice; human beings will always grapple with strife between themselves).

In particular, the questions in the book of Genesis focus upon liminal experiences like vulnerability, shame, acceptance, justice, and ultimately faith. These experiences are precisely what give definition to the space between, to the uncertainties of living and the desire to know that which is eternally certain. As we turn the page to unfold the epic drama of God's redemptive power and the potential for humanity to fulfill its covenantal responsibilities, we hold close to the liminal moments and are reminded that they form the foundation of our potential to narrow the space between ends and beginnings. The questions, then, form a sacred journey of knowing that wholeness, or *shalom*, is possible, even divine.

PART II

INTRODUCTION TO EXODUS

IF THE FIRST BOOK FOCUSES ON QUESTIONS OF IDENTITY AND ASKS, "Who are we as human beings?" the second book addresses another key question: "Who are You, God of Israel?" As God is introduced to the world, the faithful quest is paved with the discovery of laws, rituals, and ethics that emanate from the divine source. As much as it is the goal of humanity to know God, by the end of the book, God will also come to know Moshe and the Israelite people much better. Their unconditional devotion at Mount Sinai and their incessant complaints invite a relationship with God that is not merely transactional. God is not simply a commanding voice, and the Israelite people are not obedient followers with an uncertain destiny.

The book opens with the recounting of the individual children of Jacob, 70 people in total, who entered Egypt at the end of Genesis. Their descendants ultimately leave Egypt as 603,500 men at least 20 years old—more than 2 million men, women, and children! The sheer enormity of such growth is an essential part of the text. They become a nation through this growth. Exploring how one family becomes a nation is the wondrous if not preeminent miracle of the book. But more than this marvel of national growth, which spans 430 years according to the text,[1] Exodus provides the building blocks of what kind of community these people will come to emulate. We are not meant to read these verses as a story of enslavement and redemption alone, though this is the theme that animates the first half of this book. The concept of a society based on a new civility, one that feels concern for the well-being of others, deserves attention as well.

The questions of Exodus move this theme along, beginning with definitions of self and slave and concluding with the free person in their aspiration to pursue a covenantal destiny. This journey identifies the core purpose of the Jewish people: to be a light among the nations of the world, preaching tolerance for and celebrating human dignity.

Exodus

SHEMOT

1:18 "Why have you done this thing [and let the boys live]?" (Pharaoh to the midwives)

2:7 "Shall I go call for you a woman nurse from among the Hebrews and nurse for you this boy?" (Maidservant [Miriam] to Pharaoh's daughter)

2:13 "Why do you strike your fellow?" (Moshe to the Israelite)

2:14 "Who are you to be a master and judge over us?" (The man to Moshe)

2:14 "Do you mean to kill me as you killed the Egyptian?" (The Israelite to Moshe)

2:18 "Why did you come so soon today?" (Reuel to his daughters)

2:20 "Where is he?" (Reuel to his daughters)

2:20 "Why did you leave this man?" (Reuel to his daughters)

3:11 "Who am I that I should go to Pharaoh and should bring forth the children of Israel out of Egypt?" (Moshe to God)

3:13 "What is God's Name? What shall I say to them?" (Moshe to God)

4:1 "What if they do not believe me and do not listen to me, but say, 'YHVH did not appear to you'?" (Moshe to God)

4:2 "What is that in your hand?" (God to Moshe)

4:11 "Who makes man's mouth? Who makes a man dumb, or deaf, or seeing, or blind? Is it not I, YHVH?" (God to Moshe)

5:2 "Who is YHVH that I should listen to His voice and let Israel go?" (Pharaoh to Moshe and Aharon)

5:4 "Why do you, Moshe and Aharon, cause the people to break loose from their work?" (Pharaoh to Moshe and Aharon)

5:14 "Why did you not complete the prescribed amount of bricks either yesterday, or today, as you did before?" (Taskmasters to Israelites)

5:15 "Why did you do this [increase our work burdens] to your servants?" (Officers of B'nai Yisrael to Pharaoh)

5:22 "O YHVH, why have you brought evil to this people?" (Moshe to God)

5:22 "Why have you sent me?" (Moshe to God)

From the first question of this book, and in particular this portion, there is a throbbing impulse to question the authority of humanity and even of God. The entire episode of enslavement and redemption confronts the question when human beings take on the role of gods determining life and death over each other. If the final question of the book of Genesis, **"Am I in the place of God?"** is our guide, these opening chapters explore the antithesis—what it looks like for humanity to play the role of creator and destroyer. God's questions to Moshe remind us anew of the power beyond human grasp. Here our questions are those of discovery, or rediscovery, of that truth.

Conscience and Consciousness

1:18 "Why have you done this thing [and let the boys live]?"

A popular maxim attributed to American financier Henry S. Haskins as well as Ralph Waldo Emerson says that "what lies behind us and what lies before us are tiny matters compared to what lies within us."[1] This inner strength is what animates the deeply moral conscience of humanity. This inner power also becomes the subject of contention in the first chapter of the book of Exodus.

The story of Shifra and Puah, midwives to the Hebrew women, is often referred to as the first record of nonviolent resistance in history. Faced with an edict to murder Hebrew children just after they are born, the women simply refuse to comply with Pharaoh's command. Pharaoh, instead of acting on the reports of their suspicious behavior and likely taking their lives for their disobedience, asks them, **"Why have you done this thing?"**

We've read that the motivation for Pharaoh's genocidal decree is the fear that the people will become too numerous and take to war against him and his people.[2] In a devious plan to anticipate this impending threat, Pharaoh chooses to deny the Israelites their basic human rights, enslaving them and threatening to kill their children in order to prevent a future he cannot accept. This push against the throbbing consciousness of a collective body of humanity is what prompts the long and detailed narrative introducing Moshe. It is through Moshe's personal redemption and then his divine imperative to redeem the Israelite people that the Israelite consciousness is born. Shifra and Puah are actors in a divine plan that without their intervention might not have been realized.

Pharaoh's actions also teach us an important lesson about human behavior. Power isn't demonstrated by asking a question that seeks to confirm a challenge to authority. When something is correct and true, the consequences of the decision are met with certainty even if those outcomes are painful and difficult. We don't see any record of a punishment for Shifra's and Puah's disobedience. In fact, the text even rewards their behavior.[3] This moment isn't a test of our loyalty to Shifra and Puah to prove that Pharaoh's nefarious plans are inconsistent with his goal. The taking of life for political purposes should never be planned. The defiance of Shifra and Puah is a great affirmation of the power of conscience we must continue to hold onto throughout the generations.

She Took Pity On Him

2:7 "Shall I go call for you a woman nurse from among the Hebrews and nurse for you this boy?"

The text explains that a child is born to a certain Israelite man and woman. Yet Pharaoh's decree to kill the male Hebrew children hovers like an ominous cloud over the city. In desperation, the parents send their child down the river to an uncertain fate. If the child stays in the home, the forces of evil are sure to discover him and sentence him to death. On the river, in the bulrushes, the child just may have a chance to survive.

Pharaoh's daughter bathes in the waters of the river and discovers the child. Faced with the child's impending death, the princess acts with pity. She assumes the child was born to Hebrew parents and seeks to save the child. At this pivotal moment of concern, a maidservant, in Hebrew *Achot* (sister), steps forward and asks Pharaoh's daughter, **"Shall I go call for you a woman nurse from among the Hebrews and nurse for you this boy?"** It is the question that will shift the entire narrative plight of the Israelite people. Without this intervention, the circumstances of this child would have been left to chance. The choice of Pharaoh's daughter should not be quickly overlooked, nor should the bravery of the maidservant. Pharaoh's daughter responds by telling the maidservant, **"Take this child and nurse it for me,"** implying she will take the child into her care and be responsible for any circumstances of her decision.

But the question suggests there is some ambivalence in the choice the daughter of Pharaoh must make here. She could have silenced her pity with quiet resignation; she could have said that Pharaoh's decree must not be disobeyed. But she takes the fate of this child and potentially her own fate into her hands and acts with faith in the responsibility to preserve life. She could have left the child to languish in the river or even acted with genocidal vengeance like her father. By taking the child into her care and ensuring that the child will be raised in safety, perhaps even by his own mother, she illuminates the morally courageous act she makes under very dangerous circumstances.

We cannot anticipate the gravity of our choices without a moral compass. The daughter of Pharaoh is a responsible actor in a chaotic world of deceit and murder. She teaches us that moral courage is not only in her act but in her response to the throbbing pain of conscience that prompted her to take pity on the child. We learn from her that redemption begins in thought and only becomes a reality in divine action. Perhaps her inspiring choice here becomes the foundation for Moshe's concern for the treatment of the Hebrew slaves that we read of next.

Us and Them—To Whom Do We Belong?

2:13 *"Why do you strike your fellow?"*

2:14 *"Who are you to be a master and judge over us?"*

2:14 *"Do you mean to kill me as you killed the Egyptian?"*

Defining the boundaries of our identity enables us to feel a sense of belonging. The broader we define those boundaries, the greater our capacity to understand human experience. Moshe's awareness of his expanding identity, especially in relation to the Israelite slaves, is the precursor to his election as the leader of their redemption from slavery. The episode of his questioning the two Hebrew men fighting with each other is a pivotal moment of awareness and responsibility.

Moshe asks, **"Why do you strike your fellow?"** The purpose of the struggle is perhaps the focus of Moshe's intervention, but the insight behind this question is deeper. Moshe uses an interrogative to both disarm the men in their quarrel and to help the men recognize the severity of their behavior. From Moshe's perspective, two Hebrew slaves fighting against each other is even lower than the ruthlessness of the taskmaster, a condition we read of just verses earlier when Moshe took the life of the taskmaster after witnessing the taskmaster's cruel and unjust behavior toward a Hebrew slave.

Moshe's own awareness of moral responsibility may not have been evident when he struck down the Egyptian taskmaster. Here the question reveals the depth of character that Moshe possesses both in concern for his fellow Israelites and for the moral command to protect life and minimize the harm human beings can cause one another.

The man's reply to Moshe's question with another question is equally telling. When one of the quarreling men asks Moshe in response, **"Who are you to be a master and judge over us? Do you mean to kill me as you did the Egyptian?"** our impulse is to revert back to Moshe and explore the impetus behind the man's challenge. What right does Moshe have to ask about men resorting to physical violence when he just took the life of another?

This question is also the first introduction of the concept of "us" as self-identification among the class of "other." Moshe may be known to the people as the son of Yocheved, but Moshe's name was given to him by Pharaoh's daughter. At first, Pharaoh and his advisors do not question their nefarious plan to subjugate and enslave the children of Jacob. Pharaoh's proclamation **"Let us deal shrewdly with them"**[4] already defines the children of Jacob as other. Here realization of otherness is internalized by the Hebrew. Still Moshe is described as being from among his kinsmen. Ultimately this moment reaches clarity when the Israelite sees Moshe only as an other, as an oppressor to him.

When Moshe proclaims, **"Then the matter is known!"** we learn that he has acquired a moral awareness he may not have possessed before. Surely the fear he experiences is in the threat of reprisal. But it is in confirmation from the two quarreling men that his concern is not for his own life. We also see this as a defining example of the Israelites' enslavement. They have become so downtrodden as not to see this willful attempt by Moshe to disrupt their destructive behavior.

Moshe expresses a concern pulsating from his throbbing moral conscience. It is from this moment that Moshe is prepared to meet God. One message here is that when humanity and God meet in the midst of moral controversy, redemption becomes possible.

It is as if the Israelite is challenging Moshe to determine exactly who the people are as the text identifies them as **"his kinsmen."** Moshe's response is to flee. He must meet the God of Israel before returning to the people to lead them through the house of bondage to the foot of Mount Sinai. This journey begins in affirmation of Moshe's distinction as being of and separate from the people. This dichotomy makes him uniquely qualified to lead the people. These questions unequivocally locate him among the Israelites to lead them toward moral responsibility.

Radical Hospitality

> 2:18 *"Why did you come so soon today?"*
> 2:20 *"Where is he?"*
> 2:20 *"Why did you leave this man?"*

Is Yitro a priest or is he a devoted father-in-law? His role as advisor and inspiration to Moshe throughout his journey to become the leader of the Israelite people is vital to the narrative. We do not read of his professional responsibilities anywhere in the text. We do learn from Yitro that Moshe's leadership will be supported by Yitro's caring guidance and wise counsel. The model Yitro exemplifies is that of both priest and supportive parent. We'll meet him as a priest later, but he is first introduced to us when his daughters return from the well in Midian. Moshe finds the well after fleeing his narrow fate in Egypt and fends off the shepherds who seemingly prevent the daughters from drawing sufficient water for their own flocks. Yitro's immediate concern is to repay the kindness given to his daughters. And so Yitro first asks his daughters, **"Why did you come so soon today?"** in response to their unusual timing in returning from the well. He follows up his line of inquiry with **"Where is he?"** and **"Why did you leave this man?"**

In this series of questions, Yitro's character is established as a generous host. He'll even offer his daughter as a wife for Moshe! And so these questions of hospitality come into focus. Unlike Abram, whose kindness to the traveling strangers was a model for openness, Yitro has a reason to provide a home for Moshe. In the grand spaces between the verses, we believe that a strong relationship is forged between Moshe and Yitro. When he no doubt shares the story of his upbringing, Moshe will have revealed his character to Yitro and gained Yitro's trust and confidence in his purpose. Moshe has not yet met the God of Israel at this point, and we can fairly assume that Yitro's insight into the character of Moshe implies that Moshe's destiny for greatness is evident.

More than some future strategic alliance that will benefit Yitro as much as, if not more than, Moshe, the kindness Moshe receives is a crucial element of his discovery of God. After fleeing Egypt to pursue the source of justice, with this sense of comfort and support he is able to find inconsumable bushes and hear voices of divine truth. Yitro as a priest already understands this. In many ways his awareness of the God of Israel is well established by the time Moshe enters Yitro's tent.

Yitro's radical hospitality teaches us something important about the ways of our ancients and us. Wherever kindness is evident, our embrace can create redemption. Indeed, Yitro's model provides a great example of this care.

What Would Moshe Do?

3:11 "Who am I that I should go to Pharaoh and should bring forth the children of Israel out of Egypt?"

A popular mantra for Christian devotees is the phrase "What Would Jesus Do?" *Imitatio Christi,* or modeling one's behavior after the central figure of Christianity, inspires generations of young believers to walk in

God's ways. For a brief time, Judaism adapted this concept by asking, "What Would Moshe Do?" as a similar model for ethical behavior. Indeed, behavioral scientists point to the concept of play acting or modeling an ideal form of behavior as a way to inspire ethical action. Moshe atop the mountain receiving God's Torah is certainly worth emulating. His journey to that moment is an even greater inspiration to walk in God's ways within the Jewish tradition.

The opening chapters of the book pay close attention to Moshe's familial connection, to his particular circumstances of early childhood, his upbringing in the pharaoh's palace, his dramatic realization of personal and national significance, and finally his ultimate spiritual awakening and acceptance of his destiny. It becomes all the more curious and disconcerting to read of this man's ambivalence toward his elected responsibility. He questions God, **"Who am I that I should go to Pharaoh and should bring forth the children of Israel out of Egypt?"** Our first response might be "Who are you *not* to be the one to go and bring the children of Israel out of Egypt?" Even without our omniscient perspective on Moshe's fitness as a redeemer, our ethical impulse beckons us to cry out in full voice in response to the unspeakable suffering we bear witness to in this book. From Moshe we learn that the one who is empowered to respond to injustice must accept responsibility even if he is insecure in that purpose. Today we might refer to such a role as a vocation. Moshe's job is to give voice to injustice (even if the irony is that he is **"slow of speech"**).[5]

This lack of confidence and the question it prompts reveal a dimension of faith we don't readily associate with our heroes. Where the hero is customarily understood as the one who courageously steps forth to do the right thing, this hero is open and vulnerable to his weaknesses. More than a false humility, Moshe exemplifies a profoundly heroic act, sharing his uncertainty with God. Whereas the typical hero clenches his fists and bears uncertainty with an iron will, this hero opens his heart so that his voice crying for justice will be heard by the vulnerable and the oppressed too.

The Definition of God

3:13 "What is God's Name? What shall I say to them?"

The Israelites have been living in Egypt for hundreds of years. Generations have grown up with the impression that they are an inferior class of people, fated to toil and build for the Egyptian Pharaoh. In desperation they cried out to God, and God took note. Enlisting Moshe was the first great step toward liberation. But freedom will ultimately come from the hands of the people, with God's help.

First Moshe asks, **"What is God's Name? What shall I say to them?"** Moshe asks this question in anticipation of a skeptical B'nai Yisrael, downtrodden by the burdens of enslavement. The Israelites have been saturated by a foreign culture whose focus of divine energy is bound up in gods of nature and death. We must assume they are influenced by, if not participating in, the dramatic concerns of the Egyptian people in relation to the unknown. Day after day their lives are uncertain, and the Egyptian way of life has challenged their paternal instincts for divine unity. The presumption is the people will need to be persuaded that the God of Israel is appearing as redeemer. But they do not ask. *One defining feature of slavery is the absence of questions.*

God's response, **"I will be,"**[6] is strategic in this sense, because there is no simple determination of **"I will be"** that can be pointed to. It is only understood in reference to an action once it has been taken. As we learn later in the book, Moshe will seek God's face, and though his request will be denied, he will be permitted to behold the essence of God. This question of identity remains open for us. The God of Israel reacts to this inquiry enigmatically to prompt devotion, perhaps despite its illogical and irrational expression.

We can imagine what the people would have said when Moshe told them who was coming to redeem them. Maybe they would have expected a proper name for the God Moshe represented. The beauty of the question is that Moshe understands the people need something demonstrative. But God offers a quality unlike those offered by any other deity the Egyptians worship: hope.

Proving God

4:1 "What if they do not believe me and do not listen to me, but say, 'YHVH did not appear to you'?"

4:2 "What is that in your hand?"

The act of proving God would seem superfluous in a book dedicated to God's existence. God's power either *is* or *is not* present in the human drama. By comparison, there does not seem to be any doubt about the presence of God in the book of Genesis. And yet we read of Moshe's uncertainty about how to represent God's power in a world that has seemingly ignored the divine presence for generations.

When Moshe asks, **"What if they do not believe me and do not listen to me, but say, 'YHVH did not appear to you'?"** God gives Moshe the ability to turn a staff into a serpent, to turn a hand scaly white and back to normal, and to turn the Nile river into blood—impressive party tricks for a representative of the source of all life and power in the universe! This is more than the ambivalence of insufficient proof.

The request and response between God and Moshe here defines Moshe as an emissary to help the Egyptians and the Israelites, and also defines the parameters of God's power. In the minds of the Israelites, this power must be in contention with the other powers that have, they suppose (albeit mistakenly), been responsible for their subjugation and enslavement. In the minds of the Egyptians, the power must be demonstrated in distinction to the powers they wield.

Upon further reflection, the question poses a challenge to God directly. It's as if Moshe's previous question, **"What is God's Name? What shall I say to them?"** prompting the response *Ehyeh* **(I will be),** is still not sufficient proof for the people. Moshe must possess tremendous faith to return to the court of Pharaoh to advocate for a rupture in their social system with this unqualified response.

We have to wonder as well what the purpose of God's question is in response to Moshe, **"What is that in your hand?"** Not only do we wonder why God has to ask Moshe something God already knows, we also wonder how Moshe is going to respond. Moshe could have responded that the magic was an act of divine providence. Moshe could have responded with another question, something like "What is this stick you've given to me?" thus perpetuating his doubt.

There is a common parallel drawn between Moshe and the prophet Bilaam, whom we meet later in the book of Numbers. When God asks Bilaam a question that God certainly knows the answer to, the purpose is not to catch the prophet in a trap.[7] The question here opens up a dimension of God that is rarely recorded in the Bible. God is seeking truth through questions, a truth that can only be revealed in response. This is also reminiscent of God's question to Adam in the Garden, and to Cain in the field, when God is seeking the presence of the human being in the midst of their separation from God's providence and power.[8] Moshe's direct response, "A rod," is an affirmation of God's existence. We learn that even the simplest questions and answers establish the most sublime truths.

Divine Creations

4:11 "Who makes man's mouth? Who makes a man dumb, or deaf, or seeing, or blind? Is it not I, YHVH?"

Defining the limits of faith can be contentious. As the ultimate expression of the inner life, quantifying faith by measuring word and action is virtually impossible. Religions are built on and battled over limits of faith. Rarely is there peaceful acceptance when one side prevails in the argument. Coercion and crucible are tools used to shape the contours of a society. Even where the limits of faith are tested in the Bible, the divine voice, while declarative, is also inherently inadequate.

When Moshe shares his ambivalence in presenting himself as God's prophet to Pharaoh, God asks him, **"Who makes man's mouth? Who makes a man dumb, or deaf, or seeing, or blind? Is it not I, YHVH?"** The questions are a direct response to Moshe's fear that he will be incapable of speaking effectively, that his capacity to articulate the awesome message of God will somehow be inadequate. It's not a proof text here either. If so we would have expected Moshe's confirmation that God is indeed the maker of all senses. Moshe demurs instead, presumably out of a lack of faith![9] It's not that Moshe should respond with the sophisticated understanding of biological evolution or the sophistry of the theologian. As witnesses to the moment, we are supposed to nod in affirmation that

God is indeed the faithful creator of all human life and agency while watching our prophetic hero wriggle in discomfort.

Perhaps God's question isn't a blatant expression of divine power or coercion at all. The questions are an *invitation* to faith, something Moshe and B'nai Yisrael certainly have not been given permission to entertain with Pharaoh in power. In this manner, the questions are prompts to reflect on when the sense of freedom is indeed from God. While the biological origins of human life are well understood, God's questions to Moshe are a divine attempt to define the concept of freedom by basking in the glow of ultimate power and truth.

Faith is never easily defined, and yet it forms the immutable source of religious doctrine. In one sense, faith is a deliberate and willful attempt to frame our uncertainty in the language of hope. If God's response to Moshe was in the form of statements and not inquiries, we might overlook the description of faith the Bible seeks to define. To sense the world as one of God's divine creations refashions the human experience. This question evokes a transformation from a sense of self-purpose to one of divine partnership. Meanwhile Moshe's resistance to fulfilling the mission due to his inadequacies (he is **"slow of speech"**) ultimately becomes the primary subject of God's role in the palace of Pharaoh, indeed in the entire book that follows. The one who doubts his capacity becomes the most significant voice of God's Torah and one of the most significant leaders in human history.

Power and Powerlessness

5:2 "Who is YHVH that I should listen to His voice and let Israel go?"

One underlying theme of the book of Exodus is the battle between power and powerlessness. It's a battle between Pharaoh, looked on as a god by the Egyptian people, and the name of the God of the Hebrews, **Yod Hey Vav Hey.** We're learning from the theme of a human-centered God that an expansive universal deity centers around the challenge of human autonomy and self-determination. Pharaoh's narrow definition of the human being will make him incapable of recognizing sources of power outside his own, and so his question is simultaneously borne from curiosity and out of defense: **"Who is YHVH that I should listen to His voice and let Israel go?"**

The surface of the text implies that Pharaoh's lack of knowledge is not merely circumstantial. It isn't that Pharaoh has no knowledge of the God of Israel. Pharaoh's disbelief is culturally and philosophically biased. The God of Israel is not a deity who is worshiped in the Egyptian pantheon. There can be no other force in the universe that does not owe some fealty to Pharaoh. The question itself implies this relationship: **"that I should listen to His voice."** Pharaoh's deafness is willful. He could hear the voice of God as portrayed by Moshe and Aharon, but he chooses not to listen.

Herein lies one root of power over powerlessness. It is the complete disregard for any agency of power other than one's own. Some call this stubbornness. While the tactic may be successful in the short term, the persistence of Moshe and God teaches us an important lesson. Autonomy and self-determination become the cornerstones of community in the eyes of the Israelites. Power in community is defined by the source or the voice of an agency that promotes autonomy. Pharaoh's shortcoming is not in his ability to suppress the will of the people. In fact, he succeeds here. But he ultimately fails in his inability to shape and define the power of self-determination for the other, here the Israelite.

The sensitive reader knows better. It's as if we want to shout into the text at Pharoah and share with him what we know. This is the God who created the universe with word, who was revealed to Abraham when Abraham's vision was limited, with whom Jacob wrestled and sought the Name.[10]

In short, the answer to Pharaoh's question is a resounding affirmation of the entire Torah: you should listen to the voice of God. It's the only voice that really matters.

Plausible Deniability

5:4 "Why do you, Moshe and Aharon, cause the people to break loose from their work?"

Plausible deniability is a clever attempt by those in positions of power to extricate themselves from responsibility for consequences that result from their actions. When a leader employs some rationale to deny culpability for harm caused by a strategic decision, it becomes difficult to challenge the leader's position without sufficient proof. The attempt to preserve one's authority or dignity in the face of denied responsibility should give us pause and trouble our sensibilities.

When Pharaoh asks, **"Why do you, Moshe and Aharon, cause the people to break loose from their work?"** there is a note of surprise, perhaps anger, in the charge. Pharaoh does not revert to his source of power to prevent the people from fulfilling his will. Rather, he questions the motives of the defense. By asking Moshe and Aharon why they are the agents of dissent, he simultaneously relinquishes a certain amount of his own power by placing the blame on them instead. In this way, when the people cry out from the harsh labor Pharaoh imposes, Pharaoh can claim his actions are in response to efforts to incite rebellion and disrupt the order of their servitude.

Leaders employ forms of deniable action because there is uncertainty in their power and influence. By manipulating the circumstances of his influence, Pharaoh shows us that Moshe and Aharon's presence is more than a demonstration of defiance. His uncertainty is the beginning of his downfall. After Shifra and Puah defy his authority and permit the Israelite children to live, his inability to totally control the people "breaks loose" and ultimately leads to God's challenges through the plagues. Pharaoh's recognition that Moshe and Aharon can also influence the fate of his slaves reveals his weakness. Moshe's and Aharon's proclamation **"Let us go, we pray, a distance of three days into the wilderness"**[11] seems innocuous, perhaps even beneficial to Pharaoh. However, the entire project of systematic subjugation and oppression was predicated on an attempt to contain the people's fecundity, and his failed attempts cannot be stopped even by his clever attempt to shun responsibility.

The Tormentor's Remorse

5:14 "Why did you not complete the prescribed amount of bricks either yesterday, or today, as you did before?"

Moshe asks Pharaoh to let the people go. Pharaoh refuses. A holy battle between Moshe and Pharaoh is set to unfold. Leading up to this moment is Pharaoh's cruel punishment of the people by denying them access to the straw needed to make the bricks to build his cities.

It's in this moment of pain and toil that the text turns for a moment to the taskmasters, those who were assigned to be the physical instruments of Pharaoh's brutality and to ensure the work is completed. They ask, **"Why did you not complete the prescribed amount of bricks either yesterday, or today, as you did before?"**

Why would the Torah bother to record such a line of questioning? Is it to confirm that the impossible task laid on the Israelites is indeed too difficult to fulfill? Is it to record the insidiousness of oppression and that the logic of the taskmaster is too confounding for the slave?

This is indeed a most vicious question. The taskmasters must have known the answer. Moreover, the presence of a question here and not simply a punishment for disobedience introduces a certain moral violation. Perhaps the taskmasters relish their unfair advantage over the people.

Or perhaps the taskmasters are ambivalent and unwilling to enforce the harsh punishment, just as Shifra and Puah defied Pharaoh's decree regarding the death of the Israelite male children.

In uncertainty, such questions and their responses can flourish. The Torah records the question of the taskmasters to unveil the horrific consequences of enslavement. There were those who treated their slaves kindly and those who saw slaves as objects, tools to complete the lofty goals of empire expansion. The taskmasters do not have their own character. Their form is in their function, the instruments of Pharaoh's will to oppress and crush the will of his slaves. It's curious to note that the taskmasters are no longer mentioned in the narrative following this exchange.

Perhaps this question reveals a crack in Pharaoh's nefarious plans. The court of Pharaoh maintains a stranglehold of enslavement on the people, but the taskmasters dissolve into the text as agents of change. They too recognize the impossible circumstances of enslavement and may even become among the *Erev Rav*, the multitudinous crowd that leaves with the Israelites for freedom. This question, more than a taunt, is a recognition that the limits of oppression will never satisfy the desires of the master. Even the taskmasters can see this. In this awareness, liberation becomes possible for all.

Becoming Responsible

5:15 "Why did you do this [increase our work burdens] to your servants?"

The beginning of the book of Exodus portrays a world lacking in acceptance of responsibility. Through the breach, God's justice enters. We learn that Pharaoh evades responsibility when he confronts Shifra and Puah and shirks before Moshe and Aharon as God's voice resonates through the world. The people, seen first as subjects to this lack of concern, become actors themselves when the taskmasters increase the burden of their work by compelling them to search for their own straw to make the bricks to build the cities for them. The people complain to Pharaoh themselves, trying to rationalize the impossible task being laid on them, asking, **"Why did you do this [increase our work burdens] to your servants?"** Pharaoh's response is to intimidate and blame them for their own misgivings. Our sense is that the people could not even see the consequences of their outcry or their recognition that God will be there for them. Responsibility, we learn, is the acceptance of consequences even when they are potentially calamitous.

The question here reveals an important dimension of human responsibility in general and for the Israelites in particular. The harshness of Pharaoh's decree first seemed tolerable to the people. When it became intolerable, their complaint was the most accessible tool they had to fight back with. What's interesting is that Pharaoh listens to them. More than learning about Pharaoh's narrow-minded perception of the Israelites in this moment, we learn that the people themselves have much to learn about their own responsibility. The grand narrative of liberation will not be complete until the Israelites take responsibility for their own fate, brush the lintels of their doorways with the blood of sheep, and gird their loins for a swift departure from Egypt.[12]

In this challenging moment, we could not have expected more from the Israelites. They groan, they cry, and here they complain. None of these tactics will succeed until a force more powerful than Pharaoh is unleashed. Until then, Moshe and Aharon must persist. The voice of the Israelite is simply not powerful enough to embrace freedom yet.

Even Moshe Doubts

5:22 "O YHVH, why have you brought evil to these people?"

5:22 "Why have you sent me?"

In learning about leadership, we often glean wisdom from lessons of courageous action, bold decision-making, and laudable fortitude. These crucial elements of leadership narratives all emerge from challenges that must be overcome. Weakness, uncertainty, even a moral failing in the midst of critical decision-making is what perpetually lurks in the shadows of a person assuming a leadership role. As much as we celebrate the stalwart responsibility of a leader, it is their confrontation of uncertainty that we strive to emulate. Such tenacity is heroic.

To hear Moshe ask, **"O YHVH, why have you brought evil to these people?"** and **"Why have you sent me?"** is to hear the profound concern Moshe expresses in his seemingly impossible task of liberating the oppressed. This question comes after the Israelites turn their frustrations toward Moshe and Aharon and literally curse them by saying, **"May YHVH look upon you and punish you for making us loathsome to Pharaoh and his courtiers—putting a sword in their hands to slay us."**[13]

These two questions in succession return to the theme of taking responsibility, a crucial prerequisite of leadership. Pharaoh refused to accept the consequences for imposing harsh labor on the people. The people were incapable of taking responsibility for fulfilling their quotas because they did not have sufficient resources to accomplish their tasks (nor should they have been expected to do so). Now Moshe seeks God's presence in a place where he seems to have reached a limit to his influence over Pharaoh.

There is also a significant turn from blaming God to self-blame here too. Unlike the common thread of Moshe's humility in his calling to liberate the Israelites, the second question here can be read with a different tone, one of faithful curiosity. We are reminded that self-identity is the precursor to responsible action.

God's response, **"You shall soon see what I will do to Pharaoh; he will let them go because of a greater might; indeed, because of a greater might he shall drive them from his land,"**[14] doesn't seem to answer either question Moshe poses. We often read this with a tone of consternation, as if to say, "God will exact retribution upon the Egyptians." God's response is also an affirmation of Moshe's doubt by taking responsibility where no one else was willing to accept it before. Moshe's doubt has inspired faith in himself and in God.

VAERA

6:12 "How will Pharaoh listen to me since I have uncircumcised lips?" (Moshe to God)

6:30 "How will Pharaoh listen to me?" (Moshe to God)

8:5 "When shall I plead on behalf of you and your courtiers and your people that the frogs be cut off from you and your houses to remain only in the Nile?" (Moshe to Pharaoh)

8:22 "If we offer sacrifice for the abomination of the Egyptians, will they not stone us?" (Moshe to Pharaoh)

As the plagues in response to Pharaoh's recalcitrance increase in severity, the fundamental questions that help us define the limits of the self come into focus. We'll learn through Pharaoh's stubbornness and Moshe's humility that the force of the universe is crucial to whatever self-identity we create. The questions that are posed by Moshe, and only Moshe in this portion, transform from his own self-concern to a concern for the Israelite people. Moshe's ambivalence toward his own abilities is amplified by his questions in response to Pharaoh's request to stop the plagues and to justify the people's ability to leave Egypt safely. The questions that punctuate this transformation are not only emulated by the prophet and teacher, they also inspire a transformation we must undertake in our own quest for freedom. Casting off the shackles of slavery requires a confrontation with uncertainty.

When Doubt Becomes Humility

6:12 *"How will Pharaoh listen to me since I have uncircumcised lips?"*

6:30 *"How will Pharaoh listen to me?"*

One of the great ironies of the Torah is the transformation of Moshe from the man of impeded speech to the great orator of the final words given to the people on the banks of the Jordan River before they enter the land of Israel. How can someone so convinced of his inability to communicate effectively become the bold and courageous proclaimer of God's power in Egypt, the wise and discerning voice of the lawgiver, and the sagacious teacher of a new generation of free people? Either there was a misperception of ability or this was the expression of a person who possessed great humility.

When Moshe asks **"How will Pharaoh listen to me since I have uncircumcised lips?"** and later **"How will Pharaoh listen to me?"** we note first the self-doubt of the redeemer and the challenge he faces in bringing justice to a world deaf to the suffering of his people. But we also hear in this profound humility. Moshe's self-awareness is juxtaposed with his self-doubt.

As much as we celebrate or ponder the transformation of the silent one, the man **"slow of speech,"** we also hear this model of growth that the Torah preserves in its most important character. Moshe exemplifies the liberation of the slave who becomes a free person. He is the quintessential model of the uninitiated who becomes covenanted. Moshe is an inspiration for anyone who wants to break through the paralyzing fears of the bystander and become a bold and holy actor of righteousness and justice.

One lesson to glean from Moshe's humility is precisely the power to overcome doubt. One who is haughty or arrogant may have doubts, but the protective sleeve over their emotions inhibits their humility. Humility is the act that transforms the slave into the free person. Humility is the act that transforms doubt into faith and insecurity into genuine confidence.

Can You Pray for Your Enemy?

8:5 "When shall I plead on behalf of you and your courtiers and your people that the frogs be cut off from you and your houses to remain only in the Nile?"

Pharaoh's power continues to unravel as Moshe portends the fate of Egypt with a litany of plagues. After the second plague wreaks havoc on the house of Pharaoh, the tactic of asking for relief presents a vital turn in the balance of power between Pharaoh and God. Moshe asks in response to Pharaoh's cries, **"When shall I plead on behalf of you and your courtiers and your people that the frogs be cut off from you and your houses to remain only in the Nile?"** Perhaps this question could be asked more succinctly: "When do you want me to stop the frogs?"

Moshe's question here is not divinely motivated either. It is the growing awareness of Moshe's understanding that forces more powerful than one human being are at work here. Pharaoh's recalcitrance motivates the severity of the response. And so Moshe's inquiry oriented not only to the present but also to the future. As Pharaoh willfully absences himself from the fate of his people, ultimately pleading for a blessing from God for himself alone,[15] Moshe's question is the pivotal moment when logic and reason fail and the consequences of oppressing others are yet to be felt.

To be a leader only for your own benefit creates dire consequences. It's called tyranny. In the balance between "us and them," selfish motives become the stumbling block and eventually bring the downfall of despotism. Moshe's question facilitates Pharaoh's agency for change and highlights his refusal to change in future encounters. We would expect the drama of the episode to prompt Pharaoh to respond "Immediately!" instead of what he actually says, which is **"Tomorrow."**[16] Pharaoh's forceful will is still evident. He can still hold out against God's punishment and cling to the power remaining in his grasp. Hence more plagues will be necessary to reveal God's sustaining power.

There Are Differences

8:22 *"If we offer sacrifice for the abomination of the Egyptians, will they not stone us?"*

In our lofty quest to promote unity in our human experience, we inevitably stumble into the tragedy of the commons. The tragedy of the commons is when a group of people is unable to reach common ground and as a result a shared resource is left ungoverned—a sort of no one's land of resources. When an individual or group discovers their way is threatened by the ways of others, the instinct is to retreat or to defend their own position before seeking common ground with the others. Wars, economic sanctions, and social degradation ensue when we fail to see the humanity that binds us together.

In the book of Exodus, one of the undercurrents of the narrative is the religious expression of the two peoples, the Egyptians and the Israelites. According to Egyptian religious doctrine, animals are venerated. The intimation that the Israelites should offer animals as sacrifice to their God is considered taboo, an abomination. When Moshe asks Pharaoh to let the Israelites go to the wilderness to make their offering, he posits, **"If we offer sacrifice for the abomination of the Egyptians, will they not stone us?"** This is often read as a tactic employed by Moshe to facilitate the Israelites' escape from bondage. If Pharaoh lets them travel three days to offer their sacrifices, it will be that much more difficult to lure them back into slavery.

At first the Egyptians valued the shepherding wisdom the sons of Jacob brought to them. Egyptian animals were sacred much as the cow is a sacred animal in Indian culture today. Their being able to tend to flocks was something the Egyptians appreciated in the Israelites. At this point in the story, however, concern for the Israelite uprising has diminished the level of trust the Egyptians once held for them.

Pharaoh is presented with a temporary solution to his problem of a God inflicting plagues upon his people. Should he give the Israelites the ability to worship on their own, he might strengthen their loyalty in their servitude. And surely Pharaoh must know that letting the people go under any circumstances could result in a complete exodus of the community. Moshe's question appeals to the logic of Pharaoh. And when he first agrees and then changes his mind, Pharaoh's undoing is confirmed. No logic or reason will appeal to this tyrant. God's power becomes necessary.

The tragedy of the commons is never easy to overcome. Confidence-building measures are constantly needed to avert defensive or xenophobic reactions to vulnerability. The us-versus-them dichotomy is always present, and overcoming fear of the other is a persistent need. Pharaoh's recalcitrance only exacerbates the difference between the Egyptians and the Israelites. Moshe's awareness of this weakness emboldens God's efforts to step in and liberate the beleaguered people. And it will take generations to restore any confidence between these two nations.

Bo

10:3 "How long will you refuse to humble yourself before Me?" (Moshe and Aharon to Pharaoh on behalf of God)

10:7 "How long will you let this [one] be a snare for us?" (Pharaoh's servants to Pharaoh)

10:7 "Are you not aware that Egypt is lost?" (Pharaoh's servants to Pharaoh)

10:8 "Who and who will go?" (Pharaoh to Moshe)

12:26 "What is this service to you?" (Children to parents regarding the Pesah sacrifice)

13:14 "What is this?" (Children to parents about the cultural ritual life of Jews)

First readers of the Torah discover the great transformation of Abraham's family into the people of Israel in the chapters that make up this Torah portion. It is through the instructions surrounding the Passover rites and the future orientation of the questions our descendants will pose that this change is marked. Indeed, the first comment of the great Torah commentator, Rashi, on the Torah also identifies this chapter as the original document of national history.

Our lesson is that the text is rarely taught linearly. We are perpetually referring to the current and everlasting existence of the Jewish people and their contributions to civilization. The questions in this portion are the hallmark moments of this change, where we read back into these moments the origins of a people at the precise moment their redemption from enslavement is manifest.

When Is It Too Late?

10:3 *"How long will you refuse to humble yourself before Me?"*

10:7 *"How long will you let this [one] be a snare for us?"*

10:7 *"Are you not yet aware that Egypt is lost?"*

Questions posed with curiosity can deflect the intensity of emotion around issues we find difficult to resolve. Similarly, questions of a reflective nature can prompt us to respond from our better selves should we accept the challenge. However, it is more common that when we contemplate the totality or finality of a situation, heightened anxieties inhibit the curiosity found in the uncertainties.

Moshe and Aharon have appeared before the pharaoh several times by now, each time with a proclamation of God's justice through the plagues. The command by God to Moshe and Aharon is to go to Pharaoh to demonstrate God's ultimate power. There is a significant change in tactics. Pharaoh himself is being challenged to personally humble himself before God. And like the previous seven visits, we will learn that Pharaoh is incapable of responding with compassion.

Moshe and Aharon use a question to communicate the message. **"How long will you refuse to humble yourself before Me?"** Pharaoh's silence is deafening. We neither hear Pharaoh submit to the charge nor resoundingly defy the audacious claim that a pharaoh would be humbled by any force other than himself. Their departure from the presence of Pharaoh after their pointed question reinforces the arrogance of Pharaoh's silence as well.

In fact, a response to this question isn't given by Pharaoh at all but by his courtiers, who also pose questions: **"How long will you let this [one] be a snare for us?"** and **"Are you not aware that Egypt is lost?"** This response to Pharaoh's refusal to humble himself is the counsel of leadership around him that advises action contrary to his will. They foresee the end of the war between God and Pharaoh. They even begin to advise their leader to shift his perception of their fate. This has the makings of a coup d'état!

Revolutions come about when people respond to the failures of their elected or appointed leadership. Roiled by corruption, despotism, and xenophobia, the people respond with a popular uprising. Successful revolutions emerge when the inner circles of leadership refuse to abide by policies that harm the people they are supposed to protect.

We will not witness a popular uprising to overthrow the tyranny of Pharaoh, whose now unpopular policies bring widespread destruction and death. We are now painfully aware, however, that the balance between Pharaoh and God has permanently shifted here, where the lack of support from his own people prompts us to respond to God's question here too. It is too late, we learn, when you refuse to see the unbearable pain you cause by your actions.

Defining Evil

10:8 "Who and who will go?"

The grandeur of the Torah narrative ought to identify the episode in Egypt as a momentary lapse in human dignity despite the essential significance enslavement and redemption have held in the mind of the Jewish people throughout their history. The Israelites suffering for hundreds of years in Egypt cannot be undervalued. Yet the downfall of Pharaoh is quite brief in comparison to the history of the Jewish people. The moments when we witness the wavering contrition of the despotic leader seem inconsequential in light of the fundamental purpose God has for the children of Abram. And yet the timeless lessons we glean from Pharaoh establish the limits of human responsibility for us all.

We read Pharaoh's response to the questions posed by Moshe and the courtiers as a form of administrative justice when he asks, **"Who and who will go?"** More than a question of quantity, it is a subtle indication of Pharaoh's desperation. This question suggests Pharaoh still believes he has a hold on the will of the people, even on the will of God. While Moshe and Aharon answer this question directly, it is presented to reveal just how far Pharaoh is willing to go to stand in the way of God's divine justice.

Pharaoh's stubbornness is not merely a childlike tantrum of one refusing to act justly in the face of authority. This pharaoh embodies a vision of evil the Bible has carefully chosen to model so the Israelite people may aspire to a life of justice and kindness worthy of divine presence and blessing. When Pharaoh recoils from Moshe's and Aharon's response that everyone will leave to go and worship YHVH, Pharaoh accuses them of being **"bent on mischief."**[17] This is the great expression of evil, the vision of goodness appearing evil. In the nebulous reality of Pharaoh, good and evil are confused.

This is why there must be divine intervention to redeem the people and correct the injustices of Pharaoh. There are no human interventions to effectively persuade someone who conflates good and evil and refuses to seek clarity through the uncertainty between the two. Pharaoh's stubbornness is more than a refusal to let the people go. Pharaoh has willfully chosen to resist God's justice to the bitter end. It is when Moshe proclaims at the conclusion of this encounter **"You have spoken rightly. I will not see your face again!"**[18] that we understand that Pharaoh can no longer find a place for reconciliation. Thus the definition of evil and its consequences make this brief moment of the narrative the most significant of the entire sequence of slavery and redemption.

Permission to Ask

12:26 "What is this service to you?"
13:14 "What is this?"

One great contribution, if not the greatest contribution, Judaism offers to the world is the permission to ask questions and to sanctify the free exchange of wisdom through questions and answers. Curiosity and the quest to discover greater certainty through doubt is a hallmark of Jewish identity. At the heart of the Passover ritual, one that anchors the identity of Judaism and inspires connection in every generation, is a natural prompt to tell the story of slavery and redemption. Even today the practice of sanctifying time through ritual hearkens back to the exodus from Egypt to compel our holy behavior. Rather than establish this root experience as an immutable truth, from the very moments of our redemption we are guided to ask questions to confirm the truth of our day and in every generation.

When the Torah frames the questions **"What is this service to you?"** and then **"What is this?"** anticipating the questions children will ask in the future, we discover a feature of this religion unlike any other. First we marvel at the elegance of anticipation in these questions. There is a profound sense of pride and commitment to the faith and traditions of Judaism that invites the questions. When the Jewish tradition later develops the Passover Seder ritual and invites the questions of four types of children to the spiritual table, this is the question of the wise child. And to underscore its importance, we read of the wicked (or clever) child who asks the same question but closes himself off from the narrative.

But perhaps most compelling in these questions is the foundation of another essential Jewish value: hope. Implicit in the questions is a future where children will ask parents what their history is and there will be an opportunity to perpetuate the inspiration of the redemption narrative. There are countless examples of the Passover Seder taking place in the darkest corners of human history as a monumental demonstration of eternal longing for this story to move and inspire each and every generation.

Being given the permission to ask questions is more than a freedom of expression. It is a foundational ethic of identity for the Jewish people. As long as there are questions to ask that inspire authentic response, the presence of the Jewish people in the world is secure.

BESHALACH

14:5 "What is this we have done, letting Israel leave from serving us?" (Servants to Pharaoh)

14:11 "Because there were no graves in Egypt, have you taken us away to die in the desert?" (The people to Moshe)

14:11 "Why have you done this to us, to bring us forth out of Egypt?" (The people to Moshe)

14:12 "Is this not what we said to you in Egypt, saying, 'Let us be, and we will serve the Egyptians for it is better for us to serve the Egyptians than to die in this desert'?" (The people to Moshe)

14:15 "Why do you cry out to Me?" (God to Moshe)

15:24 "What should we drink?" (The people to Moshe)

16:7 "For who are we that you should grumble against us?" (Moshe and Aharon to the people)

16:8 "Since it is YHVH who will give you flesh to eat in the morning to the fullest, because YHVH has heard the grumblings you utter, what is our part?" (Moshe and Aharon to the people)

16:15 "What is this?" (The people to one another)

16:28 "How long will you refuse to follow My commandments and My teachings?" (God to Moshe)

17:2 "Why do you strive with me? Why do you test YHVH?" (Moshe to the people)

17:3 "Why did you bring us out of Egypt to kill us, our children, and our cattle with thirst?" (The people to Moshe)

17:4 "What shall I do with this people?" (Moshe to God)

17:7 "Is YHVH present among us or not?" (The people to Moshe)

The magnificent journey of the Israelite people through the desert begins in the chapters of this Torah portion. While the Promised Land is geographically a short distance to travel, the people will have to wander through deserts toward holy mountains to comprehend their unique destiny. The questions in this portion reveal quite a different story. Riddled with complaints, fears, and uncertainties about their future, the people will ultimately challenge the possibility of knowing God as the journey ahead is unknown to them. Each of the questions posed in this section may emerge from a place of doubt, and it will be the miraculous demonstrations of God's power and might that reassure the people of God's everlasting presence. These questions inspire us to reflect upon the uncertainties that exist in our lives that will be met with a confident force for good, if we seek its presence.

A Change of Heart

14:5 *"What is this we have done, letting Israel leave from serving us?"*

Ambivalence is an unavoidable expression of the human mind. People change their minds all the time, some more than others. A defining feature of the moral character is being able to say what you mean and mean what you say. Someone whose word is unmovable is someone you can rely upon even if they are your adversary. A change of heart (*V'yay'hafech l'vav*) implies deviating from your word in some way. Someone who changes their heart, at times out of whim or caprice, is a person you cannot rely upon and a person whose lack of self-confidence can infect the relationships of the people they meet. For the most dependable figures, internal conflict is a part of being alive.

The servants of Pharaoh express a sense of remorse for the decision to free the Israelite slaves. They ponder their circumstances, now bereft of the slave class they have enjoyed for centuries. How quickly their undoing has been forgotten in the midst of this upheaval!

Prompting a change of heart involves a set of circumstances or new information that compels reconsideration of a previously held position. Here the lack of a slave class in Egyptian society is what prompts a change of heart for the servants of Pharaoh. Their personal investment in the concern reveals more too. **"What is this we have done?"** implies the Egyptian elite were complicit in the subjugation and demoralization of the Israelites. This is perhaps the most tragic part of the story. The Egyptians see the glory and might of a God who celebrates and defends freedom for all and they simply cannot see beyond their personal desire for a life of ease and self-satisfaction. Their despairing attitude wants to completely overlook the previous barrage of plagues, including the death of their first-born children, to continue pursuing their goals of enslavement.

On the one hand, the Egyptians have to relearn what it means to be a society without slaves. On the other hand, the pursuit of oppression has a perpetual quality to it: once you've adopted an oppressive attitude, it is extraordinarily difficult, even in light of total loss, to change your perception. Perhaps the lesson of God's power had not been learned by the Egyptians even after the tenth plague. Perhaps the sacrifice of children could be accepted and did not have the lasting effect on them that it had on the Israelites. Death of children is what compels Abram to faith (Isaac); Jacob to despair (Joseph); and Moshe (Am Yisrael) to action.

In every possible permutation, when you change your heart to do the right thing, we call it courage.

After Despair, Do You Believe?

14:11–12 *"Because there were no graves in Egypt, have you taken us away to die in the desert?"*

"Why have you done this to us, to bring us forth out of Egypt?"

"Is this not what we said to you in Egypt, saying, 'Let us be, and we will serve the Egyptians for it is better for us to serve the Egyptians than to die in this desert'?"

There are times we can all point to in our lives when we've felt like our options are limited and our fate moving forward appears bleak. Illness, struggles with jobs or parenting, and the loss of loved ones often appear as finite destinations on a lifelong journey. The darkness and narrowness of our perception is fearsome. We're anxious for what lies ahead. Our imagination of what might yet be can be simply stultifying. There can be something profoundly hopeful in the discovery of a different approach. When it feels like there is nowhere else to go, counsel toward a new possibility is called wisdom. A text that exemplifies this narrow perception and its resolution is preserved in the Torah not only to help us reflect on what happened but to instruct us in what might yet be.

Before the sea episode and moments into their redemption, the people ask, **"Because there were no graves in Egypt, have you taken us away to die in the desert?" "Why have you done this to us, to bring us forth out of Egypt?" "Is this not what we said to you in Egypt, saying, 'Let us be, and we will serve the Egyptians for it is better for us to serve the Egyptians than to die in this desert'?"** There is a realism to their concern, and we intuitively await a response, knowing the concern is not as bleak and dire as they perceive.

The people's complaints are a symptom of their newly discovered identity. Freedom to act must include space for dissent. The complaints are included in the narrative to validate the human experience. Authentic living is not enveloped in a philosophical stoicism. Indeed, questions like these are framed by the people over twelve times in the Torah. Its recurrence isn't simply a record of the people's struggle. It is a veritable prerequisite to freedom! Freedom is difficult, and complaining becomes a Jewish virtue in the achievement of freedom.

Leadership, by comparison, is a careful adjustment from discomfort toward security and certainty. The most recent model of leadership the people knew was in Egypt, a name that now implies narrowness or limitation.[19] The people direct their concerns to Moshe, not God, and Moshe becomes responsible for broadening the horizons of the people. It is Moshe's duty, along with the elders, to broaden the perspectives of the people so they may discover God.

Limited visions do not include the capacity for God to intervene. Leadership is the act of confident planning to see divine possibility. Belief, then, is a willful act of hope despite overwhelming circumstances. Belief is a determination that the future will be better than the present.

The Independence of Questions

14:15 "Why do you cry out to Me?"

The brilliance of a well-placed question empowers both the one who asks and the one who answers. Questions are not intended to limit the relationship between the questioner and the respondent. The dynamics of questions can be exploited by power structures in ways that undermine or even destroy the potential for a sacred encounter. Authentic questions, however, enable both questioner and respondent to grow from their shared understanding. Ultimately an excellent question affirms the uniqueness of the other and commands well-deserved respect.

This respect is palpably evident in the critical moments before God miraculously parts the Sea of Reeds. Pharaoh's army presses the Israelites up to the shores of the sea, where they face certain peril, even doom. In response to the fear of the people, Moshe proclaims God's deliverance. In response to his plea that legitimately places the onus on God for protecting the Israelites after redeeming them from their enslavement in Egypt, God turns to Moshe and asks, **"Why do you cry out to Me?"** We might easily read this question as a deflection of that responsibility, that God somehow does not want to help the people in their most vulnerable moments.

This moment is far more pivotal than a momentary lapse in leadership. God's question is an egalitarian and balanced example of shared wisdom, of sacred independence. God is compelling Moshe to act here while God will take on the responsibility of punishing the Egyptians. This is God teaching Moshe through a question how to guide the people through a life-threatening moment with something they have never witnessed before: faith. Up to this moment, the people's only experience is that of Pharaoh's death-charged decrees and stubbornness that defies God and denies the potential for sacred presence to dwell among them. They may think God's power only exists in this manifestation. Even after ten plagues revealing God's power to Pharaoh, Moshe must still demonstrate the certainty of God's power. So he will raise his arms over the water, and with a cry of absolute faith the people will witness yet one more miraculous demonstration of natural, even divine, strength.

The people will continue to need proof and confidence in the power of God. This need will propel them on their sacred journey to Sinai.

Moshe: The Problem Solver

15:24 "What should we drink?"

Sometimes asking a question is easier than considering possible solutions to the problem first. In these moments, the time we ask others to spend helping us figure out the answer can even reveal to us the truth we initially sought. Yet we are impatient to contemplate the solution alone. While solving complex problems is a sign of intelligence, asking questions to avoid the mental effort is a social crutch.

There are more than a few examples of the people's impatience and prompts of questions for Moshe in the Torah. The first example of this appears shortly after the people miraculously cross the Sea of Reeds. We read, **"And all the people grumbled against Moshe, saying, 'What should we drink?'"** This question seems to ask for clarity amidst uncertainty in the desert. The people are thirsty, and there doesn't appear to be any water in their immediate proximity.[20] By keeping their eyes down, the Israelites have not yet cultivated the skill of scouting and planning. Freedom is an ability to plan for tomorrow and even to adjust one's expectations for a tomorrow that will be different from today. The tone of the text implies that their question here is narrow and small despite their visceral reaction to the environmental circumstances. Moshe could have appointed scouts to find plentiful waters just around the corner, but instead he turns to God to ask for guidance. Moshe does not yet fully understand the role of the visionary leader. So God steps in once again and instructs Moshe to turn the bitter water sweet with a magical piece of wood.[21]

The recurring narrative of this uncertainty should not be carelessly dismissed as proof that the Israelites are a stiff-necked people. On the one hand, their concern should not be underestimated. God promised them freedom and abundance, so why haven't they received such goodness? It should be that the narrative presents their dilemma of slavery and its resolution with freedom so that the people live happily ever after. The fantasy that their reality should be simple is a narrow reading of this book. Yet shrugging our shoulders each time we meet the people in distress somehow limits our truth as well.

Still, the profound acceptance that life is difficult is an elegant nuance of the Torah. Covenant and responsibility are demonstrated in weaker moments and not when there are no obstacles preventing freedom from flourishing. In this we might wonder if freedom is an ideal we should strive toward while knowing we will be constantly tested along the way. Water is a basic need of life, and the text lures us into believing that freedom is a basic need too.

Shared Responsibility

16:7 "For who are we that you should grumble against us?"

16:8 "Since it is YHVH who will give you flesh to eat in the morning to the fullest, because YHVH has heard the grumblings you utter, what is our part?"

In the beginning of the twentieth century, Franz Kafka wrote stories and novels about interminable encounters with a bureaucracy having no apparent source or destination of authority.[22] Heaping layer upon layer of interchange between characters revealed the endless turmoil in seeking truth from a nameless and faceless authority. Modern people may have contended with these circumstances in the twentieth century, but the Jewish tradition has grappled with the concerns of a formless authoritative presence from the first moments the Israelites tasted freedom.

Moments after the most dramatic demonstration of God's power before the Israelite people in the parting of the sea, and following an episode where they ask for water and receive it in abundance from God, the people begin to complain for food and sustenance. Already Moshe and Aharon's patience is tested when they ask the people, **"For who are we that you should grumble against us?"** and continue, **"Since it is YHVH who will give you flesh to eat in the morning to the fullest, because YHVH has heard the grumblings you utter, what is our part?"** They have been elected by God to lead the people, but who is in charge when the people won't follow?

Rather than point to the weaknesses Moshe and Aharon display in their discovery of their leadership roles, we can read sincerity into these questions. Who are they that the people should direct their complaints about their discomfort to them? No one has led people like this before. Who are Moshe and Aharon's models? And what does it mean to **"grumble against"** YHVH? No one has ever done that before either. Their questions do not have to be read as those of frustrated leaders passing the blame for troubles to a higher authority. They too are discovering the challenges of leadership and what role they'll ultimately play. We read in the verses not a recognition of the people's weakness but an affirmation of the real change taking place among them as a newly forming nation.

The Torah attempts to reveal an alternative model. The project of Israel is to continuously evolve an order of leadership that does not have an intangible deity as the destination of authority alone. God is, for the Jewish people, a tangible source of authority. Human leadership facilitating encounters with the divine is visceral. This has an application to every aspect of their communal experience—in sacred devotion, in witnessing God's presence, and in the distribution of responsibility. In order for the people to encounter God, their leaders will have to share the responsibility of bringing them to be with God as well.

Questions Sustain Life

16:15 "What is this?"

One of the comforts of modernity is our access to ample and copious varieties of food. Our ability to procure and consume a seemingly limitless amount of food is one of the greatest developments in human civilization. Our civilization is evolving to produce healthy and nutritious food even in laboratories as resources and supply chains become increasingly constrained. The concept of a "foodie," someone with an epicurean delight in the preparation and consumption of food, is a relatively new concept. Yet all the while, our greatest failure as a global community is the equitable distribution of that food.

The origins of a foodie's hobby can also be found in the Torah. As the Israelites journey from Egypt to Israel, the *manna*[23] God provides the people with is a vision unfettered by concerns of sustenance so they may realize their divine purpose.

The definition of the food that will nourish the Israelites during their journey is more than a question of the contents of the food. The people ask, **"What is this?"** referring to the manna[24] that will sustain them. The very act of inquiry invites an engagement, even a relationship, with the food the people consume. The Torah teaches that to be in relationship with food is to be in relationship with God.

The Sages pick up this theme when they imagine the taste of manna. It took on the flavor that people ascribed to it. If they were looking for cucumbers and leeks, they could have found such delicacies in the taste of the manna. If they were looking for a juicy steak or a piece of pizza, the manna took on these flavors and textures. In the question **"What is this?"** food becomes an implement of a relationship and not merely a means to an end.

Because God is the one providing sustenance for the people in their wanderings from Egypt to Canaan, the relationship of the people to their food cannot be overlooked. Surely we will hear them complain and pine for the **"cucumbers, melons, leeks, onions and garlic"**[25] they were given in Egypt. A food that can take on any taste in the desert requires imagination. It's not simply the imagination that inspires the taste of the food but also the imagination of the food as a point of connection with divinity. The divinity of food will take form in blessings before and after meals and the elegant and complex laws of *Kashrut* introduced in Leviticus. But the divine connection in food is found in this question too. **"What is this?"** the Israelites ask each other. We imagine the response is "It is a gift from God."

Questioning Loyalty

16:28 "How long will you refuse to follow My commandments and My teachings?"

Developing trust and cultivating loyalty is vital in a healthy relationship. Without trust and loyalty, real connections are infrequent. When trust exists between the people and God in the Torah, any obstacles in the relationship can be overcome. How wondrous it is that the need for trust and loyalty between God and the people is tested during the entire journey from Egypt to Canaan! How wondrous it is that the people lack trust after all the miraculous demonstrations of divine presence and power they've witnessed!

When God provides the people with manna to sustain them during their journey in the desert, there is a condition for its presence and bounty for the people. God instructs the people to take two portions on the day before the Sabbath so there will be sufficient rations for them on the day of rest. And yet when the people disobey this command and attempt to gather manna on the Sabbath, the confirmation of God's command is manifest in rotting food. We meet God's first expression of frustration and dismay when God asks, **"How long will you refuse to follow My commandments and My teachings?"** God wants to trust and be trusted but the people aren't ready for this.

The prompt for manna emerges from the concern of the people. Living in a settled land affords resources and tools to sustain a population based on the fundamental tenets of trust and loyalty in society. The people proclaim their loyalty to God by going into the desert, a vast desolation where access to food is limited. Their desire for food isn't a test of loyalty. It is a legitimate need! The people may not have anticipated God's response with conditions and were unaware of the limits of their needs. We should also be mindful that this is their first experience with a Sabbath day. The reader may hear some desperation in the tone of God's question, with the insight that it will be a recurring theme throughout the entire journey. However, there is legitimacy in God's question here as well. What defines the threshold of trust and loyalty to ensure any obstacle or challenge will not thwart the purpose of the relationship?

On the one hand, the Torah teaches by example that trust and loyalty are cultivated and expressed over time. The expectation that God commands and the people follow is not a core belief of Judaism because the people test their loyalty to God along the way. On the other hand, demonstrating the long-enduring patience of God during the test is a confirming feature of Jewish religion. God loses patience and then rediscovers it, whether that is by confirmation of the people's loyalty or through the eternal longing for a relationship that God desires to have with humanity. Manna teaches us that miracles don't create trust and loyalty. It must be a Torah, a covenant that commands loyalty to something greater than divine power. It will be a sacred partnership that ensures trust will be everlasting.

The Limits of Questions

17:2 "Why do you strive with me? Why do you test YHVH?"

How often do we pose a question that presumes some latent or implicit behavior without confirming it first? For example, we may ask someone, "Why did you steal that piece of chocolate?" before checking if they are even aware that something wrong has happened. What may be a line of questioning found in an interrogation room at the police station or on the witness stand in a courtroom can become a limitation of potential. Such probing may be necessary when discerning the motivations of a criminal act. But when questions are expressed with a presumption of understanding what may or may not be true, the possibility of a relationship built through genuine inquiry is narrowed.

In the Torah, questions surrounding the people's thirst and hunger shouldn't be reduced to a problem of hydration or nutrition. The fact that the people complain about their needs more than twelve times in the Torah narrative suggests that providing a sufficient, even divine, response doesn't always bring a satisfying conclusion. More than resolving the persistent complaints of a newly freed people, any response at the right time appears to be rooted in a trust the people are not yet capable of expressing for their leaders and even for God. In response to the people's complaints, Moshe asks, **"Why do you strive with me? Why do you test YHVH?"** Moshe recognizes that there is no sufficient rationale to assuage the fears and concerns of his people. If we read this cynically, we may seriously consider the proposition implicit in the people's concern: "Can we trust in a God who doesn't inspire trust?" Moshe's response to their complaints with a question in the language of a trial suggests that his tolerance has been tested to the limit and expresses a lack of trust of his own.

The strained relationship between Moshe and the people, even between God and the people, will persist during their entire journey to the land of Canaan. Perhaps an occasional trust-but-verify approach is healthy in a growing relationship. Perhaps we also learn here there is an intolerance for complaints that cannot easily be overcome. The people just can't see their circumstances differently despite all the miracles and expressions of confidence from their leaders, even from God.

These two questions remind us that even when we feel like our tolerance has reached its limit, our response should never be one of indifference. Moshe has not yet determined the fate of the people through his line of inquiry. By asking "Why?" he reminds us that a leader's patience may be finite, but their commitment to reach promised lands can be infinite.

Questioning an Ethic

17:3 "Why did you bring us out of Egypt to kill us, our children, and our cattle with thirst?"

17:4 "What shall I do with these people?"

The cornerstone of Torah ethics is the commandment to care for the stranger, the widow, the orphan, the neglected and vulnerable people among us. The sensitivity the Torah demands in this kind of care cannot be underestimated. It is an ethic that cannot simply be dictated either. It is a sense of being that can only result from a personal connection to the experience of vulnerability and the empowerment felt by protecting others from the harmful effects of neglect. Societies throughout history have been founded on this fundamental concept, and the struggle to maintain it or adhere to it among competing priorities is a sustaining value even in our days.

In the Torah the Israelites must make their journey through the desert to overcome their own experiences of powerlessness and vulnerability. They are destined to find empowerment in the divine responsibility of caring for others, but the fact that the Torah records a journey punctuated by complaint and conflict reveals how difficult and audacious caring for others can be. And so among the litany of complaints the people will continually register with Moshe and Aharon, this question emerges from a place of frustration. Their concerns for water and physical satiation easily become an argument about their own purpose as a people. They complain to Moshe, **"Why did you bring us out of Egypt to kill us, our children, and our cattle with thirst?"**

More than describing the fulfillment of the basic human need for self-satisfaction necessary before we can care for others, this question is a reflection of the people on their own condition. Did the text ever hint that their fate was to be killed? What is remarkable and even painful to read is how extreme the people's reaction is to their condition and how quickly it follows their redemption. This amplification of their feelings is a sign of stubbornness the people will rehearse at every step along the way.

They are also inadvertently questioning the ethic of care here. It is an expression of doubt that plagues anyone who cannot see past their own needs to take on their God-given responsibility to help others. As such, God's and Moshe's responses will be first to persuade and ameliorate the people's shortsightedness. Sadly, everyone's patience will be tried and even broken.

The complaint narrative continues from thirst and hunger to an existential crisis. Moshe responds, **"What shall I do with these people?"** God chooses to respond to Moshe's plea and lead the people to the rock at Horeb (the eventual location of God's revelation) to give them water either for momentary physical satisfaction or spiritual resolution.

Because we are a people destined for covenantal responsibility, we can only fulfill the responsibility of care once our basic needs are met. We cannot be a light to the nations without a lamp to illuminate our path. The people's struggles are the sparks that ignite this great ethic of empathy.

Are You There God? It's Us, the Children of Israel.

17:7 "Is YHVH present among us or not?"

Questions with binary answers are not really questions. Knowing if something is warm or cold, on or off, deep or shallow can be factually determined with a little investigation. Seeking *either-or* knowledge with an interrogative is convenient but not necessary. Perhaps implicit in the dichotomies of one or the other, the presence of *both-and* may dwell. When a question explores some definitive polarity, the space in between may be the true object of inquiry.

This dynamic could not be more evident than in this question noted in reference to the people's desperate cries for water. The text identifies the place where the people challenge both Moshe and Aharon and God as *Masah* (trial) and *Meribah* (quarrel). Trials and quarrels are never resolved in absolutes. So the question **"Is YHVH present among us or not?"** should not be understood as a query of existence. In fact, the question is whether or not God is with the people in this moment and ultimately what the definition of God's presence is at any time.

Knowing God is a continued struggle for this generation of Israelites who only felt the absence of their God while crumpled under the tyranny of an all-encompassing pantheon of Egyptian gods. Their questions here and throughout the remainder of the Torah reveal struggles in binaries. God may be present or may be absent, but God is the only absolute that defies either of these extremes. God is, by definition, the space in between, the *both-and* of existence. The people will come to learn this through a generation of experience and not by faith alone.

It is remarkable that the text places this question in the mouths of the people but does not record them expressing it themselves. Either the question was indeed posed by the people but not recorded as it happened or the people did not express this question at all. Curiously, in the latter construction the question then is not whether this was how the people felt but how it begins to identify what the people are seeking and even what will define their faith. The people are seeking the divine, and they are yet to discover where and when God dwells.

YITRO

18:14 "What is this thing that you are doing to the people?" (Yitro to Moshe)

18:14 "Why do you sit by yourself alone, and all the people stand about you from morning until evening?" (Yitro to Moshe)

The episodes recorded in these chapters, including the powerful moment when the people receive the Ten Commandments, are not riddled with questions. Indeed, the task of standing at Sinai and accepting God's revealed words expresses a confidence and preparation unlike other pivotal events throughout the Torah narrative. The two questions of this portion, expressed by Moshe's father-in-law Yitro, offer a different kind of revelation. The concept that authority is never an independent human endeavor will model for future generations what authentic and godly leadership can be. While these questions precede the moment when God speaks and delivers the commandments to the people, Yitro's intuition and Moshe's embrace of his advice have divine implications, those of shared responsibility.

Delegating Authority

18:14 "What is this thing that you are doing to the people?"

18:14 "Why do you sit by yourself alone, and all the people stand about you from morning until evening?"

What defines a leader? Charisma? Bold and courageous action? Tactical brilliance? While each of these virtues seems essential for capable leadership, the manner in which a leader communicates to the people is an unprecedented concern introduced by the Torah. We've witnessed prophetic leadership in Noah, the man who follows God's instructions without fail but never communicates to another soul beyond his immediate family. We've watched Abraham and his children contend with a tribal leadership where communication from patriarch to tribe is immutable. We've seen the tyrannical leadership of Pharaoh, whose absolute power and control is ultimately overthrown by the patient and persistent communication of Moshe and Aharon. Now we're introduced to executive leadership in Moshe. Unlike the models that precede him, Moshe's leadership is going to be based on a covenantal responsibility, a collective will to fulfill the purpose of bringing God's presence into the world.

The guidance of Moshe's father-in-law Yitro when he sees Moshe trying to solve the problems of the people alone is more than sound advice based on observation. He asks, **"What is this thing that you are doing to the people?"** and **"Why do you sit by yourself alone, and all the people stand about you from morning until evening?"** Structured leadership listens to the needs of the people and creates lines of accountability among the people themselves. It is a courageous departure from the potential despotism of a monarch or tyrant.

The people haven't needed a system of justice like this before. As slaves, they were subject to the whims of their ruling class. We imagine that they couldn't even comprehend what living as free people would require. The Torah's recognition of Yitro's role in the establishment of the people as a nation is laudable. His concern is not for administrative justice or a relief of the leader. He becomes the primary educator of human-centered justice, illuminated by God's vision and purpose. By focusing his concern on Moshe, Yitro uses his questions to establish the confederation of the people, divided equitably to ensure that all will have a place in Moshe's court of justice and are prepared to receive the covenant of God's people-centered Torah.

MISHPATIM

22:26 "In what else will they sleep?" (God to the people)

Following the moment of Revelation, the Torah turns to instructing the Israelite nation with a lengthy code of civil responsibilities and punishments for violating expected behaviors. This is not a place one would expect any questions or any uncertainty in the laws that are being written. In the singular question posed here, likely by God, there is a profound statement of ethics that the Torah conveys unlike a body of laws or simply a historical narrative. This is a teaching, the true definition of Torah, that includes a consideration for human dignity and responsibility at its core. Here is where a monumental question inspires thoughtful and sensitive consideration for every generation.

The Ethic of Questions

22:26 "In what else will they sleep?"

The nakedness the first human beings feel is not temperate. They had every need provided for them, including a climate most suitable to the unclothed body. We discover the nakedness they felt emerged from a sense of shame, an incomplete feeling. When we first understand nakedness, we locate our meaning in the presence of clothing. Now after the many generations of humankind chronicled in the Torah, the question of nakedness reemerges to express a most profound uncertainty among a litany of rules and responsibilities.

The question **"In what else shall they sleep?"** ostensibly appears as a rhetorical device to evoke thoughtful consideration. This question entices the mind and the spirit. Why did the message need to be framed in the form of a question? Is there some doubt here that the text is responding to, something that has not yet been introduced? What was God, here the speaker, even concerned about? We assume it is God, and rightfully so given the statement that follows, **"Therefore, if he cries out to me, I will pay heed, for I am compassionate."**

The question is instructive. God wants us to learn an ethic of compassion and responsibility in this Torah by God's own example. One cannot easily command compassion. More than a succession of actions that taken together can be described as compassionate, the concept, the ethic of responsibility for others becomes a foundation for the way of the Israelites.

Throughout history this ethic will be challenged, broken, and renewed. Today when the war-worn Israeli questions the act of compassionate care for one's enemy, the ethic of dignity and responsibility prevails. Our study and discovery through this question leads us to this profound truth: humanity's collective purpose is to show compassion; that is to say, we must care for the individual, one act of decency at a time. This is what God asks of us.

TERUMAH

The fulfillment of God's command that the people build a sanctuary is an extraordinary feat. Among the few chapters in the entire Torah without questions, this one, and the very notion that the instructions given to the people here are implemented without a doubt, is stunning. These are the people who complain and pine for a simpler life all along their journey toward the Promised Land. The physical completion of this divine command is unusual in the Torah. The exacting detail and the unfettered commitment to build something so definitive is inspiring given that the people have not had their own sacred space for generations and certainly never as a nation.

In a sense, the absence of questions here brings into focus the form and function of a national religion. The *mishkan*, the portable sanctuary detailed in these chapters, is built by individuals, literally, **"from every person whose heart so moves them."**[26] The collective effort will become the first public entity of the Israelite nation where it is the national duty to serve the divine. Perhaps we can surmise that when the collective will of the people is unified in creating sacred space, no questions or uncertainties are necessary.

Similarly it will be, many generations later, when the Jewish people will proclaim in prayer their duty *L'Takein Olam B'Malchut Shaddai* (to correct the world under the domain of God). Here the word "correct" could even imply building a world of certainty. The audacious dream of collective unity in every generation is reflected in the task of building a sacred space here in the Torah.

TETZAVEH

As the instructions for building the sacred space for God's presence unfold, the detailed explanations of how the people who serve the *mishkan* are recorded in the chapters of this Torah reading. The outline of their consecrated duty to serve the sanctuary and the collective will of the people is also absent any questions, implying that God's expectations for sacred behavior are both immutable and absolutely certain.

Along with the elegant and ornate vestments the priests are instructed to wear, we read about the breastplate of decision-making, the *Hoshen Mishpat*, and in particular the *Urim* and *Tummim*, two stones with some form of oracular quality. The meaning of the words is uncertain, with some translating them to assign guilt or innocence. Their function is extraordinary in terms of the questions we find in the Torah.

There are few mentions of these tools of divination in the entire Bible. We read that Eleazar, the high priest who succeeds Aharon, consults the Urim (and not the Tummim) when Moshe selects Joshua to succeed him.[27] We read of their mention at the conclusion of the Torah when Moshe is blessing the people.[28] We only read of any function of these strange objects in the stories retold in the book of Samuel, when he consults the stones as confirmation for his decision-making.[29]

The absence of questioning does not suggest that the behavior of the Israelites in the *mishkan* unequivocally existed absent any doubt. From our modern perspective, where our reliance on empirical fact to resolve our doubt prevails in the quest for certainty and understanding, the presence of the Urim and Tummim in the text is troubling. Nevertheless, infrequent mention of these objects in the civic behavior of the Israelite nation in the entire Bible affirms that the search for divine understanding does not rely on amulets or supernatural forces. It is through the preponderance of questions that we most reliably discover God's presence in our lives.

KI TISSA

32:21 "What did these people do to you that you brought this great sin upon them?" (Moshe to Aharon)

33:16 "By what shall it be known that I have found grace in Your sight, I and Your people?" (Moshe to God)

33:16 "How shall it be known that Your people have gained Your favor unless You go with us, so that we may be distinguished, Your people and I, from every people the face of the earth?" (Moshe to God)

The Torah's presentation of questioning loyalty to God is unique among works of sacred literature. The covenantal agreement between God and humanity is precarious, and these texts amplify the struggle of the people to completely fulfill what God expects from them. Indeed, the Jewish understanding of loyalty continues to evolve and sharpen in every generation because these episodes give us permission to test and expand the limits of our understanding of a divine relationship.

After a litany of communal responsibilities has been laid out for the people, the narrative returns to an active dialogue between God and Moshe. We read about the people's betrayal when they construct an idol to worship and feel the pain of the shattered tablets inscribed with words written by the hand of God. These moments sting our conscience as we pray for forgiveness as Moshe did for the people.

The questions in this portion affirm that sanctity can be achieved through doubt. Moshe wants to understand his brother's intentions in helping the people construct a golden calf as he shatters the covenantal tablets given to him by God. These questions and the narratives where they are located serve as a reminder that the command of loyal adherence to a covenant necessitates a quest for certainty as well.

Simply put, this episode unravels the certainty of revelation. The people have already lost the faith they so readily and profoundly expressed at the foot of Mount Sinai. It will be Moshe's intercession on their behalf that restores God's faith in them, demonstrating that patience and a willingness to watch the people mature will endure.

Questions as Commiseration

32:21 "What did these people do to you that you brought this great sin upon them?"

The tone of our voice reveals so much about the intent of our words. When we speak deliberately, the tone of our voice can convey accusation or express concern. We can express joy or sorrow using the same words. Reading the words in a text without punctuation prompts interpretation. How marvelously sensitive the reader of the Torah must become to plumb the depths of wisdom using the questions posed in the text!

Few questions in the Torah are as much a subject of this sensitivity as the ones we find following the episode of the golden calf. After the calf is built, the people dance in frenzied ecstasy, the tablets are smashed, and Moshe turns to his brother Aharon and asks, **"What did these people do to you that you brought this great sin upon them?"** Moshe wants an explanation, a somewhat common occurrence in the Torah, albeit typically prompted by God. The fact that Aharon responds is unique, perhaps precisely because the question comes from his brother. His desire to respond sheds light on the intent or the tone of Moshe's words. Aharon responds, **"Let not my lord be enraged. You know that these people are bent on evil."** What a dramatic turn of phrase after we learn that these people are to be a kingdom of priests!

If Moshe's question is an accusation, then Aharon's words are a defense. Aharon, after all, was left to supervise the people when Moshe ascended the mountain. He was in charge and their behavior was anything but godly. Aharon's expression was simply that the people were too powerful for him to prevent them from taking their destiny into their own hands.

If his words are expressed with concern, Aharon's response is instruction. The object of concern is the people's behavior. Moshe's absence created a distance in familiarity. He didn't know their nature while he was on the mountain. His return was one that prompted curiosity, and through his disappointment, he seeks understanding.

The traditional commentators of the Torah have taken great interest in this question. Moshe is not chastising Aharon according to Rabbi Shlomo Yitzchaki (Rashi). He interprets Moshe's question as if it were to say "How many pains must you have endured—it must be that they inflicted suffering on you, before you brought this sin upon them!"

Rabbi Moshe ben Nachman, writing a generation after Rashi, interprets the tone more subtly. He agrees that Moshe is not accusing Aharon of causing or participating in the idolatrous act, but he is questioning Aharon's silence in not reproving the people for their sinful behavior. Aharon's response, while a rationale for his own behavior, is less an apology than it is an insight into the people's character.

To commiserate through a question is incredibly sophisticated. Rather than narrating a history of acts and reactions, the brothers are exemplifying the difficulty of locating truth. The Torah is teaching us that in moments of extreme tension, like this act of idolatry and the shattering of God's Torah, the way forward is through mutual understanding. Moshe and Aharon reach this together, and their using a question to build their relationship should be a model for us as well.

Trust in God

33:16 "By what shall it be known that I have found grace in Your sight, I and Your people?"

33:16 "How shall it be known that Your people have gained Your favor unless You go with us, so that we may be distinguished, Your people and I, from every people on the face of the earth?"

Moshe's experience in defining the nation of Israel culminates in the concluding narratives of the book. The final questions of the book are found in the chapter following the episode in which the people construct the golden calf. As if Moshe is uncertain of God's presence in the world, he asks, **"By what shall it be known that I have found**

grace in Your sight, I and Your people?" It is a question that has a dual purpose. It seeks specific details with which Moshe can demonstrate his unique calling as a prophet and teacher of God's words, and it also serves a deeper purpose, one that requires emulation and exemplification by the leader of the people. What qualities shall the leader possess in order to be worthy of divine grace? More than the unique power and status of the leader in relation to God, it is the manifestation of divine influence in the people that becomes the subject of concern. **"I and Your people"** elucidates a divine relationship among the collective. Moshe is not a solitary figure whose skillful leadership rests in his unique ability to comprehend and interpret God. Moshe is confirmed as a leader when the people find divine favor as well. After aligning the people once again in their devotion and fealty to the God of Israel, he turns his attention back to God. He asks, **"How shall it be known that Your people have gained Your favor unless You go with us, so that we may be distinguished, Your people and I, from every people on the face of the earth?"**

There are two insights that arise from this question. First, this is a rare moment when Moshe aligns himself with the people. Unlike the beginning of the book where we see that the people first distinguish themselves in opposition to him,[30] he questions his own authority over the people after their redemption from Egypt.[31] Here we see him speaking in harmony with the people. Words like **"us"** and phrases like **"Your people and I"** are indicative of connection, relationship, even some form of loyalty that Moshe now engenders for B'nai Yisrael. The development of Moshe's relationship with the people evolves as the people become a nation.

The second insight, perhaps equally compelling, is how Moshe's plea for this particular nation, now covenanted with God's Word, is to be regarded in the world around them. By the end of the book, there is no question that they are a nation given a unique destiny and purpose. How will they live and contend with this role, including their seemingly incessant challenges to God and authority? God's response is to lovingly pass goodness and graciousness before Moshe. According to the Torah, end of revelation is compassion, and it is an aspiration for us in every generation.

Vayakhel and Pekudei

When the Israelites are in Egypt and Moshe asks Pharaoh to let the people go to the desert to worship YHVH, Pharaoh's persistent stubbornness motivates YHVH to bring more plagues to ensure the people's redemption. We often share Pharaoh's suspicions that once the people leave, they'll never come back.[32] And yet we witness the fulfillment of Moshe's promise to worship YHVH in the concluding chapters of the book. The intricacies of constructing a space to welcome God's presence far exceeds what Moshe beseeched Pharaoh to consider. Yet the goal is consistent throughout the entire book—the people are on a quest to meet the divine on their own terms.

This is why Moshe will find Bezalel and Ohaliab, creative artisans who gather the abundance of material used to construct the *mishkan*. They represent this quest to meet the divine without question. The act of gathering all the potential and forming something new or unique is a hallmark of creativity and reflects a certain amount of faith that what is being gathered will indeed form something new, even holy. The absence of questions here offers insight into the creative process. Creativity is more than a fulfillment of instructional steps to construct a holy structure. We learn here that anything creative is the courageous attempt to find certainty. Bezalel and Ohaliab do so with flourish!

The other significant moment in the description of the construction of the *mishkan* is the command to cease bringing gifts. Moshe instructs the people to cease from offering their gifts because they have collected more than enough material to complete the building of the *mishkan*.[33] This is always a remarkable moment to embrace amidst the complaints and drudgery the people continually express during their journey. Here is a moment when the people have offered **"more than enough,"** and it is presented without question.

The lesson remains that when the purpose of connecting with the divine is clearly understood, there are always **"more than enough"** gifts to share in the act of divine service.

CONCLUSION

If the book of Genesis presents the question of who we are as a family, the book of Exodus contends with the question of who we are as a nation. One nation confronts another in this book, and the definition of this particular confederation of tribes, more than that of being redeemed, is that of a people who grow and evolve with a unique status and responsibility. The text does not promise God's blessing simply as a gift for the obedience of the people. The text promises that in this covenantal relationship, God's favor and the blessing of the people among the nations of the world will radiate with potential for growth.

The fundamental questions of the Passover rituals are posed in this book to strengthen this newly formed identity. Posing questions for the succeeding generations is one of the great literary innovations of the Torah, even of Judaism. What will continue to bind these people together throughout the generations is a shared history and a shared destiny, both revealed by questions that define what is shared among the people and ultimately with God.

PART III

INTRODUCTION TO LEVITICUS

THE PAUCITY OF QUESTIONS IN THIS THIRD BOOK OF THE TORAH reminds us that an instruction manual of sacred service cannot be fraught with doubt. How frustrating it would be to read the directions for connecting with God if they were riddled with questions or if there were even multiple options! Unlike the vast majority of the Torah where questions help us confront our doubt and seek a faithful path in response, these chapters outline a confident explanation of sacred worship with no uncertainty. The function of sacrifices will become a cornerstone of the national ethos for the ancient Israelites because the explicit conditions for worship of God define the people's purpose. Indeed, the chapters titled "The Holiness Code," while ethical in nature, are the culmination of sacrificial worship. "Follow the rules and the reward will come as a result." The people will be obliged to make these offerings, either in praise or repentance. They will commemorate sacred occasions to reinforce their uniqueness as a people and as human beings in covenant with the divine.

The sacrificial cult no longer exists today because it was dismantled due, in part, to its overly rigid demands and even its corruption. Historically the sacrificial cult was transformed into the local practices of ritual observance in the home and communal celebration on the holidays. These adaptations to connect with God are the great innovation of Jewish tradition and form the basis of what is known as *rabbinic Judaism*.

It may also be valuable to speculate if there are consequences to legal codes or cultural norms that do not have a tolerance for uncertainty. The record of the sacrifices that were once offered is not a placeholder for the restoration of the sacrificial cult. One irony of the Torah is that questions, which are reflections of uncertainty and invitations to greater connections and meaning, are glaringly absent in the chapters that provide an explicit manual for attaining connection with the divine. The absence of questions, in light of the historical evolution of the religion of Judaism, is a compellingly positive statement that questions are a necessary communication tool to ensure connection with God is possible.

Leviticus

Vayikra—Tzav

Making an offering to something indeterminate is a profound expression of confidence. When the offerings are an expression of thanksgiving, they are the recognition that an experience of abundance is far greater than one expected to receive. Gratitude is the acknowledgment that one has more than enough. When the offerings are an attempt to take responsibility for harm caused to another or to God, they are an acceptance of responsibility and the sacrifice is an act that affirms that more is necessary.

These two opening portions of the book of Leviticus, here summarized together, outline the function and requirements for bringing offerings to the *mishkan* and eventually the *Beit HaMikdash*, the temple in Jerusalem. The absence of questions throughout this part of the Torah builds upon the certainty of sacrifice that is demanded by God and the people in their quest for sacred connection. The ultimate act of an offering is decisive. Ideally a sacrifice is the result of careful deliberation.

The presence of the priest as a mediator between the individual and YHVH is carefully explained in these chapters as well. The priest's responsibility to serve as a conduit of divine connection is something that is not saddled with doubt or even rhetorical uncertainties. The rituals a priest must undertake to be prepared for sacred service are a declaration that the potential to connect with YHVH isn't a solitary effort. YHVH is a collective expression of the people, and the priests are the representatives of that will to connect.

SHEMINI

10:17 "Why have you not eaten the purification offering in the place of the sanctuary?" (Moshe to Elazar and Itamar)

10:19 "If I had eaten the purification offering today, would it have been well-pleasing in the sight of YHVH?" (Aharon to Moshe)

This brief narrative event recorded in the book of Leviticus confronts the flaws in human action while fulfilling God's perfected teachings. The preceding chapters spend a great deal of time outlining corrective behaviors for inadvertent and willful sins of the people. The sacrificial cult is designed in part to validate human fallibility and to sanctify the process of re-connection with God. The questions that result from the fatal death of Charon's sons Nadav and Avah sharpen our ability to grapple with the fulfillment of duty while confronting the horror of a tragic loss. Sometimes the most profound answer to a difficult question is silence, as we learn from Aharon.

Intentional Disobedience

10:17 "Why have you not eaten the purification offering in the place of the sanctuary?"

10:19 "If I had eaten the purification offering today, would it have been well-pleasing in the sight of YHVH?"

Look up "unintended consequences" in a dictionary and you will find an entire school of thought on the subject. According to one source, consequences of this sort can be classified as positive, negative, or—oddly denoted—perverse. How wonderful are those moments when a new discovery emerges from a serendipitous mistake, like the discovery of penicillin to treat infections or the discovery of aspirin to help prevent heart attacks. So many lives have been saved from blunders and mishaps. There is holiness in this type of discovery as well.

In one of the rare narratives of the book of Leviticus, the introduction of Nadav and Avihu's untimely offering presents a perplexing challenge. For a text concerned with proper behavior in the temple cult, it also validates an exploration of intentional or unintentional mistakes. While we can debate whether the actions of Aharon's two sons were intentional or not, the consequences are fatal. But the unintended consequence of their death also teaches a powerful lesson in leadership.

More than a drama of divine punishment for improper behavior in the service of God, the text focuses on the responsibility of leadership. Moshe's inquiry **"Why have you not eaten the purification offering in the place of the sanctuary?"** is not simply a technical concern. He's angry. The law dictates the priest's behavior, and improper fulfillment of this responsibility can be deadly, just as it was to his other two nephews. Where Elazar and Itamar redouble their efforts to follow the law scrupulously in the wake of their loss, Moshe's question brings to light the distinction between the high priest as ultimate leader and the high priest as a prophet whose moral guidance shapes the character of the nation even in the midst of such a public trial.

Moshe's insistence on Elazar and Itamar's proper fulfillment of the priestly service is not intended to diminish the loss they must be experiencing. Rather, Moshe's adjurations advance the narrative of leadership from blind obedience to sacred duty. In short, responsibility is not divorced from the heart.

That is why, before the narrative concludes and the tension of Moshe's leadership is resolved, his brother Aharon returns with a more compelling retort. He asks, **"If I had eaten the purification offering today, would it have been well-pleasing in the sight of YHVH?"** In this Moshe is appeased.

We often read this narrative as one built on speculations of arrogance, ignorance, and carelessness. Yet these questions help us understand a much deeper and more powerful truth, that leadership is a careful enterprise. To be a leader is to endure the challenges of unintentional consequences and at the same time find a way to purposeful living and service.

TAZRIA—METZORA—ACHAREI MOT

Purity as a prerequisite of sacred worship exists in most religious traditions. Beyond the social dimensions or hygienic benefits of maintaining a certain form of bodily cleanliness, the book of Leviticus explores the spiritual dimensions of purity. The primary function of laws of purity isn't to exclude an individual from participating in the ritual life of the community if they are not fit to make an offering. Rather, the quest for purity is to enable the individual seeker an unfettered chance to encounter YHVH.

We also note that individual impurities (childbirth, menstruation, or unusual baldness), communal impurities (leprosy or other communicable diseases), and ultimately social impurities (forbidden relationships) do not elicit questions of clarification or uncertain definitions of what disqualifies a person from participating in sacrificial worship. There is a presumption here that the experience of separation is a precursor to the closeness, even intimacy, found when a good question is shared. The notion that our connection with the divine is best expressed in a purified form also suggests that the most authentic questions are asked with a similar purity of heart.

The concept of impurity connotes a negative state of being. Impurity as the separating force for divine encounter is laden with a rejection by God that isn't really present. The Torah takes great pains to outline the potentially disqualifying states of impurity so that the record can also prescribe the remedy. Though this is a culture of worship that no longer exists in practice, seeking purity to encounter YHVH remains a necessary dimension of religious continuity because the commitment to stand unimpeded before some greater or ultimate source of life is affirmative. Indeed, it is the highest form of spiritual quest. Judaism's ability to record and perpetuate this concern for purity in these chapters deserves attention despite the absence of questions along the way.

Kedoshim

This brief but consequential section of the Torah describes an ethical imperative to treat our fellow human beings with dignity. The essential teaching "Love **your fellow as yourself**"[1] is found in these chapters. There is a measure of certainty in the diverse list of interpersonal obligations, headed by the banner **"You will be holy, because, I, YHVH your God, am holy."**[2] Texts like this reinforce our impulse to read the Torah as a declaration of faithful certainty, particularly because there are no questions surrounding the complexities of preserving human dignity. Or perhaps the lack of questions in these chapters highlights the immutable theme of the Torah that human dignity is supreme. If the human being is made *"B'Tzelem Elohim"*[3] (in the image of God) and our command is to be holy, then we surmise that there is no doubt our responsibility to sustain a concern for other human beings is an act of divinity. The conditions for expressing concern here are emblematic of broadly undefined and not-yet-discovered circumstances when we may question our responsibility to show dignity for other human beings. There is a recognition implicit in these commandments that we have the ability to overcome our impulse to care for ourselves before we care for another. These texts challenge the binary between "us" and "them" and remind us there is no doubt that we must show concern for all humanity.

EMOR

The first section of this Torah portion is concerned with the circumstances in which priests should be disqualified from sacred service. It also outlines complicated limitations on the relationships priests may have with non-priests and the punishment for abusing the power of priestly duties. There is a forceful impression surrounding the priest's potential vulnerability—seen, for example, in the disqualification from service due to physical limitations. Since there are no questions in these chapters, we may conclude that the tasks of the priests are explicit and definite. There can be no deviation from the instructions God has given to them in their elected service of the people.

This section of the Torah may be confusing, with rules pertaining to vulnerability interrupted by rules for celebrating sacred occasions. There is even a short anecdote that presents a case of disobedience of the laws when the son of an Israelite mother and Egyptian father blasphemes the name of God. This episode gives us the sense of a civic duty that leaves little room for uncertainty. Whether or not the Israelite woman's son blasphemes the name of God intentionally, the outcome of the altercation is fatal.[4] Along with the rules of priestly behavior, this may remind us that questions are best expressed when greater connection with YHVH is desired.

BEHAR

25:20 "What shall we eat in the seventh year, if we may neither sow nor gather in our crops?"

The rare moment when the entire people ask a question of law is chronicled in the concluding chapters of Leviticus. Here the question is one of practicality. If the people are commanded to leave the land fallow in the seventh year, on what will they subsist? The question itself is an archetype of reason and a sacred relationship. The people are not portrayed as challenging God's authority in the law given to them. They are not defiant. They want to fulfill the command yet their concern is very real. Perhaps God wants to anticipate the anxiety in their uncertainty. How this question is presented and unfolds in the larger narrative of the growing nation of Israel confronts a powerful value: living with God.

Trust in God?

25:20 "What shall we eat in the seventh year, if we may neither sow nor gather in our crops?"

Sometimes a clarifying question uncovers a deeper conflict. Ultimately, conflict is a struggle between competing choices with the intention to move forward by doing what is right and good. Doing the right thing in the concluding chapters of the book of Leviticus means following God's agricultural laws even in the face of an uncertain future. If the Israelites were just curious to know where their sustenance would be found, the Torah would have answered plainly. Rather, faith is challenged in a process that proposes a social order based on belief, on trust. For someone who has no guarantee where their next meal will come from and whose survival is predicated on implicit trust, this question seems simply preposterous.

The Torah introduces a new ethic for the wandering Israelites and for us. Trust in God, faith in the provision of need in the future is no longer a distant reality. God's response to the question, resolving the logical dilemma of two years of abundance, is not a model the people have seen before.

Indeed, the dilemma continues as future generations grapple with the consequences of the Shemitah laws. The rabbis introduce a concept called

Prozbul, a Greek word that applies a legal fiction to obviate the circumstances of a religious quandary. They rule that in the seventh year, Jews are permitted to sell their land to non-Jews so the land can be cultivated in a legal fashion. Certainly this accommodation did not emerge from an absence of faith. It reveals a dramatic shift from divine influence in the natural order and a reliance on human agency to fulfill God's will. The Prozbul is an essential legal formula that allows the observant Jew to read the question found here in the book of Leviticus and answer, "God will provide." The bounty of God's produce isn't to be found in a supernatural cultivation of soil and vegetation. God's bounty is found in an active partnership of human and divine agency. This is perhaps precisely where divine responses to the world's greatest challenges to human thriving are to be found.

And still the question leaves us with a challenge. What concerns do we have that God can adequately respond to? Is there any inquiry that does not require human agency as part of the answer? The pleading curiosity for clarity uttered by the Israelites here is purposefully placed in the heart of a book about divine obedience to introduce the struggle with this new role human beings now take. Redemption and freedom are not agencies given by God for human fealty and loyalty. The practice of freedom as God demands requires an active response by human beings. God's response **"I will ordain My blessing for you in the sixth year, so that it will yield a crop sufficient for three years"**[5] implies a sense of physical satiation, but the freedom this God gives is one that invites the human being to act in partnership with God to feed the hungry, heal the sick, lift up the downtrodden, and bring about peace.

BECHUKOTAI

The language of the concluding chapters of Leviticus is quite distinct from the rest of the book. Where the function of sacred service is clear and determinate, these final words express a conditional relationship, beginning with the words **"If you follow My laws and faithfully observe My commandments."**[6]

The concept that obedience, mutual responsibility, even blessings are contingent upon proper behavior is a perpetual challenge that has been a guiding force of social systems throughout history. Incentives and punishments motivate the behavior of individuals and groups. But moving an entire society or civilization with conditional loyalty has never been faithfully proven. The insertion of God's conditional blessings for fulfilling the laws of the Torah is intended to inspire confidence and drive, the positive reinforcement of obedience becoming a reward in itself.

The consequences for misbehavior are outlined here as well. They are intended to dissuade the Israelites from breaking their covenantal promises and to heighten their awareness of the harrowing results of disobedience. The lack of questions in these chapters implies that God's providence can be influenced without the act of seeking. There seems to come a point when the people can no longer seek the teachings of God or the interpretations of Moshe and the elders. Observing the *mitzvot* is a standard by which the people will be measured. These chapters bring this standard into focus and remove any doubt that blessings and curses emerge depending on the collective will of the Israelite nation.

The people will fail this test again and again in the generations to come. The very notion that the conditions for worshiping God outlined in this book will be abrogated by conquest and the exile of the Israelite nation will prompt new approaches to seeking the presence of God in history and even today.

Conclusion

The book of Leviticus presents themes of sacred worship, purity, agricultural responsibility, and covenantal loyalty. Each of these concepts evolves into a comprehensive body of laws governing the behavior of individuals and society. The specific nature of the text, amplified by the absence of questions, teaches us that a society thrives best with common understandings of civic duty, personal hygiene, and ecological responsibility.

We are learning that each of the moments where we explore uncertainty is an opportunity to affirm the faithfulness of our worship of YHVH. The prerequisites for bringing an offering, the mantle of responsibility the priest carries, and our collective duty to honor the earth and the bounty it provides are reminders that when there are no questions, we are encouraged, even commanded, to act in good faith. Many of the practices outlined in this book are no longer observed today, yet the spirit of discovering and celebrating hallowed rituals continues to inspire purposeful living.

From here the text will soon return to the narrative journey the Israelites have undertaken toward the Promised Land. The foundations of behavior outlined in this book will be tested with incessant complaints, a request to change the laws, and even failures of leadership. This underscores the fragility of collective will and inspires us to renew our commitment to apply the wisdom of these laws in every generation.

Part IV

Introduction to Numbers

Now that the community has identified itself by verbally accepting the responsibility of serving as priests and a holy nation,[1] this book takes on another question of identity. Who qualifies as a representative to God for the people? Moshe alone? Aharon and the priests? The people themselves? This part of the people's journey presents the challenge implicit in such decision-making and the struggle in changing roles. The role of the leader is consistently challenged in this book: by Aharon and Miriam; by Korach; even by Bilaam (the Moabite priest). The role of God among the people also continues to be challenged through the questions expressed in this book. These encounters are recorded to help us better confront the power of the individual and the force of the people. This book teaches us that the journey to the Promised Land cannot be made without transformations of the spirit. This includes changes in the roles that have been given to us. We are meant to embrace what has been given, here a covenantal promise, and the duty to fulfill our responsibilities, actions that demand a force of will that cannot be commanded. The questions posed in this book are pivotal; they highlight a potential for new definitions of leadership, loyalty, and divine presence.

Numbers

BAMIDBAR—NASO

The opening chapters of this book read as do those of the book of Leviticus, with details pertaining to the civic responsibilities of the Israelite nation. In addition to the census, which comprises a large portion of the opening chapters, there remain essential public concerns about the conduct of individuals. These include the episode of the suspected adulteress, the laws of the nazirite, and the coordination of the construction and deconstruction of the *mishkan*.

The first seven chapters of this book do not include questions, in part due to its similarity to the instructions in the book of Leviticus. There we are reminded that collective will and civic duty are meant to be fulfilled without challenge. The certainty of these duties, juxtaposed with the fragility of the people's behavior in the remaining chapters of the book, highlights what the Torah looks like without holy doubt. The demands can become rote, and expectations can lose their impact. For example, the ritual of *Sotah* surrounding the suspicions of adultery ultimately falls out of practice precisely because the curiosity and doubt that emerges in later generations will reveal its inherent flaws.

These chapters also include the positive blessings of the people by Aharon and the priests.[1] These words are a relic of Torah behavior that is vibrant and thriving today, as parents bless children with these words in the home and they are even included in public rituals like baby namings, b'nai mitzvahs, and weddings. This too is a reminder that there can be faithful certainty that endures in every generation. The task of readers of the Torah is to immerse themselves in the uncertainties the texts reveal and then evaluate their enduring value in each generation.

B'HA'ALOTECHA

9:7 "Are we to be kept back, so as not to bring the offering of YHVH in its appointed season among the Israelites?" (Defiled Israelite men to Moshe)

11:4 "Who will give us meat?" (The people to Moshe)

11:11 "Why have You dealt ill with Your servant?" (Moshe to God)

11:11 "Why have I not enjoyed Your favor, that You have laid the burden of all these people upon me?" (Moshe to God)

11:12 "Have I conceived all these people?" (Moshe to God)

11:12 "Have I brought them forth, that You should say unto me: Carry them in your bosom, as a nursing-father carrieth the sucking child, unto the land which You swore unto their ancestors?" (Moshe to God)

11:13 "Where do I have meat?" (Moshe to God)

11:18 "Who will give us meat?" (God to Moshe, repeating the words of the people)

11:20 "Why, for this, did we leave Egypt?" (God to Moshe repeating the words of the people)

11:22 "If flocks and herds are slain for them, will it satisfy them?" (Moshe to God)

11:22 "If all the fish in the sea were caught for them, would it satisfy them?" (Moshe to God)

11:23 "Is YHVH's hand cut short?" (God to Moshe)

11:29 "Are you jealous for my sake? Who will make it so that YHVH's people were prophets, that YHVH put Spirit upon them?" (Moshe to Joshua)

11:29 "Who will be given everything of YHVH as prophets? [Would that everyone were a prophet!]" (Moshe to Joshua)

12:2 "Has YHVH only spoken to Moshe?" (Miriam and Aharon to God)

12:2 "Has God not spoken to us too?" (Miriam and Aharon to God)

12:8 "Why were you not afraid to speak against my servant, Moshe?" (God to Miriam and Aharon)

Remarkably, the most recent narrative event recorded in the Torah was in Leviticus, where we read about the tragic deaths of Aharon's sons Nadav and Avihu.[2] The retelling of the Israelite's experience in the desert through the recorded questions touch upon the limits of power in leadership. The people's cries for food prompt Moshe to grapple with his own limitations, even asking God to take his life rather than disappoint the people by not giving them what they request. The people's complaints and Moshe's impatience mount as the search for food becomes more important than their search for meaning and purpose. Finally the very question of fitness for leadership is introduced as Aharon and Miriam speak out against Moshe.

A Good Jew

9:7 "Are we to be kept back, so as not to bring the offering of YHVH in its appointed season among the Israelites?"

The core narrative of the journey from Sinai to Canaan reminds us that a change in location enables an individual to wrestle with divine presence and command. The Torah does not presume that the redemptive moment on the mountain with God's presence revealed is where the people will fully understand the role of God in their lives. Rather, the Torah continually pushes the eternal question "What's next?" and explores how a community may define their reality with a spirit of optimism and possibility along the way.

In the book of Numbers, the Israelites journey to Canaan by way of the desert. The wandering gives the people opportunities and obligations to fulfill the essential practices of Jewish living, namely offering the Paschal sacrifice. A logical quandary develops when people are incapable of making the offering, because they are impure from observing another essential mitzvah, here the care for a dead body.

In the verse we read here, these impure men appear before Moshe and Aharon and ask, **"Are we to be kept back, so as not to bring the offering of YHVH in its appointed season among the Israelites?"** This is one of those piercing questions that reveals far more about the nature of living as a Jew and the identity of a Jew in relation to God than simply resolving a matter of clear legal precedence. The question probes the role of a good

Jew who is responsible for being a servant to God but meets a religious conflict in doing so. What should someone do when they are incapable of observing a mitzvah, here an essential mitzvah, because another mitzvah invalidates their fitness for performing it? What is the identity they lose if they cannot perform the most essential act of observing Pesah as it was commanded? Or is the system itself flawed because it does not account for such gnawing and seemingly mundane complications? Either way, the quest to resolve this issue certifies that the identity of the Jew is maintained within the community, and the need to provide legal reasoning or to adjust to the law enables the Jew to remain a part of the people even when he is violating a core practice. Hence the introduction of a Second Pesah, an alternate paschal offering in the following verses.[3] It resolves the conflict of unclean corpses and establishes a new identity for the Jew at the same time. To be a Jew is to find ways to be close to God even when observing God's law forces you from your prescribed path.

The question here implies a certain maturity of the Jew and of God. The legal system is designed with the intent of meeting humanity and divinity at their best, and yet the human being is dynamic, ever growing in their understanding of the universe around them. The best interpretation implies a continual stretching and redefinition of our humanity as we grow. The Torah, and a question like this in particular, is intended to highlight the flexibility of the divine encounter to facilitate connection, not forbid it.

What Is Real?

11:11 "Why have You dealt ill with Your servant?"

11:11 "Why have I not enjoyed Your favor, that You have laid the burden of all these people upon me?"

One of the purposes of the journey through the desert is the attempt to resolve a conflict implicit in sacred duty. Complaints, resistance, and outright disobedience become the subject matter of this foundational text of identity and purpose. We may wonder how a people so mired in conflict could be worthy of divine instruction as we pore over the verses in this book. The people's concerns for physical sustenance are likely manifestations of a deeper conflict of faith, of loyalty, of obedience to divine command. What results is known as drama.

Drama is defined as a struggle between conflicting ideas. What we identify as drama is the fantastic imagination toward resolution of conflict. But it is not real. It is important to note that the origin of drama is the Greek word for action. Knowing we must act and how we choose to do so are the subjects of great theater and political philosophy. Drama is the unfolding conflict toward what becomes real.

The drama of the Israelites is no more poignant than the episode of complaint found in this rapid succession of questions. The people are complaining for the food they don't have, God is angry at the narrow-minded Israelites who cannot think beyond their next meal, and Moshe is upset at his inability to change the people's behavior whether by the teachings he received on Sinai or by his experiences of leadership.

Moshe asks, **"Why have you dealt ill with Your servant?"** and **"Why have I not enjoyed Your favor, that You have laid the burden of all these people upon me?"** The litany of these questions reveals the anxiety and urgency of his concern. We don't ask multiple questions when we're calm. And yet his exhaustion in this moment of leadership is not unfamiliar to those who accept the mantle of responsibility.

We cannot underestimate the anxiety of the people here. Rather than dismissing their concern as a sign of petulance uttered by redeemed slaves lingering with the residue of their oppression, their concern prompts us to entertain the seriousness of their cries. How can anyone enter sacred service when their basic needs are not met?

We cannot disregard Moshe's frustration either. More than the length of experience we have shared with his leadership of the people from Egypt to the Promised Land, we imagine that he has tried every leadership trick in the book up to this point. Facing yet another example of failure, he also breaks down in his impatience, a recurring theme for him throughout the book.

Finally we imagine God's frustration. That God has spoken or God's anger is felt in some palpable fashion implies a certain openness to hear. Herein may be the insight to the episode. More than the drama of the people's complaints, the capacity to hear God's voice even amidst frustration is a model worth emulating. Conflict is unavoidable. But hearing the other through the conflict can be the foundation of sacred connections. If only the people would listen!

Questions Help Us Grow

11:12 "Have I conceived all these people?"

11:12 "Have I brought them forth, that You should say unto me: Carry them in your bosom, as a nursing-father carrieth the sucking child, unto the land which You swore unto their ancestors?"

Now we focus on Moshe, who is constantly exploring his own identity, both in relation to the people and in relation to God. The desert is fraught with a persistent reality of what community is, a collective tasked with reaching a common destination safely. We cannot presume everyone is satisfied by the experience all the time. It's why the text takes note of the people in this moment by adding, **"Moshe heard the people weeping, every clan apart, each person at the entrance of their tent."**[4] The challenge of community is to satisfy the majority as the frustration mounts when there is no foreseeable consensus.

Turning our attention to Moshe's experience as a leader provides a lens into the identity of the individual precisely at the moment when covenantal loyalty appears to be a secondary concern. When the people rally against Moshe in discontent for their meager provisions, Moshe asks, **"Have I conceived all these people? Have I brought them forth, that You should say unto me: Carry them in your bosom, as a nursing-father carrieth the sucking child, unto the land which You swore unto their ancestors?"**

It's clear we have two distinct expressions here. The series of questions in this part of the text are superficially read as an emotional unloading of stress on God. Probe deeper, and the questions focus on identity too. Here the psychology of stress and an apparent threat to identity is explored. To be a Jew is to grapple with responsibility and identity. Moshe took the job, after all, and the acknowledgment of its seemingly unbearable moments is a recognition that being in covenant with God does not guarantee implicit obedience. Moshe's expression is self-identifying too. He is testing his limits. Such defining moments shape who we are and who we ought to be.

This moment in the narrative also helps us shape and define the contours of the people. Rather than fading into the background of the unfolding drama, the people are coming into focus! While we see them here cast in a shadow of self-centeredness and corporeal desire, their vocal response is a call to the leader of the people and to God that the experience of becoming is a process. Through the expression of discontent, the leader and the people have an opportunity to grow.

Nostalgia—The Ache of Memory

11:4 "Who will give us meat?"
11:13 "Where do I have meat?"
11:18 "Who will give us meat?"
11:20 "Why, for this, did we leave Egypt?"

There is a distinction between memory for the sake of survival and memory for the sake of self-preservation. What often feels like a life-or-death experience may only be an uncomfortable situation. What is truly detrimental to one's health can be overlooked when the danger is not imminent. For those with young children, helping a child recover from a small scratch is quite different than rushing them to the hospital after a serious injury has occurred.

Accessing our memory and constructing our present based on past experience is vital to our survival. We call this "nostalgia," a sometimes painful sense of the past in relation to our present experience. Through the aches of memory, we are prepared to confront the challenge to change.

The people's complaints in the desert legitimately border on questions of survival. The uncertainty of their wandering is understandable. And yet they have a promise from God their survival will be assured, while the manna appears to demonstrate God's commitment to them.

One thing is certain: when genuine survival is on the line, questions are not the most effective tool to elicit a response. What sounds like a cry for survival is really an expression of doubt. Will God provide for them as promised? The people cry for the food and comfort that they once enjoyed even if it came at the price of their dignity. Is God a reliable partner?

One more piece of this puzzle is the clear distinction between "the people" and the "leader." The people ask, **"Who will give us meat?"** **"Why, for this, did we leave Egypt?"** and even Moshe asks, **"Where do I have meat?"** to underscore the complete degradation of trust between him and the people. Moshe is pitted against them and once again is forced to mediate between the people and God.

Nostalgia can be a powerful force for change in the present. It inspires us to create anew a security we felt before. It can also compel us to return to the way things used to be, as if the comforts we seek only existed once upon a time. This episode and the memories of Egypt it evokes for the people is not existential. God has provided sustenance for them all along the way! But the people are clinging to an identity that prevents their embrace of freedom. Their nostalgia is a pain far greater than their momentary discomforts.

Here the challenge is over a basic necessity. In the chapters that follow, the challenge is rooted in the very nature of leadership and privilege. Aharon and Miriam, and Korach and his followers, challenge the authority of Moshe based on a clear distinction between those who are privileged with God's presence and those who are not. This expression of doubt prompts God to affirm their faith in the questions that follow.

It's Never Enough

11:22 *"If flocks and herds are slain for them, will it satisfy them?"*

11:22 *"If all the fish in the sea were caught for them, would it satisfy them?"*

11:23 *"Is YHVH's hand cut short?"*

Modern spirituality wrestles with definitions of "enough." This is particularly acute when we have access to more-than-necessary quantities of food, shelter, clothing, healthcare, and so forth to sustain us. Even time is a resource that can be sufficiently quantified. While there are places with an abundance of most basic human needs, there are even more with inadequate access to those very same resources. When we acknowledge such disparities exist even on the fundamental level of basic survival needs, the question of enough becomes a value statement.

A crucial lesson of the desert narrative in the Torah demonstrates how the Israelite nation will contend with the measure of enough. Their incessant complaints and continual tests of leadership remind us that for the generation that was redeemed from slavery in Egypt, there will never be enough to satisfy their physical and spiritual hunger.

Moshe asks, **"If flocks and herds are slain for them, will it satisfy them?"** and **"If all the fish in the sea were caught for them, would it satisfy them?"** probing the very concept that the people's cries for food and water have a limit. He senses that all that has been provided to the people to sustain them on their journey is indeed sufficient and their complaints are extreme and unreasonable.

Yet God will respond with something greater. In fact, there may be an implicit test in the people's complaints to see if the God of Israel can truly act beyond the limits of human understanding. It is why God responds to Moshe's logical concern with a powerful reminder. God asks, **"Is YHVH's hand cut short?"** or as some interpretations read, **"Is there a limit to YHVH's power?"**[5] God's question isn't self-reflective. God's response to Moshe's question with another question underscores a fundamental tenet of monotheistic belief. The God of Israel is unlimited. There is never enough to contain the God of the universe. This moment of challenge for the Israelite nation is like a drop in the limitless ocean of God's power. This will be a lesson we continue to learn in every generation.

Confident Questions

11:29 "Are you jealous for my sake? Who will make it so that YHVH's people were prophets, that YHVH put Spirit upon them?"

Impulsive responses to a sense of powerlessness are natural, even instinctual. When our impulses are misguided or overloaded, we call that "anxiety." Overcoming any form of anxiety involves both self-awareness and a measured expression of confidence from others—especially when the feelings of powerlessness are strong. The Torah takes on this concern for anxiety powerfully in the concluding episode at a place called Kivrot HaTaavah (Graves of Desire).

Moshe gathers the elders to help confront a litany of complaints from the people regarding their culinary deprivations. When a young person rushes to Moshe informing him of Eldad and Medad's prophetic ecstasy, Joshua, Moshe's trusted protégé, urges him to quell their insubordination. Moshe responds to Joshua by asking, **"Are you jealous for my sake?"** He follows the question with an essential qualifier: **"Who will make it so that YHVH's people were prophets, that YHVH put Spirit upon them?"** At first it appears that Moshe is inviting anyone whose spirit moves him to act as a prophet among the people. When we read this pointed question, our instinct is to see the leader of the people softening his authoritative grip and allowing the inspired youth and others to share in the vision of his leadership. Indeed, the episode is centered in the midst of the elders with whom Moshe is consulting, presumably on the fitness and focus of the community.

Moshe asks the question to quell Joshua's anxiety. Where Joshua sees an insurrection, Moshe sees a desire to connect with God. The people of Israel are intended to be a holy people. "Holiness" by this definition is a capacity to share a vision of God and God's word in the community. The gift is not reserved to one person alone even if that one person is Moshe, who has the most lucid interactions of all the people with God. We learn that holiness is felt in sacred communities, and the amelioration of concern is an invitation to experience divine encounter. Moshe's additional question, **"Who will make it so that YHVH's people were prophets?"** is sincere. Overcoming anxiety seems to be a vital step in the right direction.

Is God Really for Us All?

12:2 "Has YHVH only spoken to Moshe? Has God not spoken to us too?"

Priests and a holy nation do not imply holiness is reserved for the select few. Each and every person has the potential to encounter God. So Aharon and Miriam ask, **"Has YHVH only spoken to Moshe? Has YHVH not spoken to us too?"** to raise the question, in part, of where the perception of divinity begins. More than a singular plea from the closest individuals to Moshe, this represents a challenge to the nature of this community, this people. And yet the response to these questions is not an examination of the structure of leadership or the well-being of the community under this new social order alone. The response is taken personally and responded to by God as a challenge.

The impact of the questions is found in the responses within the text itself. The text first describes Moshe as a most humble human being.[6] Then God clearly says to Miriam and Aharon, **"With him I speak mouth to mouth plainly and not in riddles, and he beholds the likeness of YHVH."** There is a unique status and relationship we can hold with God, but there is a singular uniqueness Moshe enjoys with God that is sustained throughout the Bible. The questions themselves are placed in the context of a personal attack. Moshe married a Cushite woman, and Aharon and Miriam react to the less-than-perfect character and private life of the prophet and teacher.

At first the entire episode troubles us because our supporting heroes are so forcefully scrutinized and punished for their insolent criticism. Yet the concern opens up for us a sensitivity to our purpose as a people. Our privileged status as a holy people is not predicated on direct access to the presence of absolute holiness. Our leaders are elevated because they have humility and an access to God that most of us cannot attain. The point of the moment isn't to quell internecine jealousy; rather, the point is that there are those whose perfected states of being give them greater access to the divine presence than others. Moreover, a determination for divine access is a combination of human perfection and divine election. Aharon and Miriam's complaint implies there is some special decision-making process or that human privilege can be changed by divine entreaty.

There are examples in the text where there is a change, perhaps a clarification, in God's mind when questions of humility are present. For example, the people express their desire to fulfill the responsibilities of the Passover sacrifice though they are unfit to do so because they are physically impure. Another example we will explore further are the questions surrounding the request for land inheritance by the daughters of Zelophehad. In both cases, the desire to fulfill the responsibilities of divine command emerge from a sincere, even humble, request for clarity. And in these cases, God responds. How poignant that God does not entertain Aharon and Miriam's complaint here!

Divine Intimacy

12:8 "Why were you not afraid to speak against My servant, Moshe?"

Visions of divine intimacy are painted with delicate brushstrokes on a canvas fashioned by human beings. Even our most esoteric imagination of what true intimacy with divinity might be like will always be perceived through the hand and ink of our corporeal limitation. When we envision what true intimacy with God might be, it's not surprising to find our visions approximate the experience of human intimacy. More than a physical bonding, the emotional connections that define closeness transcend a sense of formal structure. Intimacy at its core dissolves form and function. As such, true intimacy is vulnerable. The Torah captures this intimacy in this pivotal yet easily overlooked episode in the book of Numbers.

God asks Aharon and Miriam a question unlike any other question God poses to humanity, **"Why were you not afraid to speak against My servant, Moshe?"** Our first instinct is to interpret the motivations and actions of Moshe's siblings as brazen attempts to unseat their brother and devalue his special relationship with God. After all, the subtext of the entire book of Bamidbar is a challenge to Moshe's authority and to a lesser extent a challenge to God's authority. But God's question here is more than a suggestive inference derived from the presumed behavior of these two individuals in some respects equal and worthy of respect by God.

What is it that God is seeking from them and their response? Is it that they should be apologetic for even intimating that Moshe is somehow inferior in his capacity as God's friend? After Miriam is stricken with leprosy, Aharon's pleas for clemency imply as much. What's transpiring in this episode is far more complex. God's frustration is like that of an angry parent. We read God's reply: **"If her father spat in her face, would she not bear her shame for seven days?"**[7] It's human logic from a divine point of view.

What makes this moment so pivotal is not Aharon and Miriam's protest. In a sense their objections to Moshe's special relationship with God are legitimate, just as Korach's protest will carry a certain measure of validity later on. But the shift in how God relates to the three of these prophetic figures exemplifies God's vision for intimacy with humanity. God's infallibility does not make God inaccessible. Rather, the closeness his beloved servants feel allows them to question God's actions and for God to react in a manner that is only possible in a loving partnership. God doesn't simply decree punishment without engagement. God hopes Aharon and Miriam will be in awe of their brother. But they are not. God's disappointment, even frustration, undergirds the ultimate truth of human behavior. We imagine that God does not totally know the thoughts and feelings of his beloved partners. So God must ask for their rationale. The lack of a response, and God's dramatic departure from the encounter, leave us with a sense that the questioning is not only natural but even emblematic of intimacy even with the divine. It's unknowable. It's frustrating and threatening. It's vulnerable. It's totally human.

The book of Numbers will dance between form and function in the divine encounter. Indeed, if the people are to truly stand worthy of God's presence in their midst, they must break through the limitations of their visions of intimacy. We learn from this question and the episode in which it is situated that the bilateral intimacy of humanity and divinity implies uncertainty only questions can resolve.

SHLACH LECHA

13:18 "What kind of land is it?" (Moshe to the scouts)

13:18 "Are the people who dwell in it strong or weak, few or many?" (Moshe to the scouts)

13:19 "Is the country in which they dwell good or bad?" (Moshe to the scouts)

13:19 "Are the towns they live in open or fortified?" (Moshe to the scouts)

13:20 "Is the soil rich or poor?" (Moshe to the scouts)

13:20 "Is it wooded or not?" (Moshe to the scouts)

14:3 "Why did YHVH bring us to this land to die by the sword?" (The people to Moshe and Aharon)

14:11 "How long will these people spurn Me?" (God to Moshe)

14:11 "How long will they not believe in Me, for all the signs which I have wrought among them?" (God to Moshe)

14:27 "How long shall I bear with this evil congregation that keeps murmuring against Me?" (God to Moshe and Aharon)

14:41 "Why do you transgress the mouth of YHVH?" (Moshe to the people)

The vacillations between narrative and law in the chapters of this portion are a reflection of a dynamic tension between faith and function as the people journey toward the land of Canaan. The questions that appear here prompt a fatal unraveling of the steadfast connection between God and the Israelite people consecrated at Mount Sinai. The ultimate value of the scouting episode and the condemnation of the generation to perish in the desert is more than a cautionary tale. The permission to question isn't ever silenced. But we also learn there are limits to our questions, and pushing too far has lasting consequences.

Binary Questions Are Not Questions at All

13:18 "What kind of land is it?"

13:18 "Are the people who dwell in it strong or weak, few or many?"

13:19 "Is the country in which they dwell good or bad?

13:19 "Are the towns they live in open or fortified?"

13:20 "Is the soil rich or poor?"

13:20 "Is it wooded or not?"

We've learned that the process of inquiry through questions is more than a check for knowledge. When an interrogative is used in the Torah, the response or the development of the narrative is always focused on a greater understanding of both our humanity and our understanding of the divine. In this way, expressions that merely seek knowledge aren't really questions at all. They are expressions of a binary form. The knowledge is either true or false. There is no uncertainty one way or the other. That is why there are almost no expressions in the entire Hebrew Bible that simply ask for knowledge.

The questions Moshe asks the scouts are not merely binaries either. While on the surface the questions that ensue appear to seek answers of an either-or nature, we also hear an underlying premise that will ultimately test the people and determine their fate to remain in the desert for the rest of their lives. Moshe asks,

"What kind of land is it?"

"Are the people who dwell in it strong or weak, few or many?"

"Is the country in which they dwell good or bad?"

"Are the towns they live in open or fortified?"

"Is the soil rich or poor?"

"Is it wooded or not?"

These questions might be a guide for ascertaining knowledge about an unknown land. The scouts simply have to return with the answers. However, they interpret the knowledge they've gained upon their return and conflate their findings in a moment of crisis. Their understanding of their findings unravels into a campaign of misinformation, portraying a perception that has no grounding in reality: **"we looked like grasshoppers to ourselves, and so we must have looked to them."**[8]

There is an important lesson here. Expressions that check for knowledge require only a response confirming or invalidating the premise. But questions that prompt a binary response will almost certainly invite a deeper connection, a relationship that will endure long beyond the momentary inquiry. Moshe's hope was that the people would bring excitement and hope to the next stage of their journey. While the majority of the scouts fell short of this expectation, Joshua and Caleb's sense of promise is redemptive.

Making Uncertainty Certain—Do Not Try This at Home

14:3 "Why did YHVH bring us to this land to die by the sword?"

14:11 "How long will these people spurn me? . . . How long will they not believe in me, for all the signs which I have wrought among them?"

14:27 "How long shall I bear with this evil congregation that keeps murmuring against me?"

Crying out as a response to fear, concern, and doubt is a reflex in the face of an uncertain future, especially one that appears perilous and fatal. When our anxieties outweigh the realities of the moment, we do well to embrace words of confidence from partners, friends, and our leaders to instill faith or comfort. But tensions mount and fears are amplified when the words shared are hollow and insincere. Capturing this tension in the literature of the Bible is more than dramatic license. It's a model for holy behavior.

The people's cries to God are quite familiar during the journey from Egypt to the Promised Land. For example, when the people cry out after leaving Egypt, Moshe mollifies them and promises divine protection as Pharaoh and his armies pursue them to the shores of the sea. Now, years after the people have journeyed with their God, the demonstration of faith and love in God's presence should be certain. Yet their fear is still unassuaged. Whereas Moshe was able to comfort and inspire them in circumstances before, here there is an absence of Moshe's voice that cannot be overlooked. So the people ask, **"Why did YHVH bring us to this land to die by the sword?"** They have no idea what their fate might be. They even hear from Joshua and Caleb, who attempt to instill confidence in the people even before they express their doubt through this question. They're exhausted, physically and emotionally, and their questions are less about seeking certainty than they are an expression of their faithless condition.

At this moment, even God is recorded as losing faith. God intervenes and responds with more questions, **"How long will these people spurn me? . . . How long will they not believe in me, for all the signs which I have wrought among them?"** **"How long shall I bear with this evil congregation that keeps murmuring against me?"** The project of forging a covenant with a holy nation seems more distant than ever at this moment. So much uncertainty. So little faith.

The questions reveal more than the narrative itself. There is a point when a response to uncertainty ceases to be about fear and becomes something insidious, even destructive. More than anxiety, the lack of faith the people express here is the great disappointment of the book. Fear of and anxiety for the unknown are natural. Narrow resignation that forecloses the future is the antithesis of faith. The Torah recognizes this impulse in human beings and introduces divine influence to counterbalance its terrible effects. We learn from this terrible moment that when the faithful voice is ignored, the punishment is banishment to the desert.

The reward for the faithful commitment of Joshua and Caleb is justified. The punishment for the generation to wander in the desert is valid too. Faith is sown in the comforting words of leaders and in a courageous recognition that uncertain futures aren't easily solved with overtures of certainty. While the future remains unknown, it is the confidence to face the future that defines a true faith. Both the people and God will need to find this confidence on the journey.

Changing the Future by Changing the Past Never Succeeds

14:41 "Why do you transgress the mouth of YHVH?"

Remorse is a powerful response that becomes more sophisticated as we mature. The word itself suggests a gnawing or grating of our conscience when past choices have negative consequences in our present and future. We express remorse when a negative reaction prompts us to change for fear of future reprisal. Over time we learn to recognize the severity of a punishment to deter our future actions . . . to a point. Too often, though, we choose to act in ways that are contrary to our nature despite the consequences. When the negative response becomes too great to bear, remorse is often the expression that indicates our awareness that our behavior has to change. Sometimes that awareness lasts a lifetime, even a generation. But what happens when it doesn't?

This is perhaps the key to the episode of the people scouting the Promised Land. When they succumb to their fears and faithlessness in response to the reports from those who see the dangers present in their future, God condemns their generation to wander the desert. We might have thought the punishment was enough to quell their rebellious ways, but their response is the painful recognition that even God's words cannot prevent people from choosing to harm themselves. When Moshe asks the people, **"Why do you transgress the mouth of YHVH?"** he is responding to his desire to head to the Promised Land even after God has condemned them to wander. The people tell Moshe, **"We are prepared to go up to the place that YHVH has spoken of, for we were**

wrong.[9] Moshe's sage guidance is completely ignored as the people become entrenched in their belief that their remorse is sincere.

This episode elucidates an important spiritual practice. Trying to change the future by changing the past will never succeed. Where the people have the opportunity to express *Teshuvah* (repentance) or true remorse, their fear of wandering, or of disappointing God and Moshe, clouds their desire to change their behavior. Accepting their fate is too great a punishment to bear and so they respond with a sense of resolve where remorse would be more appropriate.

Accepting responsibility is a sign of maturity and spiritual depth. The truly penitent person recognizes that failures are the building blocks of healthier and holier futures. We experience sadness for this generation that endured slavery and witnessed the grandeur of revelation but could not accept responsibility.

KORACH

16:3 "Why do you lift yourselves above the assembly of YHVH?" (Korach to Moshe and Aharon)

16:9–10 "Is it but a small thing unto you, that the God of Israel has separated you from the congregation of Israel, to bring you near to the divine self, to do the service of the tabernacle of YHVH, and to stand before the congregation to guide them; that God brought you near, and all your brothers, the sons of Levi, with you?" (Moshe and Aharon to Korach)

16:10 "Will you seek the priesthood as well?" (Moshe and Aharon to Korach)

16:11 "Who is Aharon that you murmur against him?" (Moshe and Aharon to Korach)

16:13 "Is it a small thing that you brought us up out of a land flowing with milk and honey to kill us in the desert, but you need to make yourself also a prince over us?" (Datan and Abiram to Moshe)

16:14 "Will you put out the eyes of these men?" (Datan and Abiram to Moshe)

16:22 "Shall one person sin, and you will be wrathful with the entire congregation?" (Moshe and Aharon to God)

These chapters chronicle the quintessential challenge to authority staged by Korach, a cousin of Moshe and Aharon. The larger question of recovering faith within doubt is presented in a rebellion that appears to be a logical response to a lack of power. We would have expected Korach, indeed the entire nation of Israel, to conform to and obey the division of leadership. After all, God speaks from the mountain and Moshe appears with the tablets written by God's hand. What else do they need? Where acceptance and defiance intersect, the questions posed by Korach—and Moshe and Aharon in response—remind us that challenges have lasting consequences. The questions here grapple with the very nature of doubt and the tragedy of submitting to fearful impulses. Confidence will be restored by supernatural events as the ground swallows up Korach and his followers. But the mistrust has already plagued the people in their growing defiance of authority.

Challenge by Question

16:3 "Why do you lift yourselves above the assembly of YHVH?"

We occasionally interpret questions as a challenge to the truth or authority we hold. Most of the time a question does not have such conviction behind its purpose. Our sensitivities are heightened when any questions are asked because they can imply a lack of trust or a sense of doubt in our motives. Resolving that doubt with dignity is one measure of the holiness we aspire to achieve.

Part of our sensitivity to the purpose of questions emerges from situations like the one we read about in the story of Korach. The episode of Korach and his band challenging the authority of Moshe and Aharon simmers with this potential defensiveness and the thoughtful consideration of the consequences before reacting upon that defensive impulse. Korach asks, **"Why do you lift yourselves above the assembly of YHVH?"** The tone of this question, which seems contentious, is what heightens the sensitivity. The question could have been a genuine expression of curiosity about the behavior of Moshe and Aharon. Instead Korach preempts his inquiry with the invective **"You have gone too far!"** The questioner already has an answer in mind.

How Moshe responds is indicative of the nature of the question. By falling upon his face, a symbolic act of humility, Moshe is creating space between Korach's attack and his response. He is symbolically lowering himself to disarm the thrust of the question. As a result, Moshe's response has little to do with him directly and everything to do with a connection to God.

If someone expresses a curiosity about the behavior or actions we take, we might contend with our emotional response defensively before we contemplate the efficacy of our feelings. Acting on impulse in any event prompts a harsh response, sometimes even resulting in violence.

There is a model worthy of emulation here. When a question seems to challenge one's authority, a sacred pause before responding is vital. After a moment to properly align our reaction with the value concern behind the question, we can respond with the ultimate goal of serving the divine and maximizing human dignity.

A Sufficient Question

16:9–10 "Is it but a small thing unto you, that the God of Israel has separated you from the congregation of Israel, to bring you near to the divine self, to do the service of the tabernacle of YHVH, and to stand before the congregation to guide them; that God brought you near, and all your brothers, the sons of Levi, with you?"

16:10 "Will you seek the priesthood as well?"

16:11 "Who is Aharon that you murmur against him?"

There is a growing body of research that validates the strength and veracity of first impressions and has changed the way we approach difficult situations. While we may be wracked with self-doubt or feel that our judgment in the moment is incomplete, there are more examples when our first thoughts are more accurate than our measured attempts at a best second guess.[10] Learning to trust our instincts and not to act upon our first impressions prematurely is a mark of wisdom, even sanctity. The Torah will confront this lesson in the dramatic narrative of Korach and his challenge to Moshe and Aharon's authority.

When Korach and his followers question the hierarchy of God's communications with the people, Moshe falls upon his face and confirms that the challenge will be addressed by God. There is a coda to this moment, however, when Moshe must add some questions of his own to Korach's troubling inquiry. Moshe asks within a few short verses:

"Is it but a small thing unto you, that the God of Israel has separated you from the congregation of Israel, to bring you near to the divine self, to do the service of the tabernacle of YHVH, and to stand before the congregation to guide them; that God brought you near, and all your brothers, the sons of Levi, with you?" The language of sufficiency is repeated frequently in this brief interlude. Moshe and Aharon are accused of going too far. Moshe and Aharon identify Korach as going **"too far"** as well. The questions that Moshe asks in response to Korach's accusations here underscore the very concern of sufficient service to God. Is there enough when it comes to God?

On one hand, Korach's question is quite valid. If our ultimate goal is to be in service of the divine, what does it mean that only some of us have the ability to fully serve or to be privileged by God's divine response face to face? On the other hand, there is nothing that limits Korach's or anyone's ability to serve wholeheartedly. Each of us has a unique role to serve in the quest for divine encounter, each of us with our proper and sacred duty placed before us.

The first impression that remains is that Korach and his followers are challenging the structure of authority for their own aggrandizement. While we can wrestle with the legitimacy of their complaints, the manner and the ultimate outcome of their challenge does not inspire sanctity. Yet it is Moshe's questions and responses, charging them with going too far, that remind us that a sufficient question has the potential to be a holy question.

When Questions Distort the Truth

16:13 "Is it a small thing that you brought us up out of a land flowing with milk and honey to kill us in the desert, but you need to make yourself also a prince over us?"

16:14 "Will you put out the eyes of these men?"

Testing hypotheses and expressing curiosity are necessary for discovering truth. But what happens when our conclusions don't match the questions we ask? A truth-seeking value judgment can easily be twisted if it is not measured against a greater truth. Overcoming false beliefs is an exercise in humility and an unrelenting commitment to honesty. These qualities are not innate to human experience and must be learned from someone else.

The Torah grapples with humility and honesty in the book of Numbers, specifically in the verses that confront the challenge to Moshe's authority by his cousin Korach. Among the rebellious band are two characters from another family, Datan and Abiram, who typify a challenge to Moshe based on false premises. When Moshe calls for their presence to account for their rebellious actions, they ask, **"Is it a small thing that you brought us up out of a land flowing with milk and honey to kill us in the desert, but you need to make yourself also a prince over us?"** The land of Egypt was never said to be one flowing with milk and honey. Datan and Abiram use this expression, one used to describe the Promised Land, so they may twist God and Moshe's intentions and lead the people astray. Their unfounded challenges go further when they also ask, **"Will you put out the eyes of these men?"** When questions conflate the truth or even create unverified truths by their implications, the breakdown of trust has catastrophic consequences.

Datan and Abiram's objections cause Moshe great concern. This is why God's response is all the more surprising: **"Pay no regard to their offerings."**[11] We've been trained to hear God's voice through command. Truth-telling and verification are exercises of faith. God's assurance to Moshe is an assurance to us that our unrelenting commitment to honesty will be godly too.

Abraham's Legacy

16:22 *"Shall one person sin, and you will be wrathful with the entire congregation?"*

At this point in the Torah, the stories of Genesis seem distant from the dramatic unfolding of the Israelite nation and their wanderings in the desert. Family origins and the promise to be a blessing are as much a part of their identity as they are a point of instruction around the campfire. Where instinct and intuition are formed, the stories of our heroes affirm and educate our choices for the future. For example, the righteous challenge to God by Abram in the moments leading up to the destruction of the cities of Sodom and Gomorrah takes focus again many generations later.

When Korach and his rebellious band question Moshe and Aharon's unique privileges with God, the punishment for their disobedience is instant death. Moshe and Aharon's question to God is reflexive and emblematic of the growing ethic of these people. Before God has a chance to exact the decree, Moshe and Aharon supplicate themselves and ask, **"Shall one person sin, and You will be wrathful with the entire congregation?"**

At first we feel that Moshe and Aharon should stand by quietly as God metes out punishment. After all, Moshe tells Korach it will be God who chooses whom to welcome into the tent. Instead Moshe and Aharon attempt to intercede and challenge God's expressed will. Reminiscent of Abraham's pleas for God's mercy before the destruction of the cities of Sodom and Gomorrah, the limit of human understanding of or tolerance for the loss of innocent life is tested. There is even a connection in the language when Moshe warns the people, **"Move away from the tents of these wicked men and touch nothing that belongs to them lest you be wiped out for all their sins,"** and the language Abram uses, **"Will You wipe away the innocent along with the guilty?"**[12]

When we make the connection between these two moments, a new understanding of our role as emissaries of God is sharpened. Our responsibility is to challenge authority when we feel that the punishment is far too severe for the sin that was committed. How ironic that the thrust of the argument in this episode is the limits of our challenges as we read repeatedly **"You have gone too far!"** While those words are no longer lodged against God, the test of God's vengeance becomes an ethical imperative for our biblical heroes and for us.

HUKKAT

20:4 "Why have you brought YHVH's congregation into this wilderness for us and our beasts to die there?"(The people to Moshe)

20:5 "Why did you make us leave Egypt to bring us to this wretched place, a place with no grain or figs or vines or pomegranates?" (The people to Moshe)

20:10 "Hear now, you rebels, are we to bring forth water for you from this rock?" (Moshe to the people)

21:5 "Why did you bring us up out of Egypt to die in this desert?" (The people to Moshe)

The people's defiance of Moshe's leadership and their lack of trust in God's protection culminate in these chapters. Moshe's patience is ultimately broken when he can no longer hear the commanding voice clearly enough to lead the people. In the heartbreaking question expressed by Moshe, he even calls the people rebels, describing them as what might be the opposite of the priests and the holy nation God envisions they will become. Meanwhile the death of Aharon and Miriam in these chapters marks a significant transition for the people, who experience a tremendous loss that coincides with the conclusion of their rebellious behavior and their quest to become the holy nation consecrated at Mount Sinai. We will no longer hear of any seditious acts or of any complaints first-hand after the episode when Moshe strikes the rock.

The Questions We Don't Want Answered

20:4 "Why have you brought YHVH's congregation into this wilderness for us and our beasts to die there?"

20:5 "Why did you make us leave Egypt to bring us to this wretched place, a place with no grain or figs or vines or pomegranates?"

Following the fragile confederation of Israelite tribes through the desert teaches us a poignant lesson in the human dimensions of change and transformation. We bear witness to the people's woes and their faithless wanderings. We grow weary of their incessant cries. Like the boy who cried wolf, our ability to take their complaints seriously wanes after so many recapitulations of the same fears are expressed.

We hear the familiar refrain expressed in two questions: **"Why have you brought YHVH's congregation into this wilderness for us and our beasts to die there?"** and **"Why did you make us leave Egypt to bring us to this wretched place, a place with no grain or figs or vines or pome-**

granates?" If we read the people's complaints as yet another cry of hopelessness, we can also read their reactions here with a sense of detachment.

Among the many commentaries that churn through the texts in this narrative, we return to one essential perspective. This is the line of questioning that prompts Moshe to strike the rock. Shall we infer that there came a point for Moshe when the people had simply asked too many questions?

The people are expressing nostalgia here, albeit under duress, that reflects a certainty for which they yearn. The intention of the desert journey was to both shatter their slave mentality and introduce a new condition of certainty, a certainty found in the eternal quest for freedom. The people will be called "stiff-necked" for questions like these. We don't even want to answer the question because we know that any answer we devise won't give honor to the path toward the Promised Land they're meant to forge. The ultimate lesson is that change is not possible if our ties to the past are stronger than our bonds to the future.

The Most Tragic Question

20:10 "Hear now, you rebels, are we to bring forth water for you from this rock?"

While we often think answers to questions are a response to the concern of another, there are questions that can shape and alter the future of the questioner too. These questions may even become the ultimate expression of free will. In other words, we shape our fate through our curiosity as much as through our certainty. The Torah's lessons in these types of questions guide us and instruct us to balance and anticipate the outcomes of our choices so we may ask wise questions and choose with the free will God hopes we'll wield rather than be subject to.

For this, the episode of the rock frames the most tragic of all questions in the Torah. Not only does it reflect Moshe's complete lack of faith in the people at a pivotal moment in the desert narrative, but it also demonstrates how misplaced curiosity can result in catastrophe. When Moshe asks, **"Hear now, you rebels, are we to bring forth water for you from this rock?"** the thrust of the question is emphasized by the direction of the request. **"You rebels"** and **"for you"** imply that Moshe is not desirous of the result of his actions at all. There is an implication that the force of Moshe's question is punitive, that what will come next affects the community and not the leader. The tragedy is that it is the leader who will suffer from the consequences of his defiant tone.

The moment hinges on the quality of listening. Here it is as much Moshe listening to the sound of divine guidance as it is the tone of the question he asks. God's punishment following Moshe's actions is often connected to the confusing instructions given to him (to speak to the rock when earlier he was told to strike the rock).[13] Moshe's punishment is also associated with the fact that he strikes the rock not once but twice, indicating his rage is beyond the pale of responsible behavior. In this latter explanation, the leader's failure is in his inability to hear the consequences of his actions, most likely drowned out by his rage and disappointment in the people's incessant cries.

Perhaps we learn that harsh punishment is a consequence for responding with an action that isn't connected to the question itself. Moshe is formally prohibited from entering the Promised Land not for acting in contrast to God's words alone but for his ultimate loss of patience with the incessant questions of the people. The punishment derives from a betrayal of the trust God places in us to handle unsettling feelings that emerge from uncertainty.

This is a well-placed question in the Torah and vital to our understanding of ourselves, our impulses, and the divine imperative to subdue those impulses for a greater good. Even the best among us are subject to a certain deafness in the face of threats and a repressed faith. While there is ample debate whether Moshe was worthy to enter the Promised Land despite his outrageous reactions here, the Torah is also outlining a path to moral and ethical goodness, one that demands acute listening skills and a heroic sense of restraint. Moshe's inability to live up to that lofty standard isn't as much an indictment of his humanity as it is a model for the Jewish hero, one worthy of entering the Promised Land because they have been able to conquer their instincts and listen wisely to their own questions too.

Same Question, Different Result?

21:5 "Why did you bring us up out of Egypt to die in this desert?"[14]

When the same question, or slight variations of the same question, is asked on multiple occasions, we must consider the underlying motivation for repeated inquiry. The question children will ask during a long journey, "Are we there yet?" comes to mind as a classic example of a question pleading for something more than the definitive answer. Similarly, questions that are often self-reflective and repetitious like "Why is this happening to me?" reveal a deeper insecurity in the moment and not a concern for the circumstances that may have prompted the inward turn.

One question is asked throughout the people's journey from Egypt to Israel, and it is shaped and molded by their location, their proximity to the Promised Land, and their endurance of this forty-year trek. **"Why did you bring us up out of Egypt to die in this desert?"** is a question asked approximately ten times in the Torah, either by the people or as implied by Moshe when he argues with God. After one or two times, we cannot read this question as a complaint worthy of address. The people's incessant cries are less about their perceived threat of mortal danger than they are a plea for reason. The people seek faithful inspiration in the face of something they cannot see, touch, or sense at all.

It's not unreasonable to hear their concern expressed in the form of a question this way. Perhaps the lesson that doubt and uncertainty are an essential feature of faith is what the people's experience teaches us. The repetition of the inquiry, though, reveals a characteristic of the people that even the divine presence cannot comprehend! When we read this question multiple times in the narrative, our lesson is not simply gained from the petulance and narrow-minded perspective of the people. We learn that difficult circumstances cannot be met with questions that aren't meant to be truly answered. To ask a question knowing the correct answer is contrary to one's perception of the moment is to play act, to dramatize an experience even to the point of the absurd.

Of course God and Moshe do not bring the people to the desert to die. What a terrible story that would be! But if this is a story of how to change our behavior and how to learn the way to walk in the path of

God, then these doubts and uncertainties are leading indicators toward that faithful journey.

This is the last time the people will ask a question in the Torah. At this point, Moshe has been banished from entering the Promised Land, Aharon and Miriam have died, and the people's journey now begins to move at a quicker pace. The response to this last question is immediate and severe. God sends snakes to punish them for their insolence. Moshe's staff becomes an amulet and an icon. Perhaps it reminds the people that asking the same question but expecting a different result will never succeed.

BALAK

22:9 "Who are these men with you?" (God to Bilaam)

22:28 "What have I done to you that you have struck me these three times?" (The donkey to Bilaam)

22:30 "Have I been in the habit of doing this to you?" (The donkey to Bilaam)

22:32 "Why have you beaten your donkey three times?" (Angel to Bilaam)

22:37 "Why did you not come to me?" (Balak to Bilaam)

22:37 "Am I not able to honor you?" (Balak to Bilaam)

22:38 "Now, do I have any power to speak at all?" (Bilaam to Balak)

23:8 "How shall I curse whom God has not cursed?" (Bilaam to Balak?)

23:8 "How shall I doom whom YHVH has not doomed?" (Bilaam to Balak?)

23:10 "Who has counted the dust of Jacob, numbered the dust cloud of Israel?" (Bilaam to Balak?)

23:11 "What have you done to me?" (Balak to Bilaam)

23:17 "What did YHVH say?" (Balak to Bilaam)

On the surface, the fantastic tale of Bilaam and the Moabites seems to provide entertainment for the reader. It may have even been amusing to the Israelites, who at this point must have been weary of their long journey toward freedom. But beneath the surface of talking donkeys and curses turned into blessings, an important shift is taking place. The people are now a nation among the nations. They are not Jacob's children nor are they nomads from Haran. They are a covenanted people on a journey with a purpose. How they are regarded by and interact with the world around them comes into focus.

The Torah takes up the concern of the nations of the world now as the Israelites have become a force to be reckoned with among them. The fact that there are so many questions in this single narrative, none of which are expressed by Moshe or the people, also expands the consciousness of the text. These questions explore divine encounters outside the covenant—Bilaam is ostensibly the only non-Israelite character whose encounters with God are recorded in the Torah—and reveal that God's concern is universal.

Does God Care about Everyone and Everything?

22:9 "Who are these men with you?"

The Torah presumes God's omnipotence from the first moments of creation. When we read of moments where God asks a question, we might think that God's divine knowledge is uncertain or incomplete, or we might re-imagine God's questions as acts of seeking out a truth someone has not yet discovered. But these moments reveal more about divine knowledge than divine uncertainty.

God asks Bilaam, **"Who are these men with you?"** We have already learned the identity of these men: **"the elders of Moab and the elders of Midian, versed in divination."**[15] God's question isn't about occupations. God is asking Bilaam to consider something completely unique. On the surface, the men are asking Bilaam to perform a curse typically used to thwart the designs of an invading force. Given his limited knowledge, Balak's fear of the throngs of foreigners traveling through his land and concern for his own people are legitimate. God's question to Bilaam is expressed to help him and ultimately the nations of the world understand that the act of cursing should not be performed for this particular people, nor for any particular group of people at any time. In short, this entire episode highlights the value of human dignity.

That is why the conversation recorded between Bilaam and God is the essential text of this incredulous tale. The question of the men who summon Bilaam attempts to uncover their intent, a purpose that God as a force for justice in the world cannot endure. This culminates in God's response after a repeated attempt by Balak to bring Bilaam to him. God says, **"If these men have come to invite you, you may go with them. But do whatever I command you, that you shall do."**[16] While the exchange may begin to help Bilaam's awareness grow, it will take a talking donkey and a heap of blessings to ultimately teach him God's truth.

Here is one message to consider from God's question. When we ask about another person and their identity, we have permission, maybe we are even obliged, to ascertain the purpose and intention of those whom we encounter. Having this sensitivity doesn't limit our power. In fact, like God it accentuates our potential power. Here the intention is that power be used for a blessing and not a curse.

Questions and Answers

22:28 "What have I done to you that you have struck me these three times?"
22:30 "Have I been in the habit of doing this to you?"
22:32 "Why have you beaten your donkey three times?"

When we ask questions that prompt a response, we risk receiving an answer that defies our expectations. In a careful analysis of the questions we ask, we might assume that the one who incorrectly responds to our questions fails to see what we see, or we might surmise that the unanticipated response is a reaction to a poorly formed question. In healthy communication, any lack of clarity is addressed so that a proper response is given.

Perhaps the entire episode of Bilaam and the donkey is meant to explore inconsistencies between the questioner and the answerer. Even so, the episode of the donkey is a fantastic digression from the real narrative of the Torah, which is meant to elucidate two core principles. The first is that God has blessed Israel, despite their lack of faith, and no harm is to come to them on their journey. The second is that God's quest for faithful adherence is predicated on healthy communication. This is something that Bilaam must learn—here from a simple donkey.

The donkey is given a divine voice to question Bilaam's abusive behavior: **"What have I done to you that you have struck me these three times?" "Have I been in the habit of doing this to you?"** These questions from the mouth of a donkey convey a desire for response, some sort of acknowledgment that the abusive behavior does not make sense. Bilaam's insistence that the donkey's resistance is an embarrassment (**"You have made a mockery of me!"**[17]) is the crux of the story. He doesn't see his actions have repercussions beyond himself. His eyes need to be opened so that his curses may become blessings.

Or perhaps this narrative is meant to reveal inconsistencies between human and divine will. The angel asks Bilaam directly, **"Why have you beaten your donkey three times?"** a question posed after Bilaam's eyes are opened. Bilaam's deference to the angel is not a sufficient response to his revelation. The question also demands a response, one where the conventional understanding of power dynamics (between human and donkey, human and angel) are irrelevant in the face of dignity for all living beings. Bilaam's treatment of the donkey prompts the question, and his deference to the angel prompts the question of him.

This episode playfully and crucially brings into focus a new definition of faith. Our capacity to answer questions faithfully demands a sense of humility, one that will be forced on us if we cannot see it on our own.

Human Questions and Divine Answers

22:37 "Why did you not come to me?"

22:37 "Am I not able to honor you?"

The faithful person recognizes that something or someone is always greater than they are. Whether it is a biological recognition that our existence is contingent on the ontological capitulation of a parent or that it is a social construct that recognizes the vastness of the universe and its grandeur existed long before the first human beings, faith is a profound statement that what is now unknown can be known. To reduce our existence to the sole power of our own hands and the fate that we construct with our actions is to deny the reality of experience. It's a fantasy that the essential themes of the Torah constantly challenge.

When Balak summons Bilaam to curse the Israelites, he is not aware of, or ignores, the power of YHVH and the loyalty that God will demonstrate to the people. Balak believes that some clever conjuring can thwart the destiny of an entire nation and that his power as a king can affect the will of nature, even the will of God.

Balak's presumptuous questions **"Why did you not come to me? . . . Am I not able to honor you?"** imply that Balak believes he can influence the fate of the Israelite nation. While the questions suggest uncertainty, we also wonder what honor he could possibly be speaking about. Bilaam has already declined the invitation, so what is it that Balak can provide that would make it worth his while?

Bilaam, while not a prophet of YHVH, can speak with God. The text even suggests that Bilaam speaks with God, face to face, as directly as the ancestors of Jacob.

Another powerful undercurrent of the Torah is the influence that other tribes and nations will bring to bear on the destiny of the Israelite nation. God's powerful indictment of the Israelites in the final chapters of the Torah and future books of the Bible is that foreign nations will conquer them, and it will be because they have defiled themselves and rejected their God.[18] The student of the Torah who has for a lifetime read the beginning and end and everything in between will be reminded that the power to transform curses into blessings is divinely inspired.

The Prophet's Question

22:38 "Now, do I have any power to speak at all?"

The job description of a prophet does not include an ability to ask good questions. Wisdom and humility, perhaps. A sense of justice and certainty, likely. But doubt and curiosity? Typically those are reserved for the uninitiated. Whether the prophet is a conduit of the divine voice or a wizened sage conveying truth from experience, we expect the prophet to be a force for certainty in the world. Questions may help us approach the truth, but they are never truth in themselves.

With this the presence of Bilaam has become a curious phenomenon in the Torah. He is able to speak with God, face to face, and yet he is oblivious to the presence of God. He is angry and cantankerous when he reacts to the donkey and he is apprehensive when the messengers of Balak come for him. But once Bilaam appears before the Moabite king

Balak and asks, **"Now, do I have any power to speak at all?"** we sense a shift in the character of Bilaam that will alter his destiny and the curse that he has been tasked with uttering against the Israelites.

The question itself suggests a kind of humility. Bilaam has to recognize that what comes forth from his mouth will not be influenced by his own experience. In the authentic posture of a prophet, he is merely the conduit of God's will here. If God wills the people to be cursed, Bilaam will be the voice to make it so. Similarly, if God's will is to bless the people, Bilaam will express the words as they have been given to him, without any filters.

Ironically, such power seems to be the most liberating. And where the translation here may influence our understanding of what Bilaam is asking of Balak,[19] the question invites us to consider what truly free speech is and perhaps even to deeply explore the true prerequisites of a prophet. We bristle when the unfiltered expressions of another rest uncomfortably on our shoulders. Often we shut down our ability to see the person who is speaking and focus on the person's words and motivations to speak in such a manner. The prophet is simultaneously completely free of and totally beholden to the divine voice, and our acceptance of the prophet's voice can also be divinely inspired.

This question opens up for us a deeper understanding of how we interpret the words of others and who defines freedom for whom.

A Perfect Faith

23:8 *"How shall I curse whom God has not cursed?"*

23:8 *"How shall I doom whom YHVH has not doomed?"*

23:10 *"Who has counted the dust of Jacob, numbered the dust cloud of Israel?"*

As much as the book of Numbers presents the definition of a community, the book also contends with the perception of the other nations of the world when they are confronted with the massive exodus of Israelites from Egypt back to their homeland. In the first of the three messages Bilaam delivers in the presence of Balak, we are presented with his questions: **"How shall I curse whom God has not cursed. . . . How shall I doom whom YHVH has not doomed?"** While the implication is that he is referring to the people of Israel and not just a group or individual from among the people, we also read the conclusion of his first inquiry, **"Who has counted the dust of Jacob, numbered the dust cloud of Israel?"**

In a rare moment for the Torah, this set of reflective questions posed from the outside looking in is as much a definition of how other nations perceive the Israelite nation as it is a definition of the people themselves. The Israelite nation has possibly experienced a social dysmorphia whereby their defiance, disobedience, and disloyalty have condemned them, the older generation, to wander the desert for the rest of their lives. Yet this question introduces a sense of wonder and awe into the narrative, one that propels the Israelite people toward a preferential or selective status.

Despite their shortcomings and even the looming perception of a God who dooms an entire generation, this question opens up a dimension of identity that has not yet been expressed: dignity. There is something in the dignity of the people that merits the awe and respect of the nations around them. Surely there are those who repudiate the nation of Israel for its uniqueness. The text generously reminds us that God's blessing for these people is greater than any attempt to provoke anger or curses among the nations. The people will be blessed by God. That is their covenant.

It's Not about You!

23:11 "What have you done to me?"

We are constantly struggling with our sense of self-importance, especially in relation to the circumstances of our lives. A push here or an encouragement there seems to confirm that what we do matters. An essential part of being human is believing we can make a difference. And part of the joy of being human is seeing and celebrating the differences we can make. The moral life is one that takes this responsibility seriously and influences the world around us for good, for the dignity of all, and for a sense of justice. Within us is an inexorable capacity to serve ourselves, to satisfy urges and desires that care not for differences in the world or for others.

Whenever we read in the Torah a first-person reflection, it is always and without exception an expression that serves the self and not the other.[20] There is no "I" or "me" in the Torah that endures as a responsible and moral position of the human being. The entire project of building a nation is to subsume the desires of the self and frame the experience of being in the collective. Questions that come from another leader, here in the voice of Balak, amplify this distinction. When Balak asks, **"What have you done to me?"** we want to say in response, "It's not about you!" Balak will need two more fanfare-filled occasions to understand this on his own.

The question here also narrows the intention of this Torah episode. As we read of this local king who perceives an existential threat in a nation of people traveling through his land to their own land, we learn that it is futile to attempt to change the will of God. Future statements in lyrical prose will confirm that Balak's efforts, while perhaps the responsible actions of a monarch protecting his sovereignty, are misguided in the face of divine imperative.[21] This question and its place in the narrative affirm that YHVH has a will that supersedes any human force.

Failing to Listen to the Answer
23:17 "What did YHVH say?"

Intense focus, even to the point of ignoring everything else, is considered a valuable ability if not a spiritual practice. But although such focus is a celebrated function of productivity, single-mindedness can be a fatal flaw. Part of the absurdity of the story in this portion of the Torah is how Balak's sole determination to curse the people prevents him from hearing Bilaam's simple and consistent statement. Bilaam will only speak what God instructs him to say. After Bilaam utters words of praise and not curses as requested by Balak, the king moves his altars multiple times to gain some different advantage over the people.

The words Bilaam utters won't deter Balak from trying to accomplish what he sets out to do. When Balak sets up the second altar space and Bilaam returns from conferring with God, Balak asks, **"What did YHVH say?"** Eager to receive a response somehow different than before, Balak isn't really interested in what Bilaam has to say. But this is asked for more than a clarification of information. We should not overlook how Balak refers to the God of Israel. He is not like Pharaoh, who considers the Israelites a separate nation with a separate God. Even so, despite his direct acknowledgment of God, Balak's extraordinary determination to curse the people deafens him to Bilaam's repeated claims that he will only speak what God instructs him to say.

The irony of the story is, in part, that Balak never acknowledges this awesome demonstration of God's power. For Balak, YHVH is a tool, one he should be able to use in his own plan for power and domination.

So we learn at the end of this ordeal, **"Balak also went his way."**[22] This strange tale makes its way into the Torah to reveal that the God of Israel can be for anyone, if only they will listen.

PINCHAS

27:4 "Why should the name of our father be diminished among his family because he had no son?" (Bnot Zelophehad to Moshe)

The singular question of this portion overshadows a critical moment when God publicly and explicitly changes the rules in order to preserve the integrity of one family. The book of Numbers has many challenges to authority, usually without any fundamental change to God's Torah or the spirit of God's relationship with the people. Here the existential challenge isn't a general or all-encompassing concern. Instead we begin to see and celebrate the people embracing the commands of the Torah. They now ask questions not to undermine the very purpose of forming a nation, a family of families so to speak, but to validate and strengthen the bonds between those families and ultimately with God.

Questions Change God's Mind

27:4 *"Why should the name of our father be diminished among his family because he had no son?"*

By definition the Torah's message of covenantal relationship between divinity and humanity cannot be unilateral. One essential insight this document shares with all humanity is its recognition of our capacity to influence or participate in a divine unfolding of reality. In other words, one of Judaism's great contributions is humanity's everlasting quest to bring God's presence into the world, even if that means redefining what that presence is. There are rare moments when changing the divine mind isn't a result of recalcitrance but of measured and reasoned concern. In these moments, the permission to inquire and the capacity to change God's mind are what make Judaism a valued expression of human potential. They serve as the basis of the rabbinic tradition, the audacious and enduring belief that God's will can and does evolve, even today.

This potential comes into focus once again in the latter chapters of the book of Bamidbar. The daughters of Zelophehad are faithful and compliant citizens of the Israelite nation. Seeing that the rules established by God and conveyed by Moshe potentially undermine their dignity and autonomy, the daughters present themselves to Moshe and ask, **"Why should the name of our father be diminished among his family because he had no son?"** While the circumstances that prompt this question are legal and part of the structure of the social order, the notion that human beings can, indeed must, challenge the divine vision of human order is a totally unique contribution to human understanding.

The responses of Moshe and God are also powerful examples of the validation of human curiosity. If the daughters had not challenged the social order, the response from God would not have established their claim to their heritage. A different social order would have emerged, one in which the subjugation of women and a disparity of familial legacies would have narrowed human experience. It may not be so much that the mind of God was changed here as it was the mind of humanity evolved in this nascent stage to make room for the dignity, the prosperity, and the protection of all. In that sense, changing God's mind is always a change for the betterment of humanity.

MATTOT

32:6 "Shall your brothers go to war and you stay here?" (Moshe to Gad and Reuven)

32:7 "Why will you hinder the hearts of the Israelites from entering into the land YHVH has given them?" (Moshe to Gad and Reuven)

The book of Numbers turns toward a conclusion in these chapters as the nation of Israel prepares to enter the Promised Land. One defining feature of this moment is how deeply sensitive the people, and especially Moshe, have become through their arduous and awesome journey in the desert. A new generation, unfettered by the shackles of slavery their parents wore in Egypt, is prepared to enter a land they have been dreaming of. The questions in these chapters uncover a new test of loyalty and allegiance. While the children of Reuven and Gad will remain on the east plains of the Jordan, their affirmations of protection and defense assure the unity of the Israelite nation, even opening the possibility that location will not define or limit their devotion to God and their brethren.

Questions Teach Patience

32:6 *"Shall your brothers go to war and you stay here?"*

32:7 *"Why will you hinder the hearts of the Israelites from entering into the land YHVH has given them?"*

It is common and slightly embarrassing to ask a question only to learn later that we would have never asked it had we known more of the truth beforehand. Indeed, patient teachers and loving friends will often indulge a short-sighted inquiry for the opportunity to share in the learning of truth together. There are moments when a question in the Torah may be based on limited understanding. In those moments, we too are like the patient teachers and loving friends who seek to learn the truths of the Torah together.

The scene is set in the final chapters of Numbers as the Israelites are about to enter into the Promised Land. Two of the tribes, the Reubenites and the Gadites, ask to settle the land on the eastern banks of the Jordan River. The land is plentiful, and there are sufficient resources to help their families thrive. It's even close to the rest of the family. What's not to like?

Moshe does not respond kindly to this request. His first response is in the form of two questions, **"Shall your brothers go to war and you stay here?"** and **"Why will you hinder the hearts of the Israelites from entering into the land YHVH has given them?"** Moshe's questions aren't unreasonable. While the expectation that the entire nation of Israel will inhabit the Promised Land has never been explicit, this exchange and the questions it contains question the purpose of geographic limits.

The Reubenites and the Gadites promptly respond to affirm their loyalty to the people and to help the rest of the Israelite nation settle the land of Canaan. Moshe then gives them permission on condition they fulfill their promise. The exchange is rapid and God is not involved. This is a novel understanding of the role of allegiance and commitment to the Israelite confederation. With this we are reminded the nation of Israel has never, nor will ever be, a people exclusively dwelling within specific boundaries. They will always be among the nations of the world.

Patient teachers understand that short-sighted questions, with guidance and understanding, can reveal deeper truths than those that might have originally appeared. While Moshe would have liked the family to live together, the strategic position and the qualitative choice the Reubenites and Gadites occupy and make only builds on a grand vision of the nation of Israel as "a light among the nations."[23]

MASEI

Good travel planning includes a balanced amount of situational awareness and just the right amount of spontaneity. For the experienced traveler, effective planning is dependent upon one's tolerance for uncertainty. For example, having a destination for lodging, respite, and nourishment can offer direction and purpose to a journey. At the same time, being open to unforeseen opportunities along the way can uplift the spirit and create a sense of adventure. The journey narrative for the Israelite nation focuses upon both these experiences. As the book concludes, the people's journey from the base of Mount Sinai to the plains of Moab and the borders of Canaan leaves us with a sense of adventure for what comes next.

The people have had a very specific destination for nearly forty years. Along the way, they have acquired the Torah, they have built the *mishkan*, and they have instituted a system of sacrifices to assume personal and communal responsibility. The people have challenged their leaders, even YHVH, and have endured the consequences of their disobedience. These chapters do not introduce any questions because they are primarily reflective of these experiences. The concluding words of this book imply that the people are prepared to reach their destination, the Promised Land of Canaan, to assume their national responsibilities. Perhaps the spontaneity of the journey recedes into the background of this definitive and specific fulfillment of their purpose to reach their destination safely.

CONCLUSION

For scholars and devoted students of the Torah, the symmetry of this book has always been a crucial tool in understanding it. Yet the inconsistent interplay between the narratives and the instructions leave us, perhaps intentionally, wandering in the desert along with our ancestors. The questions of this book reveal a different truth, one that endures in every generation. One lesson we glean from this text is that every religious quest demands mutual understanding. When matters of authority and ritual adherence come into focus, the presentation of questions helps both YHVH and the Israelite nation grapple with the distance between them and ideally draws the other near.

The Israelite nation, unlike the family of Abraham, is instructed to build a central space to encounter YHVH. The *mishkan* is a focal point and a radical departure from previous understandings of religious encounters. Its specificity and the guidelines for behavior surrounding and within the space become foundational for an innovative expression of sacred connection. No longer will the people be nomadic, making offerings to YHVH when the spirit moves them. In recalling the first question God asks humanity, *"Ayeka?"* (**Where are you?**), the fulfillment of the commandments here result in a positive *Hineni!* (**Here I am!**).

The narrative will turn toward Moshe in the final moments of his life and the concluding lessons he will impart to the people as they enter the Promised Land. As the final speeches begin, Moshe will remind the people of the push and pull of their questions and complaints, but with an eye toward the potential they possess, the potential to be a nation of holy priests, to be sacred servants of YHVH.

PART V

INTRODUCTION TO DEUTERONOMY

THE OPENING CHAPTERS IN THE BOOK OF DEUTERONOMY PRESENTS themselves as a summary of the entire journey of the Jewish people. With this concept looming in the background, it is once again curious that questions are introduced in the narrative. This book is more than a summary of experience, though. It is the culmination of the people's journeys from slavery to freedom. It is also the record of a later generation admiring the triumphs and defeats of their spiritual ancestors. The text is riddled with moments where the questions surpass the momentary force of inquiry and are transmuted into a voice of identity. In this book, the questions move from an immediate call for reaction and response and enter the palace of eternal questing.

Like the beginnings of the Torah in the Garden of Eden, the Jordan River is more than a definition of location. In a valley flanked by mountains, the people prepare to cross over, their preparations a towering image and a great metaphor for change and transformation. With this image in mind, the people become fully prepared to enter the Promised Land. Their purpose is to assume the responsibility of living their lives in the kingdom of priests and holiness they are destined to become. It may even be a model of inquiry wherein the questions of this book will teach the people to ask good questions themselves in every generation.

Deuteronomy

DEVARIM

1:12 "How can I myself bear your cumbrance, and your burden, and your strife?" (Moshe to the people)

1:28 "Where are we going up?" (Moshe to the people)

The point where we begin to tell our stories reveals so much about our experiences of the present and even the futures we envision. Small details like location, time of day, who is part of the story at the beginning, and so forth can all play a significant role in the unfolding narrative. When we pay close attention, even to the smallest details, our understanding of the stories we tell becomes a rich tapestry of meaning.

The Torah's storytelling power comes into focus in the opening chapters of the final book. That is why the first words of Moshe's great soliloquy as the people are about to enter the Promised Land reveal that the struggle, the stubbornness, and the shortsightedness of the people will become the practical foundations of a new identity once the people finally enter the Promised Land.

Who Might We Yet Be?

1:12 "How can I myself bear your cumbrance, and your burden, and your strife?"

When we're building relationships, a rhetorical question can draw the other close or it can stun them into silence. For a parent, rhetorical questions are often punitive expressions of uncertainty to their child. "Did you do that?" can be either a request for accountability or an attempt to shock the child into awareness. Rhetorical questions have an implicit power dynamic that can often occlude a connection even in the attempt to clarify a shared experience.

In the final episodes of the Torah, Moshe begins by recalling the forty-year journey that led the people to this moment. He asks, **"How can I myself bear your cumbrance, and your burden, and your strife?"** The use of a question by Moshe should not be understated. We could simply resolve that Moshe is a tired leader, frustrated by the years of the people's struggle and defiance. Angered and dismayed, he simply asks the people something he already knows the answer to. Since we heard this expression before when the Israelites wandered in the desert, the question is more than an expression of exhaustion. Moshe has typified the people here in a way that will persist throughout the generations. The Jewish people are "stiff-necked." Even their leader thinks so!

And still there is a deeper message in the question and its untimely expression, because Moshe is hoping to inspire the people to enter the Promised Land. Moshe might have begun his epic tale with adulation before descending into criticism and then returning, hopefully, to the promise. Rather, the entire narrative of preparation to enter the land begins with this critique. While the sobriety of the moment might dissuade the listeners (and us, the readers), there is something instructive in Moshe's capitulations. His characterization of this stubborn, recalcitrant people is not simply an indictment of their being. It is a powerful and instructive framing of their incredible capacity to transcend their own negativity.

Consider this: the generation that fled Pharaoh and Egypt was incapable of envisioning the Promised Land. Their spite and disbelief were genuinely more than any one leader ought to carry alone. Meanwhile they were instilling in their children both the promise of a brighter future and the horror of their afflictions. Ambivalence was transmitted, even vicariously, from one generation to the next. Moshe's account of this challenging behavior to the new generation about to enter the Promised Land is more than a cautionary tale. This question defines the relationship between leader and people and even between the people and their God. This nation was never meant to enter the Promised Land complacent and blindly obedient. The very quality that brings anger and frustration to their leader has become the cornerstone of the very identity that will strengthen them and endure in the Promised Land for many generations to come.

Ironically, although Moshe has complained of his incapacity to lead the people, he seems quite capable by the end of the story. Perhaps Moshe has a touch of stubbornness himself?

Narrowing the Field
1:28 "Where are we going up?"

Flowcharts are an effective tool to graphically depict a series of information and our responses to it. When we're making decisions about crucial matters in our lives—relationships, careers, and health, to name a few—the use of flowcharts enables us to more readily anticipate and understand the consequences of our actions. Flowcharts also induce anxiety when the "what if"s of our choices become overwhelming and shut us down.

The story of the people and their scouting of the Promised Land presents a kind of flowchart of choices that the people will refer back to once their wandering ceases. The command to go up to the Promised Land and bring back reports as they prepared to enter it long ago proved to be a pivotal moment in the history of the generation. When Joshua and Caleb returned to the camp, their expressions of confidence were summarily dismissed.[1] The outcome of the people's fear and disbelief was condemnation to live out their years in exile, in the desert.

At that moment, the people narrowed their field of vision. They only saw one possible outcome to the report that the land was forbidding: their failure.

Moshe recounts this episode for the people to help them see the consequences of narrowing the field. When Moshe summarizes their experience in the desert by asking **"Where are we going up?"** he is trying to convey the potential curiosity such a question evokes and even more so reflecting the rigidity of the people's choices based on a report of limited knowledge. Under ordinary circumstances, the majority opinion is the appropriate one to follow. This episode teaches us that when the majority favor a point of view limiting human potential, the results can be detrimental and even fatal to the life of a community. Joshua and Caleb's reaction to the moment is the other line of connection, the unified voice that will bring the people to the Promised Land.

So Moshe reminds the people of this decision and the limitations of flowchart thinking to reveal a deeper truth: **"Have no dread or fear of them. None other than YHVH your God, who goes before you, will fight for you."**[2] These are a people in covenant with a God who will protect them.

VA'ETCHANAN

4:32 "Has anything as grand as this ever happened, or has its like ever been known?" (Moshe to the people)

4:33 "Have any people heard the voice of God speaking out of a fire, as you have, and survived?" (Moshe to the people)

4:34 "Or has God ventured to go and take for God's Self one nation from the midst of another nation, by trials, by signs, and by wonders, and by war, by a mighty and an outstretched arm, and by awesome power, as YHVH your God did for you in Egypt before your very eyes?" (Moshe to the people)

5:23 "For what mortal ever heard the voice of the living God speak out of the fire, as we have, and lived?" (Moshe to the people)

6:20 "What is the meaning of these testimonies, statutes, and ordinances that YHVH our God has commanded you?" (Moshe to the people)

Now that the telling of the Israelites' story begins in the desert with an eye toward the nation they are destined to become, Moshe is able to reflect back with them on the awesome and miraculous events that confirm their unique destiny. The chapters of this portion include a reiteration of the Ten Commandments and the text that has become the central expression of Jewish identity, the *Shema*. The questions posed here inspire an eternal quest for truth within the guidelines of the people's destiny. Who the people might yet be is framed by their sense of wonder and awe for the presence of God, who was with them before and will be with them in the succeeding generations.

Remembering a Miracle

4:32 "Has anything as grand as this ever happened, or has its like ever been known?"

4:33 "Have any people heard the voice of God speaking out of a fire, as you have, and survived?"

4:34 "Or has God ventured to go and take for God's Self one nation from the midst of another nation, by trials, by signs, and by wonders, and by war, by a mighty and an outstretched arm, and by awesome power, as YHVH your God did for you in Egypt before your very eyes?"

The Bible has a memory on its own. There are moments when the narrative reflects backward to portray a brighter future, as if to teach that tomorrow's possibilities are carefully built upon the experiences of yesterday's failures and triumphs. It is commonly noted that when the Bible mentions a location or a circumstance that existed in the past but has relevance for the present—for example, **"as is the case today"**[3]—this is more than a point of reference for the reader. It reveals a crucial technique of biblical storytelling. The text is not meant to be simply a historical record of past events. It has a divine purpose as a projection into the future. The book of Deuteronomy frequently wavers between tenses to bring us closer to the history of the Israelites and to inspire within us the awesome potential for God's presence in the future.

The series of questions that end Moshe's first teaching to the people exemplifies the memory of miracles. Moshe poses the questions the people may ask in the future.

"Has anything as grand as this ever happened, or has its like ever been known? . . . Have any people heard the voice of God speaking out of a fire, as you have, and survived? . . . Or has God ventured to go and take for God's Self one nation from the midst of another nation, by trials, by signs, and by wonders, and by war, by a mighty and an outstretched arm, and by awesome power, as YHVH your God did for you in Egypt before your very eyes?"

We're not quite certain what miracles this generation witnessed. In fact, the book will make great efforts to mention that divine revelation occurs with those present and those absent from before or who are not yet born in the future.[4] Moshe's expressions of amazement at this moment transcend the literal experience and introduce the power of memory. More than a recollection of past events, the framing of the questions here is an opportunity to affirm the remarkable character of the people and the uniqueness of their destiny.

Moshe reminds the people that any relationship they have with the God of All will be through their historical and circumstantial connection. They will always be a people who have been redeemed. Their salvation will forever be manifest **"by trials, by signs, and by wonders, and by war."** Not by miracles. Through this blessed status they are not to enjoy the riches of the world by divine gift or fiat. Rather, their covenantal responsibility begins with an acknowledgement that they are taken to be God's hands in the world.

Remembering a miracle is more powerful than witnessing a miracle firsthand. To remember acts and circumstances that defy the natural order is both to say that our present experiences are a gift and to say that a potential for divine presence is always possible.

Moshe poses these memories as questions to reveal the delicate nature of memory and hope. Whether or not the answers to his questions points to the divine election of the Jewish people, he is identifying the very nature of potential as an aspiration situated between the past and the future. And if his people are to enter the Promised Land, they will need to recognize and celebrate their heritage as well their legacy.

Radical Amazement

5:23 For what mortal ever heard the voice of the living God speak out of the fire, as we have, and lived?

The Bible records moments that take our breath away. Creation; the birth of humanity; Abram and Isaac on the mountaintop; Moshe at the burning bush; the revelation of Torah on Mount Sinai; Korach's death when the ground opens and swallows him; and so much more. The Bible's purpose is to describe how things have come to be, which is mythology, as well as to describe how the world ought to be. Something as powerful as the narrative of the giving of the law through the Ten Commandments is not simply a didactic primer in moral behavior given in a classroom. The smoke, the *shofar* blasts, and the awesome voice of God all convey that lawful behavior is a total body experience.

The book of Deuteronomy consistently focuses on this dynamic not only to remind us of the historical events and the codes of law that prepare the people to enter the Promised Land but also to instill in us a sense of awe that God is present with humanity. Rabbi Abraham Joshua Heschel coined the term "radical amazement" to describe the posture of the seeker in the midst of Biblical history and the potential for future truths to be revealed. This is best understood in Moshe's question to the people after he reminds the people of the revelation at Mount Sinai.

Shortly after reiterating the Ten Commandments spoken by God on Mount Sinai, Moshe asks the people, **"For what mortal ever heard the voice of the living God speak out of the fire, as we have, and lived?"** Even if succeeding generations may never see the living God with their own eyes, they have a myth that identifies the direct revelation of the God of Israel to the Israelites. Amazement, then, isn't temporal. It has an eternal quality. Such revelations were lovingly passed to each succeeding generation.

Redeemable by Reason

6:20 "What is the meaning of these testimonies, statutes, and ordinances that YHVH our God has commanded you?"

In formal schools of education, there is a helpful distinction made between indoctrination and inculcation. Indoctrination, by definition, involves the transmission of knowledge without any explanation. There may very well be a good reason for the shared information, but the process of transmission is absolute. Inculcation, in contrast, is the transmission of knowledge with reasons to support the purpose of the shared wisdom. Inculcation has a quality of learning unlike indoctrination because it gives permission to the recipient to determine the rationale and the validity of the shared knowledge on their own. Inculcation is a superior form of teaching and learning, by comparison, because the transmission of knowledge is as much about the information as it is about permission to apply critical thinking to the exchange between teacher and student.

The most significant questions and transmission of knowledge in Jewish tradition are centered around the retelling of the enslavement and redemption of the people from Egypt. As Moshe is preparing the generation of Israelites about to enter the Promised Land, he guides the people and their children to address questions of behavior with good reason. Implicit in the question **"What is the meaning of these testimonies, statutes, and ordinances that YHVH our God has commanded you?"** is the recognition that the Israelites' children and succeeding generations will have a natural curiosity about their origins, seeking explanations for particular behavior. One's impulse might be to say as justification, "Because God said so," or more accurately, "Because I said so." Moshe's rationale for this question and the anticipated response is one of the greatest gifts Jewish thinking contributes to humanity. The redemptive power of God's involvement in human destiny is a gift both of reason and of hope. **"God freed us from there, that God might take us and give us the land that God promised on oath to our ancestors. Then YHVH commanded us to observe all these laws, to revere YHVH our God, for our lasting good and survival, as is now the case."**[5]

The spirit of the Passover Seder endures in succeeding generations not only because the cultural experience of retelling our history can bind us to the present and future but also because the experience of question and response, of curiosity and rationale, is accepted and celebrated. Indeed, this quality of reasonable knowledge is inspirational. If there is one rationale that is so clear throughout all of Jewish tradition and practice, it is that the redemption of our ancestors was indeed a promise of our redemption in future generations. Moshe's rationale here is wise and challenging. If we take God's role to heart, then our behavior and actions according to the laws that govern the Israelites will have meaning.

EKEV

7:17 "How can I dispossess them?" (Moshe to the people, anticipating what the people will ask themselves in the Promised Land)

9:2 "Who can stand before the Anakites?" (Moshe to the people, anticipating what the people will ask themselves in the Promised Land)

10:12 "And now, O Israel, what does YHVH your God ask of you?" (Moshe to the people)

Inspiring the courage of a nation is unlike bolstering the bravery of an individual or even a small group. National courage is built upon shared history and a common understanding of a destiny greater than any one person. Moshe's final words to the Israelites are focused upon this effort, helping to provide the people with some common history, shared experience, and ultimately proven tests of their courage as reflected in the questions of this Torah portion. Equally important will be the message that God is central to the pursuit of wisdom. It will be an everlasting commitment, one that will be tested and will also flourish in the succeeding generations.

We Could Be Heroes!

7:17 "How can I dispossess them?"

9:2 "Who can stand before the Anakites?"

Expressions of uncertainty are as certain as expressions of confidence. We celebrate those heroes who fearlessly transcend doubt and courageously face the unknown. Most of the time, though, we all need some encouragement. Even the hero is not so much self-motivated as inspired by the confidence of others. We can identify this quality in individuals, but the project of the Torah is to inspire heroism within an entire nation.

Moshe will occasionally employ a question to inspire heroic action in the generation about to enter the Promised Land. We'll see that he anticipates what the people may ask when they enter the land by musing, **"These nations are more numerous [than we are]; how can [we] dispossess them?"** Moshe continues the theme shortly later with a second question: **"Who can stand before the Anakites?"** At the same time he is attempting to instill confidence in the people's ability to succeed with the support of God, he is also revealing questioning as a way of conveying meaning and purpose.

One of the themes of the book of Deuteronomy is that the people have the power within themselves to achieve success in the Promised Land. Questions that are posed by Moshe to reflect the minds and hearts of the people in their uncertainty are always prompts for expressions of confidence and inspiration. We won't read the responses to questions like these with a cold, hard pragmatism as if to proclaim, "You can defeat the inhabitants of the land, but only if you have a strong army." Moshe presents these questions to inspire the people. They are meant to challenge the doubt that naturally exists in the face of uncertain futures and to instill in the Israelites' heroic courage on their journey into the Promised Land.

This style of motivation is a powerful tool in the rhetoric of inspiring courageous action. The Torah captures these moments in Moshe's voice to remind both the generation entering the Promised Land and to inspire us, the readers of their legacy, that our fears of uncertainty can be faced with the confidence found in God's supportive presence.

Conditional Love

10:12 "And now, O Israel, what does YHVH your God ask of you?"

When a question is used to cultivate responsibility, it is as much a literary tool as it is the foundation of a deep connection or relationship. When Moshe asks, **"And now, O Israel, what does YHVH your God ask of you?"** the response that follows is more than a litany of rules. Demands like **"Revere YHVH your God"** and **"Walk in God's ways"**[6] are incredibly open-ended. In constructing this part of his speech, Moshe is describing requests from God that transcend specific actions or precise behaviors. It appears that God is asking for the loyalty of the people's souls.

Theologically, this relationship makes sense. Divine authority in its perfection is a commanding force. Human beings in their fallibility respond. Philosophically, though, this entire teaching from Moshe is defining a relationship future generations will have with the God of their ancestors, in itself an abstraction of perfection. This question has an exquisite quality to it that only emerges from a relationship that has already withstood challenges, tests, and triumphs. This question defines love. To know that love has an iridescent and transcendent quality of reverence and movement suddenly makes qualities like love quite tangible. It is only after a journey like the Israelites have endured with their God that a request or a demand for love is even possible.

In essence, God's request, as framed by Moshe, is more covenantal than the introduction of *mitzvot* on Mount Sinai. The Torah teaches us more than a specific path of behavior. In fact, Jewish tradition will continue to evolve from the glimpse into holy behavior that the Torah reveals for all generations. The demand for love or reverence is ephemeral, unbound by time or space. The real quality of being in love begins after the request or demand for love has been met. Yes, there are demonstrable acts that support and nourish loving relationships. But the quality of being in love is something that can only be deepened after all the demonstrations are established. We act lovingly so we may be loving.

The book of Deuteronomy powerfully captures this aspiration. Here a question typifies the ultimate goal: sharing one's soul fully with the God of All.

RE'EH

12:30 "How do those nations worship their gods?" (Moshe to the people)

This Torah portion outlines many of the unique laws the Israelite nation is commanded to observe. The single question in these chapters will bring into focus one of the looming concerns that will persistently torment the people during their life in the land: idolatry of and loyalty to other divine forces. Moshe's question is not modeling ways to avoid the allure of false gods. Instead, we learn that responding to the natural inclination of questions will establish a new ethic, one that proposes abstinence from the outset.

Don't Even Ask!

12:30 "How do those nations worship their gods?"

Anticipating a question can be a sign of prophecy. More than a logical conclusion to a series of premises and conclusions, a question to be asked in the future is brimming with promise. Moshe has already envisioned Israelites in succeeding generations asking about their identity and their ancestors' history in Egypt. His portrayals are as much an affirmation of the unique relationship the Jewish people will have with God as they are a projection of the essential forms of identity for generations to come.

Preparing the people to avoid asking questions is another skill entirely. Moshe is responding to what will be the Israelites' natural and perhaps dangerous curiosity about the inhabitants they have been commanded to dispossess. When Moshe poses the question **"How do those nations worship their gods?"** it is more than the people's imagination that concerns him. The question is posed to reveal a certain anxiety for the Israelites' future behavior. Moshe is trying to shape the narrative of the future by curbing their curiosity. And still, if questions embrace the holiness of doubt, why would Moshe ask a question to encourage the people to avoid further inquiry?

Moshe's goal is to prevent interest in false gods and to simultaneously inspire the people's faith in God's divine providence. We the readers will come to learn that this natural curiosity and the inclination to imitate the ways of others is unavoidable—even if we were commanded by Moshe to avoid them. We already recognize this flaw in the people's capacity to live in perfect faith, and Moshe's anticipation here may be fruitless. It is as if the people were told to eat all the fruit in the Garden of Eden except from the tree in the middle. We remember what happened then and are reminded of this futile request as the people are about to enter the Promised Land. But instead of commanding the people to avoid their curiosity (e.g., "Don't ask about their gods, ever!"), Moshe opens up a dialogue that will help the people evolve in future generations.

One of the goals of the psalmist is to respond to this question again and again: **"They have eyes, but do not see, ears, but cannot hear, lips but cannot speak."**[7] Without validating their curiosity, the people would never reach their own conclusions.

Herein is a fundamental truth of faith. Faith isn't so much about blind obedience. Faith is reflection upon a range of thoughts that may deviate from a sense of higher purpose and truth. Making the choice to act in alignment with the truths the Torah prescribes is an active response. Moshe's intent is to guide the people toward this choice. Like a loving parent who wants their child to choose wisely, with this question Moshe equally anticipates curiosity and prompts the deeper thinking that the behavior of others may be inconsistent with or contradictory to the wisdom of the Torah.

SHOFTIM

18:21 "How shall we know the word that YHVH has not spoken?" (Moshe to the people)

20:5 "Is there someone who built a new house and has not dedicated it?" (Moshe to the people)

20:6 "Is there someone who planted a vineyard and has not used the fruit thereof?" (Moshe to the people)

20:7 "Is there someone who was recently betrothed and not yet married?" (Moshe to the people)

20:8 "Is there someone who is fearful and faint hearted?" (Moshe to the people)

The formation of a nation requires a system of justice to determine its proper behavior, as the eponymous beginning of this Torah portion suggests (*Shoftim* means "judges" in Hebrew). In addition to the laws guiding the structures of organization and adjudication of God's laws, the questions of this Torah portion affirm a code of behavior that cannot easily be written down and codified. The laws of the heart or spirit are understood without extensive description, here in relation to preparations for military service. The implication of the questions posed in the text is that duty to family and one's well-being take precedence over service to the greater cause of national identity.

False Prophets

18:21 "How shall we know the word that YHVH has not spoken?"

Today there is no shortage of predictions and prophecies. There are even competitions to celebrate the formation and articulation of future circumstances, with rewards going to those who are close enough. One can even study to become a "futurist." With so many purveyors of information, prophecy seems to be an avocation and not a divinely inspired gift. It is increasingly more complicated than ever before to sift through this barrage of knowledge, to balance the commentary and insight of pundits and experts, and to ultimately choose which path to follow.

The Torah was keen to identify who might be a prophet and how we might address the heretical nature of falsely speaking in the name of God. Moshe frames the concern in a question, **"How shall we know the**

word that YHVH has not spoken?" to emphasize a deeper concern. It's not for lack of information that a prophet speaks with authority, but it is with an abundance of information that we may find our confusion. The response in the Torah is both honest and unsatisfying: **"If the prophet speaks in the name of YHVH and the oracle does not come true, that oracle was not spoken by YHVH."** In other words, we'll only know after the fact if the prophecy was true or not.

This form of "Monday-morning quarterbacking" is not what builds and sustains a healthy society. It reveals a significant weakness in the system of information sharing. While there are metrics and trends to analyze when making a prediction, the future is always uncertain. The difficulty with the Torah's definition of authentic prophecy is the lack of time constraints. It would be easy for a presumed prophet to make a prediction, and should it not take place as predicted, the prophet could simply say it hasn't happened yet.

It seems impossible to truly ascertain what knowledge is effective until it actually becomes relevant. George Santayana is quoted as saying "Prayer is poetry, believed in." So many words are thrown into the common discourse every day, but it is only when those words take on a prophetic quality, a quality of belief, that they do indeed become true.

The honesty of the statement in response to the question is helpful. When that which is prophesied does indeed become real, then the propheseer's insight is validated. If not, then society has a responsibility to stamp out the falsehood and remove it from their midst.

We might wonder: if such rigorous measurements were applied today, how much information that flows into the world would be lifted up and how much more would be disregarded?

Leading Questions

20:5 "Is there someone who built a new house and has not dedicated it?"

20:6 "Is there someone who planted a vineyard and has not used the fruit thereof?"

20:7 "Is there someone who was recently betrothed and not yet married?"

20:8 "Is there someone who is fearful and faint hearted?"

Defining ethical behavior in the public or private space is an essential feature of a thriving society. The Torah as a foundational text is replete with guidance and instruction to shape the new Israelite nation according to a unique ethical model based on interpersonal integrity and divine responsibility. Similarly, how a people conduct themselves in times of war is equally fundamental in the shaping of a society. The absence of ethical behavior can devolve into chaotic anarchy in which violence or physical power may be the only way to restore a sense of order. Concern for proper behavior in war is a hallmark of civilized society, which is why the ethics of warfare are woven through the pages of the book of Deuteronomy. In particular, this section of the Torah, titled *Shoftim*, is focused on the theme of a just society, not only within the boundaries of the new nation but in relation to the nations of the world as well.

The series of questions to be prompted by the leader in preparation for war are an exquisite glimpse into the care and concern the Israelite people have for each other. In preparation for war, the leader is prompted to ask, **"Is there someone who built a new house and has not dedicated it?" "Is there someone who planted a vineyard and has not used the fruit thereof?" "Is there someone who was recently betrothed and not yet married?" "Is there someone who is fearful and faint hearted?"**

These questions posed in succession are more than a checklist of readiness for war. While the implication may be a sensitivity to the potential fate that awaits the soldier as he marches into battle, these questions establish a prerequisite for protecting and defending the nation. The concern is for a sense of contentment and the understanding that life is incomplete if these goals and others similar to them are left unfulfilled. The underlying concern of these chapters in the grand narrative of the Jewish people is cultivating loyalty, and even a sense of love, for the nation of Israel. Defending the people from foreign invasion or preserving the integrity of the land must come from a place of love and not from a place of coercion. A society loyal to a king or a structure of leadership that doesn't take into account the fundamental needs of citizens isn't a society worthy of God's presence.

KI TEITZEI—KI TAVO

The book of Deuteronomy envisions the culmination of the Israelite journey. There is a sense of finality looming in Moshe's final words to the people here that expresses a summary of their experience, as if their travels are complete. It is also through this lens that the promises of the future are introduced. On the surface, we would not expect new laws to be announced in a moment of reflection like this. Certainly there are many laws, guidelines, adjurations, and celebrations that are repeated in this book. Yet these chapters epitomize the inclusion of new laws, perhaps in relation to the many laws the people have received before. Their framing is unique and explicit nonetheless.

These are no questions that emerge from the legal codes recorded here. This reasserts the determinate role of a legal system in the function of Israelite society. In addition, we have learned before that there is no uncertainty when vision and mission are in alignment with the collective will of the people.

These chapters also include a myriad of blessings for adherence to and curses for disobedience of the law. Unlike the use of the Urim and Tummim[8] to determine blessings and curses from a supernatural source, the language of certainty here is troubling and not empirically proven. The blessings and curses are presented more as a threat or a cautionary tale than a promise. The presence of explicit blessings, and more succinctly shuddering curses, is to dissuade the Israelites from behavior that deviates from the covenantal promise made at Mount Sinai.

These chapters are essential in the preparations for the people to enter the Promised Land and assume the responsibilities of governing as a nation. There are ethical and civil laws that dictate behavior and they serve as the standard by which punishment or correction will be necessary. There is also a vision of a future replete with blessings or scorched by curses—depending on the people's choices. As the final chapters truly do summarize the journey of the Israelites and expand this vision beyond behavioral expectations, we will refer back to this wisdom in generations to come to glean from them a code of behavior that transcends blessing and curses altogether.

NITZAVIM

29:23 "Why has YHVH done this to the land?" (Moshe to the people)

29:23 "What is this great anger?" (Moshe to the people)

30:12 "Who shall go up for us to heaven, and take it for us, and make us hear it, that we may do it?" (Moshe to the people)

30:13 "Who shall cross over the sea for us, and take it for us, and make us hear it, that we may do it?" (Moshe to the people)

The beauty of questions is evident in the resolution of the doubt they reveal. We've now learned that our curiosity can lead to confidence and our confidence can lead to faith. In these chapters and the concluding moments of the Torah, an expression of future hesitancy is a powerful lesson in the life of faith. A faithful life does not approach the present or the future without any uncertainty. On the contrary, the natural and humane reaction to the world is that what is seen is not always what is felt, that what is perceived is not always real. The confidence Moshe instills in the people through the questions he asks is not to prevent any sense of doubt but to ensure that in the face of doubt, the people will have all the confidence necessary to confront even the most devastating of possibilities: exile.

Why? Because . . .

29:23 *"Why has YHVH done this to the land?"*

29:33 *"What is this great anger?"*

It is a rare circumstance in the Torah when a question is posed and an explicit answer is given. The goal in the use of a question is as much to evoke interest and curiosity in the subject being discussed as it is to open up a realm of possible interpretations. When an answer is given, however, it narrowly defines the purpose of the question. It concludes a conversation and provides one explanation for the uncertainty. When answers like these are given, the Torah ceases to be a source of inspiration and becomes more like an instruction manual.

The comfort of answers is that there is certainty where once there was doubt. The unsettling nature of answers is that there is a presumption of trust that may not be warranted. Moreover, the tone of answers may not be inclusive; they may even paralyze our thinking.

In Moshe's third and final discourse to the people, the tone shifts from guidance of the present generation to promises (and threats) for future generations. Questions dance between certainty and speculation to paint a picture of the life the Israelites will now lead as they enter the Promised Land. When Moshe reflects on the projected destruction and exile of the people in future generations, he asks, as though from the perspective of a foreigner, **"Why has YHVH done this to the land? What is this great anger?"**

The answers that follow imply the destruction of the land will be a direct consequence of the people's betrayal of their covenant with God. Scholars have pointed to the parallel nature of these verses and those of another society that existed at the time, namely, the Assyrians.[9] Describing a parallel between earthly and divine rule may have been one purpose in the text, but perhaps the very nature of the questions expressed in this way can expand our understanding of reasonable inquiry altogether.

Moshe could have simply explained that the consequences of the people's betrayal would be desolation of the land and their expulsion from it. There are several examples to support that style of communication between a leader and a people. When the message is conveyed by future inquiry in the voice of foreign nations, the intention behind the message becomes equally complicated. The intent is not so much prophecy as it is to instill caution and fear in the minds of the people and inspire them to maintain their loyalty to God.

We will learn this method of instilling fear is ineffective. The questions are not merely descriptions of how people in the future will respond (the argument "What will people think if you do this?" can be very compelling). This is an invitation to be self-reflective. Moshe's inspiration is not to chronicle historical moments from a vantage point in the future but to inspire the people to recognize their actions do indeed have implications for their future.

Such thinking is familiar. Moshe uses the refrain to contend with God on Mount Sinai when the people rebel.[10] There Moshe changes God's mind and God does not destroy the people. If only this generation who did not witness the awesome power of God in the desert might be compelled to change their behavior to avoid the scorn of the nations who will witness their failures!

Can You Do It? You Can Do It!

30:12 "Who shall go up for us to heaven, and take it for us, and make us hear it, that we may do it?"

30:13 "Who shall cross over the sea for us, and take it for us, and make us hear it, that we may do it?"

Epic tales of heroes often begin with a feat that few of us would ever think of attempting. Heroes have the courage to confront improbable outcomes and discover a more direct and effective way to overcome challenges. Motivating someone, let alone a nation, to place their confidence in their own capabilities and face the unpredictable cannot be commanded. Here a question is precisely the right form of inspiration to help doubters find all the courage they need within.

Moshe asks, **"Who shall go up for us to heaven, and take it for us, and make us hear it, that we may do it?"** and **"Who shall cross over the sea for us, and take it for us, and make us hear it, that we may do it?"** Moshe frames these questions as those one should not ask, prompting the obvious response, which is to tacitly ask these very same questions! By engaging the senses and giving validity to the ambivalence the questions capture, Moshe is able to offer encouraging wisdom for a people swept up in divine providence as they enter a land that has been promised to them.

Moshe responds, **"No, the matter is very close to you, in your mouth and in your heart, to observe it."**[11] Moshe's goal isn't to create a mercenary force willing to place themselves willingly in the line of danger to protect a system of values and a deity they cannot see or touch. The goal is to instill in the people a sense of confidence that whatever challenges they confront in future generations, their heroism will not be ossified in some ancient text or entombed in a vault. **"It is not in the heavens,"**[12] Moshe proclaims! The heroic life is something each and every one of us has the potential to live.

VAYELECH

When do we stop asking questions? After every possible uncertainty has been explored and our doubt has been alleviated, the absence of a question embodies a certain kind of calmness, maybe even serenity. There are also times when we stop asking or even answering questions because we feel like the search for any resolution of doubt is impossible. In this dichotomy of unasked questions, we focus on the moment God stops asking questions of the Israelites to reveal insights into the prophetic vision of damning futures.

In this single chapter that comprises an entire weekly portion of the Torah, Moshe announces the concluding moments of his life, and God affirms the plan to elect Joshua to succeed Moshe as the leader of the people. Whereas questions invite a future of sacred partnership between YHVH and the Israelites, the pronouncements that the people will break their covenant with God and that God will punish them are deflating. The transformative experience the family of Abram has endured for hundreds of years is replete with questions and opportunities for greater relationship and connection. Yet God has reached a conclusion about the people. God proclaims, **"They will eat their fill and grow fat and turn to other gods and serve them, spurning me and breaking My covenant. . . . For I know what plans they are devising even now, before I bring them into the land I promised on oath."**[13] Their defiance is no longer worthy of holy doubt. The paralyzing statement by YHVH **"I will abandon them and hide My countenance from them"**[14] may invoke a sense of guilt in the reader. Either the people are not worthy of divine presence because they disobey the laws of God's commandments or there simply will never be enough devotion and commitment expressed by the people to assuage God's concerns.

In a way, we are glad the book does not conclude at this moment. There will be yet more questions asked as the people reach the Promised Land. There is a powerful lesson about questions and their ability to continue a conversation and a relationship. When we stop asking questions and envision catastrophic futures, we lose hope, even purpose. Our goal is to always be ready to ask more questions to bring us to places of calmness, serenity, even faith.

HA'AZINU

32:6 "Do you thus requite YHVH, O boorish and mindless people?" (Moshe to the people)

32:6 "Is not God your father that acquired you, made you, and established you?" (Moshe to the people)

32:30 "How could one chase a thousand, and two put ten thousand to flight, except their rock had given them over and YHVH had delivered them up?" (Moshe to the people)

32:37–38 "Where are their gods, the rock in whom they trusted, who ate the fat of their sacrifices and drank the wine of their offering?" (God)

Shifting between poetry and prose is a hallmark of biblical literature. There are as many great truths to be discovered in the faithful refrains as in the narrative events that bring the people into the land of Israel. These varieties of expression leave enduring impressions of what our ancestors heard when the commanding presence spoke. It can also be confusing to distinguish between the two, especially when the two forms of expression occur from one chapter to the next. While poetry deliberately invokes the imagination to coax the reader to uncover a kaleidoscope of meaning in its message, prose is more direct and shapes the imagination to uncover the depth in a single message. The final poem Moshe expresses for the people in the one chapter that makes up this portion is filled with questions that expand the people's consciousness of the role God has played and will continue to play in their national confederation.

Did You Forget Something?

32:6: "Do you thus requite YHVH, O boorish and mindless people?"

32:6 "Is not God your father that acquired you, made you, and established you?"

With all the focus upon memory and the inspiration that comes from a triumphant past replete with redemption and revelation, there isn't much conversation about forgetting. Striving to remember something that is easily forgotten is a prodigious task. It prompts us to erect monuments and record histories not merely for posterity but to guide our present and future actions.

The adjurations of Moshe in the closing chapters of the Torah shake our confidence. We'll learn from them that the people will not succeed in sustaining their loyalty and responsibility to God—and the history of the Jewish people will affirm this in the centuries that follow. Asking questions to evoke memories will be even more important many generations later. These adjurations do not simply foreshadow the future of the Israelite people; they are codified to inspire within us the powerful connections we can forge with the God of Israel in our midst.

This is why we read the following questions with concern and hope. **"Do you thus requite YHVH, O boorish and mindless people? Is not God your father that acquired you, made you, and established you?"** The text is simple. The questions here imply a concern for a people who will eventually disobey the religion given to them on Mount Sinai. It is also possible to read the questions as a reflection of the opening chapters of the book: that the generation yet to inhabit the Promised Land has still not yet appropriately responded to the grandeur and magnificence of living with God present among them.

We may also conclude the challenge is perpetual and that a covenantal relationship with God will be in constant turmoil between the command and the response. A book of faith that commands memory must also command the act of not forgetting. They are two distinct functions. In between not forgetting and remembering we discover the powerful lessons of personal growth. Who we were and who we may yet become lives precisely in the space between these two.

It Is Awesome

32:30 "How could one chase a thousand, and two put ten thousand to flight, except their rock had given them over and YHVH had delivered them up?"

It isn't simple to express wonder without using an interrogative. When what is natural appears to us as extraordinary, curiosity is most easily reflected in the form of a question. Wonder touches the limits of imagination and identifies that there does indeed exist more than what was understood before. Awe expressed in the form of a question, then, is poetic. It is an expression not meant to be answered, an expression refracted by a spectrum of interpretations. Even if there is a reasonable explanation for a wondrous phenomenon, a question always asks something deeper. How can I see something that wasn't seen there before?

In the concluding chapters of the Torah, Moshe posits a question the enemies of Israel will ask in the midst of their victories over the people: **"How could one chase a thousand, and two put ten thousand to flight, except their rock had given them over and YHVH had delivered them up?"** To read this as an Israelite is to stand in awe of Moshe's premonitions. It is also to recognize that without God's presence, the Israelites fail. Their failure is a consequence of God's absence and not the strength of the nations of the world.

The arc of the Torah envisions the triumph of God and God's particular influence over the Israelite people. It is the celebration of an everlasting commitment to the people through moments of defiance, rebellion, and weakness. There are also many uplifting moments of unconditional devotion and quests to be worthy to stand in God's presence that define this uncommon relationship. This question is a reminder to the people that without the relationship with their God, with whom they have a covenant, they cannot succeed. Or more succinctly, only with the presence, support, and inspiration of their God will the Israelite people become the inheritors of the Promised Land.

Where Did You Go?

32:37–38 "Where are their gods, the rock in whom they trusted, who ate the fat of their sacrifices, and drank the wine of their offering?"

When God asks the human beings in the Garden of Eden **"Where are you?"** commentary helps us understand that God isn't asking for a location. Rather, he is challenging the human beings to explore their identity. Now at the end of the Torah, God asks a similar question and even in similar language,[15] but it is directed toward other nations of the world. Even God has come to understand that not every human being is prepared to respond to the commanding question.

So God is curious. **"Where are their gods, the rock in whom they trusted, who ate the fat of their sacrifices and drank the wine of their offering?"** This question may connote a dimension of antagonism—especially if we read these words in light of the psalmist.[16] But we may also read this question as Moshe's poetic expression in the final moments of his life and leadership. On one level this is a very direct question. **"Where are their gods?"** implies that the beliefs of other nations dissolve in the faith of YHVH.

On another level, this question presents a challenging role and identity for the Jewish people. To be priests and a holy nation suggests their value is in distinction to that of other peoples. While there are countless examples of the admiration and respect found among the nations of the world for Israel, there are also countless examples of the hatred and animosity with which the world regards Israel and the people's proclaimed status of having the One True God in their midst. This question may be seen as a challenge and not a nullification of their striving for divinity, as an opportunity to meet other visions of God in the world. This question, when read with such sensitivity, is an invitation to conversation.

V'ZOT HA'BERAKHA
33:29 "Who is like you?"

The last chapters of the Torah are simultaneously fulfilling and frustrating. The people do not actually enter the Promised Land and so return home—a journey hundreds of years in the making. We have to begin the book of Joshua to learn more about the history of the Jewish people. We realize that the Promised Land, being somewhat elusive, is as much a state of mind as it is a location on a map. These final chapters and the final question of the Torah leave us with yet one more expression of curiosity that inspires this state of mind. As Jewish custom has us read these last words and immediately return to the beginning in our annual reading of the text, the question profoundly asks us to consider who the main character of the Torah is. Moshe? The people? God? Like all great questions in the Torah, this one also has many answers to cultivate sacred and purposeful relationships.

A Question for God
33:29 "Who is like you?"
In his book *God: A Biography*, Jack Miles astutely observes, "God's attempt to shape mankind in his image, would be far more comprehen-

sible if God had a richer subjective life, one more clearly separate from, more clearly prior to, the human object of his shaping."[17] By framing the subjectivity of God in the quest to be a godly image, we are given permission to know ourselves better. If God has a history, then so do we. If God has a destiny, then we do as well.

This kind of thinking does not foreclose the awesome and unknowable power of divine potential and it encourages our experience of being human and located in a divine presence we can actually know. The confluence of divine and human understanding through subjective knowledge is what leaves the student of the Torah craving deeper understanding. It is why Jewish tradition doesn't ever really end the reading of the Torah. We roll the scrolls back to the beginning precisely at the moment when the last verse is read. In this spirit, the last question piques our curiosity to go back to the beginning to learn more about God so we may learn more about ourselves.

The final question of the Torah, which some interpret not as a question but as an exclamation, presents the same sense of wonder and even uncertainty with which all the previous questions contend. We read, "**O happy Israel! Who is like you, a people delivered by YHVH?**" The question is reminiscent of the awe in God's power in the "Song of the Sea."[18] But now the awesome power of the people is in focus as they complete their journey. It is yet one more moment of triumph for the people to behold as this question expresses the perpetual wonderment of who the people are and might yet be.

Because this is the last question of the Torah as well as Moshe's final message to the people, we may want to summarize the entire experience through the lens of these brief words. Such effort is indulgent because it assumes that one phrase, one sentence, indeed one question could capture the entire purpose of the Torah. If we ask ourselves, however, whom the Torah was written for, this final question is an inspiration for each of the leading figures. It is a celebration of God, who has created an entire nation with the potential to walk in godly ways. It is a triumph of Moshe, who has brought the people from the lowest slums of enslavement to the majestic and royal palaces of priests. And it is an affirmation of the people, who are both redeemed by God and have become worthy of awe among the nations. As a culmination of a never-ending book, this question seems to capture best the Torah's wisdom. It offers us, the readers of this book thousands of years later, permission to discover the divine image within ourselves and to seek out the path of righteous and holy action in our age.

CONCLUSION

The questions in the concluding book of the Torah do not close the chapter on the history of Judaism, because they ultimately ask, "Who might we yet be?" God, who first asks, "Where are you?" marvels at the possibility that human capacity is limitless, searching further and deeper into the vastness of existence, physical and spiritual, ever seeking truth, and the oneness of all. The final question of Israel, "Who is like you?" exemplifies this search for identity, a search clothed in wonder and awe.

Conclusion: The Holiness of Doubt

WHEN THINKING OF FAITH, WE HAVE THE IMPULSE TO CONJURE THE valor of warriors and piety of religious leaders as manifestations of absolute confidence. Yet the courage of a military general or the inspiration of a priest is momentary, even ephemeral. The beauty of our humanity is to capture glimpses of faith throughout our lives, moments that inspire us to continually pursue divine encounters all the while knowing that the times we do not feel inspired or confident aren't punishments or lapses of good judgment. Rather, the ability to seek deeper understanding and truth from that which does not seem clear or certain is precisely the faithful path.

Even if we do not define ourselves as religious people or believers in any one particular faith system, we can all identify moments when we sense clarity or certainty in our purpose. Moments like these often appear from expressions of wonder or curiosity or in the confirmation of a hypothesis. But if the Torah teaches us anything about faith, it is that all experiences of certainty are rarely enduring. The patchwork of tales and encounters with divinity throughout the book are intended to be snapshots of a faithful life. The book affirms that none of our spiritual founders experienced total certainty. In truth, it is the questions of the Torah that reveal the evolution of our ancestors' faith. We even discover an understanding of the faith God places in humanity to inspire our own faithful devotion through the questions recorded in the text.

What makes doubt holy, then, isn't the audacious claim that uncertainty has some power to evoke divine attention. God loves the answers if not more than the questions. The holiness of doubt is found in the prism through which a resolution of uncertainty is refracted. A spectrum of interpretation and understanding illuminates the seeker's path, leading us in every generation toward greater truths. Good questions will always forge stronger bonds than didactic proclamations of certainty. The Torah does indeed highlight the powerful moments when God commands and the people obey. The entirety of the Torah, however, grapples with all that occurs before and after those moments of revelation.

Indeed, one great treasure of Jewish wisdom throughout the generations is the honor and value placed on the question. Questions are the foundation of the most important storytelling recorded in the thousands of years of Jewish tradition. We have faith that all the questions and stories woven between them prepare us to receive certainty or truth when it is revealed. The holiness of doubt is a sacred process in which curiosity is celebrated, awareness grows, and relationships are sown.

"Ask good questions," the Torah teaches. The reward for a good question and even better answer is an encounter with holiness, even with the divine.

Study Guide to *The Holiness of Doubt*

THERE ARE MANY WAYS TO ENJOY THIS BOOK. I HOPE YOU DISCOVER them all and even more than I could have imagined! This book was written in a spirit of study by following the questions through the text. Stitching together the moments when some form of the interrogative is used reveals what makes doubt holy. The Torah prepares us to learn from our experiences of doubt and guides us to achieve our most sacred visions of meaning and purpose through the answers we discover together.

I envision two frameworks that would be useful in a classroom or book group setting to study this book. The questions in the Torah can first be studied as a general subject with the themes of uncertainty and doubt winding their way through the complicated and inspiring narratives of the text. The second path of learning begins by exploring the meaning of questions in the Torah through broadly defined themes, as described below. These two models are designed to facilitate understanding and inspire discussion around the questions themselves. Both models follow Bloom's taxonomy of questions, each question evolving from an understanding of information as knowledge and an interpretive concept that has present and even future relevance.

TWO PATHS TO STUDY THE QUESTIONS OF THE TORAH

1. Read the questions in a particular portion or selected questions of an entire book and analyze their meaning relative to the portion and the entire Torah narrative.

a. Follow the weekly reading by studying the questions each portion contains. You will notice that the majority of the portions have at least one question, but there are several that do not (sixteen, to be exact!). One recommendation is to extend the learning of those portions with more than enough questions over a period of time, like a study unit, so that when you encounter weeks without questions, the only subject you may choose to discuss is "Why aren't there any questions here?"

b. You will discover in your study that there is not an abundance of classical commentary on the questions posed in the text. My attempt in this book is to provide some commentary to spark discussion. You can use the commentary to apply the more complex forms of analysis of Bloom's taxonomy or it can inspire your analysis and discussion.

2. Develop a thematic approach to the study of the Torah and use the questions as a guide. Identify ten or a handful of questions that address a theme and explore what the Torah may be teaching us about the theme. These themes guide the seeker toward paths of meaning and purpose; in essence, a life of faith.

a. Here are five broad themes I have identified.
   i. identity
   ii. relationships
   iii. power and authority
   iv. hope and aspiration
   v. faith

b. Develop your own theme and present a series of related questions to explore this theme.

MODEL 1—SAMPLE LESSON FOR WEEKLY STUDY
Parshat Bereisheet
Bloom's Taxonomy

- Knowledge—What are the questions in the portion?
- Comprehension—Why are the questions a part of these chapters?

- Application—How do the themes of the questions apply to our lives today?
- Analysis—What might have been other ways to convey the message in the questions?
- Synthesis—What questions might you have wanted to be asked?
- Evaluation—Why is this question an essential part of the text?

Here's a suggested sample lesson for a weekly study using questions as the theme.

Goal
By the end of this study group or class, the learner will be able to

1. Identify when and why questions appear in this portion.

2. Interpret the levels of meaning in the questions.

3. Define the value of doubt that emerges from the questions.

4. Synthesize and evaluate the meaning and value of doubt raised by the questions.

Objective
Learners will engage the questions and discuss how doubt is a crucial feature of faith.

Process of Study

1. Review the questions of the portion. Take note of specific details that situate the question in the text. (Knowledge)

2. The questions respond to a level of uncertainty. What is the uncertainty? (Comprehension)

3. How do the questions highlight or respond to the uncertainties the text reveals? (Application)

4. Why is there a need to confront the uncertainty of this moment? How does the concern raised by the text relate to the overall growth of Jewish consciousness? (Analysis)

5. Have you confronted a similar uncertainty before? How did you resolve the conflict? What does the Torah teach you in response to this conflict? (Synthesis)

Evaluation

After discussing some or all of the questions in the portion, explore the larger concepts of uncertainty and doubt as they relate to faith. Do the questions here inspire trust or faith? Do they limit or negate faith? If the latter, why are they written in the book?

Vayishlach

32:18 "Who are you, and where are you going, and who are these before you?" (Jacob to his servants, anticipating the questions Esau will ask them)

32:28 "What is your name?" (Angel to Jacob)

32:30 "What is your name?" (Jacob to angel)

32:30 "Why did you ask for my name?" (Angel to Jacob)

33:5 "Who are these to you?" (Esau to Jacob)

33:8 "Who is this whole camp that I am meeting [in relation] to you?" (Esau to Jacob)

33:15 "Why is this, have I found favor in my lord's eye?" (Esau to Jacob)

34:31 "Should one deal with our sister as with a harlot?" (Simon and Levi to Jacob)

MODEL 2—SAMPLE LESSON FOR THEMATIC STUDY
Goal
By the end of this study group or class, the learner will be able to

1. Identify when and why questions appear in this portion.

2. Interpret the levels of meaning in the questions.

3. Explore the theme that is evident in the questions.

4. Synthesize and evaluate the meaning and value of doubt raised by the questions.

Objective

By choosing a theme (or several themes during a course of study), learners will discover and discuss the purpose of a theme in the Torah and how the theme applies to a life of faith.

SAMPLE TEN-WEEK COURSE

Session 1—Introduction: What Is a Question?

Session 2—Questions for the Seder Table

Session 3—Questions Imply Doubt

Session 4—Questions Invite Relationship

Session 5—Questions of Power and Authority

Session 6—Rhetorical Questions and Why They Are Used

Session 7—The Absence of Questions

Session 8—Questions Inspire Faith

Session 9—When We Stop Asking Questions

Session 10—Conclusion: What Questions Will You Ask?

SAMPLE THEME: IDENTITY

Use the selected questions to explore the theme of identity.

Genesis 4:9, 24:23, 25:23, 27:32, 32:30, 50:19

Exodus 3:11, 3:13, 5:22, 10:8, 32:26, 33:16

Numbers 9:7, 11:12, 12:2, 20:5, 23:8

Deuteronomy 5:22, 32:6, 33:29

Process of Study

1. Review questions either from this list or of your own choosing. Take note of specific details that situate the questions in the text. (Knowledge)

2. The questions respond to a level of uncertainty. What is the uncertainty? (Comprehension)

3. How do the questions highlight or respond to the theme of identity? (Application)

4. What is the conflict in identity the text is struggling to define? (Analysis)

5. Have you confronted a similar questions of identity before? How did you resolve them? What does the Torah teach you in response to this conflict? (Synthesis)

Evaluation

The theme of identity is something we discover, explore, cultivate, and share. The Torah presents the concept of identity through questions. Indeed, many of the times we read about identity in the Torah, it is surrounded or punctuated by questions. How do questions help us define ourselves? How do questions define our relationships to others?

Learning is a constantly evolving process. Please share your experience with me at www.rabbijoshuahoffman.com or rabbijoshuahoffman @gmail.com.

Notes

ACKNOWLEDGMENTS
1. Ex. 20:18 Pirke d'Rabbi Eliezer 41:16.
2. Babylonian Talmud Yevamot 62b.
3. Babylonian Talmud Ta'anit 7a.

INTRODUCTION
1. Psalm 34:13.
2. Zohar, Bamidbar, Behaalotecha 58.
3. Genesis 18:23–32, Numbers 11:10–24, Numbers 16:1–15.
4. Genesis 3:9, 4:9.
5. Babylonian Talmud Menachot 29b, https://www.sefaria.org/Menachot.29b?lang=bi.

GENESIS
1. Genesis Rabbah 85:2, https://www.sefaria.org/Bereishit_Rabbah.85.2?lang=bi.
2. Genesis 2:16–17.
3. Genesis 3:10.
4. Genesis 3:11.
5. Rashi, comment on 3:10.
6. Genesis 1:31.
7. Genesis 4:7.
8. Genesis 4:9.
9. Genesis 8:21.
10. Genesis 11:7.
11. Genesis 15:5.
12. Genesis 16:14.
13. Genesis 21:7.
14. Job 42:2.
15. Genesis 12:1–3.
16. Genesis Rabbah 39:1, https://www.sefaria.org/Bereishit_Rabbah.39.1?lang=bi.
17. Genesis Rabbah 38:13ff, https://www.sefaria.org/Bereishit_Rabbah.38.13?lang=bi.
18. Genesis 19:12.
19. Genesis 14.

20. Rashi, based on Genesis Rabbah 61, https://www.sefaria.org/Rashi_on_Bereshit _Rabbah.64.4.2?lang=bi.
21. Genesis 21:29–31.
22. Genesis 22:8.
23. Rashi, commentary on Genesis 23:15, https://www.sefaria.org/Rashi_on_Genesis .23.15?lang=bi.
24. Sforno, commentary on Genesis 23:15, https://www.sefaria.org/Sforno_on_Genesis .23.15?lang=bi
25. Ethics of the Sages, 5:3, https://www.sefaria.org/Pirkei_Avot.5.3?lang=bi.
26. Genesis 24:1.
27. Genesis 24:3–4.
28. Genesis 24:8.
29. Genesis 18:2, 19:2, 43:24.
30. Genesis 24:31.
31. Genesis 24:31.
32. Genesis 24:31.
33. Based on Song of Solomon 3:4.
34. Genesis 25:23.
35. Genesis 25:23.
36. Genesis 12:10–20.
37. Genesis 20:1–18.
38. Genesis 26:28–29.
39. Genesis 26:34–35 .
40. Genesis 27:39–40.
41. Genesis 29:14.
42. Genesis 29:14.
43. Genesis 25:22.
44. Genesis 30:14.
45. See Genesis 50:19.
46. Babylonian Talmud Megillah 13b, https://www.sefaria.org/Megillah.13b?lang=bi.
47. Genesis 30:8. *Naftali* literally means "my struggling."
48. Genesis 30:2.
49. Genesis 12:10 and 27:38.
50. Genesis 32:23ff.
51. See previous comments.
52. Midrash Genesis Rabbah 38:13, https://www.sefaria.org/Bereishit_Rabbah.38.13 ?lang=bi.
53. Talmud Sanhedrin 106b—ליבא בעי הקב"ה.
54. Genesis 33:9.
55. Genesis 33:10.
56. Genesis 32:32.
57. Harold M. Schulweis, "Consolation," https://www.vbs.org/worship/meet-our -clergy/rabbi-harold-schulweis/sermons/consolation.
58. Genesis 27:36.

59. Genesis 34:2.
60. Genesis 37:14.
61. See Rashi, Ibn Ezra et al. on this verse.
62. Genesis 37:27.
63. Genesis 25:23.
64. Psalm 116:12.
65. I am grateful to Rabbi J. B. Sacks for translation help here.
66. Genesis 37:22.
67. Exodus 1:8.
68. Genesis 42:9.
69. Genesis 42:10.
70. See Genesis 43:10.
71. Genesis 43:23.
72. Genesis 43:8–9.
73. Genesis 42:7.
74. Genesis 38:25.
75. Genesis 46:34.
76. Genesis 44:4–5.
77. Genesis 47:4.
78. Exodus 1:8.
79. Genesis 47:7.
80. Genesis 48:10.
81. For examples see Genesis 19:12, 24:23, 24:47, 27:18, 27:32, 32:30.
82. Genesis 48:11.
83. Genesis 30:2.
84. Genesis 2:3.

PART II: INTRODUCTION TO EXODUS
1. Exodus 12:40–41.

EXODUS
1. The source of this quote is uncertain. See for further study https://quoteinvestigator
.com/2011/01/11/what-lies-within/.
2. Exodus 1:9.
3. Exodus 1:21.
4. Exodus 1:10.
5. Exodus 4:10.
6. Exodus 3:14.
7. Numbers 22:9.
8. Adapted from Louis Ginzberg, *The Legends of the Jews*, 2nd ed. (Philadelphia, PA: Jewish Publication Society, 2003), 3:6.
9. Exodus 4:10.
10. Genesis 18:14, 32:30.

11. Exodus 5:3.

12. Exodus 12:22.

13. Exodus 5:21.

14. Exodus 6:1.

15. Exodus 12:32.

16. Exodus 8:6.

17. Exodus 10:10.

18. Exodus 10:29.

19. "Egypt" in Hebrew is *Mitzrayim*. One definition of Mitzrayim is "limit in motion."

20. Later we can infer that there was indeed water a short distance away in Elim. See Exodus 14:27.

21. Exodus 15:25.

22. See, for example, Franz Kafka, "Before the Law," trans. Ian Johnston, https://www.kafka-online.info/before-the-law.html.

23. "Now the manna was like coriander seed, and in color it was like bdellium [a semi-transparent and fragrant resin from certain trees]" (Numbers 11:7).

24. See n. 23 and also Exodus 16:31, "It was like coriander seed, white, and it tasted like wafers of honey"; as well as Exodus 16:14, "a fine and flaky substance, as fine as frost on the ground."

25. See Numbers 11:5.

26. Exodus 25:2.

27. "But he shall present himself to Eleazar the priest, who shall on his behalf seek the decision of the Urim before YHVH" (Numbers 27:21).

28. "And of Levi he said: Let your Thummim and Urim be with your faithful one" (Deuteronomy 33:8).

29. 1 Samuel 14:41, 28:6.

30. Exodus 2:14.

31. Exodus 17:4.

32. See Exodus 5:8 and 10:10 where Pharaoh calls the people "shirkers" and "bent on mischief."

33. "So the people stopped bringing, their efforts had been more than enough for all the tasks to be done" (Exodus 36:6–7).

LEVITICUS

1. Leviticus 19:18.

2. Leviticus 19:3.

3. Genesis 1:27.

4. Leviticus 24:10–23.

5. Leviticus 25:21.

6. Leviticus 26:3.

PART IV: INTRODUCTION TO NUMBERS

1. Exodus 19:6.

NUMBERS

1. Numbers 6:22–27.
2. Leviticus 10:1–20.
3. Numbers 9:10–13.
4. Numbers 11:10.
5. Jewish Publication Society, ed., *JPS TANAKH: The Holy Scriptures (Blue): The New JPS Translation According to the Traditional Hebrew Text* (Philadelphia: Jewish Publication Society, 1985), 308.
6. Numbers 12:3.
7. Numbers 12:14.
8. Numbers 13:33.
9. Numbers 14:40.
10. See, for example, Daniel Kahneman, Olivier Sibony, and Cass R. Sunstein, *Noise: A Flaw in Human Judgment* (Boston: Little, Brown Spark, 2021); and Malcolm Gladwell, *Blink: The Power of Thinking without Thinking* (New York: Back Bay Books, 2007).
11. Numbers 16:15.
12. Numbers 16:26 and Genesis 18:23. The Hebrew root word *Samech Pay Heh* means "to sweep away."
13. Exodus 17:6.
14. This question is also found at Exodus 14:11, 17:3, 32:12, 32:21; and Numbers 11:20, 14:3, 16:13, 20:4, 20:5.
15. Numbers 22:7.
16. Numbers 22:20.
17. Numbers 22:29.
18. See, for example, Deuteronomy 32:19–28.
19. See Ovadiah Sforno, *Sforno: Commentary on the Torah, Complete Volume* (New York: Mesorah Publications, 1997); *M'Umah* (freely) could also imply Bilaam has no free will at all.
20. Compare Genesis 12:18, 27:37 and Exodus 5:2.
21. Numbers 23:18 et seq.
22. Numbers 24:25.
23. Isaiah 49:6.

THE BOOK OF DEUTERONOMY

1. Numbers 14:6–10.
2. Deuteronomy 1:29–30.
3. Deuteronomy 4:20, 6:24, 8:18, passim.
4. Deuteronomy 29:14.
5. Deuteronomy 6:23–24.
6. Deuteronomy 8:6.
7. Psalm 115:5, et cetera.
8. Exodus 28:30.
9. Jeffrey H. Tigay, *The JPS Torah Commentary: Deuteronomy* (Philadelphia: Jewish Publication Society, 1996), 282.

10. Exodus 32:12.
11. Deuteronomy 30:14.
12. Deuteronomy 30:12.
13. Deuteronomy 31:20–21.
14. Deuteronomy 31:17.
15. Here the Hebrew word is *Ay*. In Genesis 3:9, the Hebrew word is *Ayeka*.
16. See Psalm 115:2.
17. Jack Miles, *God: A Biography* (New York: Vintage Press 1996), 87.
18. Exodus 15:1–21.

Index

About the Author

Rabbi Joshua Hoffman has studied and practiced as a pulpit rabbi in the Southern California area for the past twenty-five years. He was recently appointed president and CEO of the Academy for Jewish Religion California, a transdenominational seminary training future cantors, chaplains, and rabbis. He proudly served Congregation Valley Beth Shalom in Encino from 2003 to 2021. As an ordinee of the fifth class of the Ziegler School of Rabbinic Studies, he received prestigious awards and achieved an MA in rabbinic studies in 2003. He also received his MA in education from the American Jewish University in 1999 and his BA in English and American literature from Brandeis University in 1996. Over the years he has cultivated extensive experience with the Los Angeles and North American Jewish communities, serving in positions of leadership with the Rabbinical Assembly; the Board of Rabbis of Southern California; the Sandra Caplan Community Bet Din; and the JFNA Rabbinic Cabinet. Joshua teaches in the greater Los Angeles Jewish community and has been a lecturer in courses on liturgy and essential Jewish texts at the American Jewish University. He publishes widely, including a series of Torah portion commentaries for the *Los Angeles Jewish Journal*. Joshua is married to Rabbi Becky Hoffman and lives with their three children in Sherman Oaks, California. This is his first book.

Made in the USA
Las Vegas, NV
11 August 2024